The Affair of the Poisons

THE
Affair
OF THE
Poisons

⋘§⋙

Louis XIV, Madame de Montespan, and One of
History's Great Unsolved Mysteries

⋘§⋙

FRANCES MOSSIKER

ALFRED A. KNOPF
NEW YORK 1969

THIS IS A BORZOI BOOK
PUBLISHED BY ALFRED A. KNOPF, INC.

FIRST EDITION

For my brother, EVERETT SANGER,
and for FAE

ACKNOWLEDGMENTS

I NOTE my primary debt of gratitude to Mr. Douglas Schneider, cultural attaché of the American Embassy in Paris, and to Mme Anne-Marie Degory, special assistant to the attaché in 1964–5, when research on this book began. Through their good offices, my work in the libraries, archives, and museums of France has been facilitated and expedited. I appreciate the courtesy extended me by the staffs of the Bibliothèque de l'Arsenal and the Archives Nationales in Paris. At the Bibliothèque Nationale, I enjoyed once again, as often in the past, the cooperation of Mme Janine Roncato, *archiviste paléographe* and *bibliothécaire*, and of Mlle Nicole Villa, *conservateur*, Cabinet des Estampes. Mme M. Odier-Lesourd, *documentaliste* at l'Office Français de Relations Publiques, has aided me in assembling the iconography for this volume. I express my profound appreciation for the gracious assistance rendered me by M. Gérald Van Der Kemp, *conservateur en chef* of the Musée de Versailles, and for the special consideration shown me at the Service de Documentation Photographique de la Réunion des Musées Nationaux at the Château de Versailles. Mr. Gallaher of the staff of the California Palace of the Legion of Honor assisted in an inquiry into the provenience of the Largillière portrait of the Marquis de Montespan in the Collis P. Huntington Collection. I profited from the rich resources of the New York Public Library, where many courtesies were offered me by Mr. Edward Di Roma, Economics, Chief, and by members of his staff. Access to the vast collections at the University of Texas libraries was made available to me through the many courtesies of Dr. Warren F. Roberts, director, Humanities Research Center, and of Mrs. June Moll, librarian, Stark Library. At the Fondren Library of Southern Methodist University offers of assistance came unfailingly from Miss Anne Bailey, periodicals librarian, and Miss Elizabeth Glaab, librarian. Thanks to the Dallas Public Library, to Mrs. Lillian M. Bradshaw, the director, and to Miss Erma McClure, professional assistant, General Reference Department, the interlibrary loan was put into operation in my behalf: rare books requisite to this study were obtained for my use in Dallas from the Library of Congress and from university libraries across the land. My thanks go to Dr. Laurence Perrine for his translations from the French of the several stanzas of verse included in these pages. And I owe warm thanks, as well, to Judge Irving L. Goldberg,

ACKNOWLEDGMENTS

United States Court of Appeals for the Fifth Circuit, for generous assistance in interpretation of *Ancien Régime* legal procedure. As for *Ancien Régime* medical theory and practice, the light of modern medical science has been effectively directed upon that field by two eminent members of the twentieth-century faculty: I have Dr. Harold W. Kimmerling and Dr. Arthur G. Schoch to thank for their patience in dealing with my many questions. And I have Dr. Robert T. Long to thank for a most interesting experiment in the analysis of a dream dreamed three centuries ago. I was most fortunate to have had the opportunity to consult—during this investigation into the Poisons Affair—with Dr. Morton F. Mason, Professor of Forensic Medicine and Toxicology, University of Texas, Southwestern Medical School at Dallas, and I mark here my gratitude to him for his time and attention. I greatly appreciate the skilled and zealous services of Mrs. Esther Swift in the preparation of the several drafts of the manuscript of this book. First and last, I reiterate my special thanks to my editor, Mr. Robert Gottlieb, for invaluable directives and ineffable understanding.

CONTENTS

CONTENTS

ILLUSTRATIONS

NOTE ON CITATIONS

IN MOST INSTANCES, quotations are identified within the text: the contemporaries speak for themselves, in their memoirs, diaries, letters; detailed information on the source of such citations is to be found in the Contemporary Sources (pp. 330–1). The citations from the Duc de Saint-Simon, the Abbé de Choisy, the Abbé Le Dieu, the Marquis de Sourches, the Duc d'Antin, the Marquis de La Fare, and Primi Visconti are from their published Memoirs. Those of the Marquis de Dangeau are from his Journal. Citations from Mme de Motteville, Mlle de Montpensier (the *Grande Mademoiselle*), and the Duchesse de Mazarin (Hortense Mancini) are from their Memoirs. Those from the Comtesse de La Fayette are from either her *Histoire d'Henriette d'Angleterre* or her *Mémoires de la cour de France*. Quotations from Mme de Caylus are from her *Souvenirs*; those of Louise de la Vallière are from her *Reflexions sur la Miséricorde de Dieu* and from letters. The quotations from Mme de Sévigné, the Duchesse d'Orléans (the second *Madame*), Mme du Noyer, Mlle de Scudéry, Mme de Maintenon, the Marquis de Feuquières, Ezekiel Spanheim, and the Marquis de Saint-Maurice are from their letters, varied collections of published correspondence. A quotation from the Duchesse de Longueville (p. 65) comes from a letter published by Victor Cousin in the collection entitled *Madame de Sablé*. The citations from Colbert and Louvois are frequently taken from their official correspondence. Quotations from the Comte de Bussy are from his letters, his Memoirs, and his chronicle, *L'Histoire amoureuse des Gaules*. When Bishop Bossuet is cited, it is either from his published sermons and funeral orations, or from the Memoirs of his secretary, the Abbé Le Dieu. Quotations from Nicolas de la Reynie are taken from either the Archives de la Bastille or from La Reynie's own personal notes and papers. Quotations from the prisoners involved in the Poisons Affair are taken verbatim from the official trial dossier in the Archives de la Bastille, or from La Reynie's notebooks. Quotations from the letters of Mme de Montespan are from a collection of her correspondence and poetry published in the Appendix of Pierre Clement's *Madame de Montespan et Louis XIV*. Quotations from Louis XIV are from his *Mémoires*, his *Oeuvres*, and his *Lettres*, further identified in the Contemporary Sources.

All translations of quotations are by the author.

The Affair of the Poisons

Prologue

G LORY IS THE WORD by which to evoke him: Louis XIV, King
of France and of Navarre, Louis the Great, the Sun
King, Rex Christianissimus.

He appears in all his glory in the Council Chamber of his
palace—thousand-windowed, golden Versailles. He has summoned
his councilors of state into session; nothing unusual, nothing to
attract attention in such an occasion since council meetings are
daily occurrences in this palace, since this King is his own Prime
Minister, and a diligent one.

What does attract attention is the bulky, imposing black leather
coffer—under lock and key, and conspicuous with seals, all intact,
unbroken since the date affixed in 1681; this is the chest which is
delivered ceremoniously by Chancellor Pontchartrain's own hand
into His Majesty's.

What is unusual is the fire which His Majesty has ordered laid
and lit in the cavernous hearth of the ornate bronze and marble
fireplace—for the season is not the season for fires; it is summer,
midsummer, July 13, 1709.

The King is burning evidence, though the official minutes of
the meeting do not state it quite that bluntly; evidence which
threatens tarnish to his glory, blemish to the name of his onetime
official mistress—and through her name, to his; as well as to the
names of their four children, favored by him over his legitimate

offspring: two bastard daughters and two bastard sons, integrated by marriage into the royal family; the males legitimized by edict of the Parlement of Paris; and, by a second edict, shortly to be declared full Princes of the Blood: in the line of succession to the throne in the event of the extinction of the legitimate Bourbon line, which by 1712 would loom as a grim possibility.

Louis XIV, in that summer of 1709, could afford no further diminution of his glory: "All his glory," in that first decade of the 1700's, was not all the glory it had been in the mid- and late 1600's when he had stood in the prime of his manhood, and France at the zenith of her power and prestige.

Glory was his own favorite word, the word forever on his lips and forever on his pen: "Love of glory is assuredly my dominant passion," he wrote in his Memoirs; and again, in his series of instructions for the Dauphin, his throne-heir. ". . . Above all other things, above life itself, I would prefer a lofty and a glorious reputation," he declared, sounding like the hero of a Corneille drama (as he and most of his aristocratic contemporaries fancied themselves), and using the word in the classic sense of great and honorable fame, honor beyond honor, supreme self-triumph. In Louis's own excellent definition: "My dignity, my glory, my grandeur, my reputation"—meaning his own and that of France; man and monarch one, indistinguishable, inextricable; monarch and state indivisibly, indissolubly one, one and the same: *L'État ç'est moi,* "I am the State"; whether or not he actually spoke the words, it was the truth.

In 1709, monarch and state stood hard-pressed, at bay: a pack of enemies, the nations of Europe in coalition, closing in on France, threatening invasion at every border. "France was ruined long before she had ceased to be victorious," in Alexis de Tocqueville's most frequently quoted quotation; a half century's military rampage, even though victorious, had drained the nation of manpower and exhausted her resources.

By 1704, she had ceased to be victorious; French military supremacy shattered on the battlefield of Blenheim, although no one dared report it to Versailles. "The news that he was no longer invincible" (in Voltaire's famous line) had to be broken to His Majesty by Madame de Maintenon, the Favorite of that era (for, even in his seventies, he could not do without a woman in his life).

French naval supremacy was shattered in that same month of August, 1704: with the capture of Gibraltar, the Mediterranean became an "English lake," as it would remain until well into our time (thereafter, "No more great French fleets were to be seen upon its waters or upon those of the Ocean," as Voltaire noted sadly; "the French fleet would shrink back into the state in which Louis XIV had found it; another example of the many extraordinary enterprises which had both their origin and their conclusion in his reign").

In 1706, the Sun King must have shuddered at the solar eclipse which darkened the European Continent—the sun, only recently established by the Copernican theory as the center of the universe; the sun, adopted by Louis as his personal device, his heraldic bearing, his sign, symbol, emblem. The eclipse occurring on May 11 was one to terrify a credulous and superstitious age, a credulous and superstitious monarch: Was it the dark and sinister omen of France's defeat at Ramillies, that spring, and subsequent loss of Flanders? Was it the dark portent of France's defeat at Turin, in the autumn, and the subsequent loss of Italy?

It seemed an irony of fate that after a half century of clear-cut, outright, unabashed, and victorious aggression, France's arms should meet their first grave defeat in the War of the Spanish Succession; for, if ever a war could be said to be understandable, it might have been this one. Louis XIV was fighting—France was fighting, against all Europe—to maintain Louis's grandson on the throne of Spain,* bequeathed to the young French prince by his

---

* All twenty-three crowns of Spain had been bequeathed to Louis XIV's second eldest grandson, the seventeen-year-old Duc d'Anjou, by the last will and testament of the young Duke's great-uncle, Charles II, the late King of Spain. Charles, dying without issue, had turned to the issue of his sisters, the elder wed to the Bourbon King of France; the younger, to a Habsburg Emperor of Austria. Had Charles II's French (his Bourbon) great-nephew declined the Spanish crowns, then his Austrian (Habsburg) great-nephew

great-uncle, Charles II of Spain. Had Louis XIV refused to accept the Spanish Empire for the French house of Bourbon, the Austrian house of Habsburg had next claim to it. In the dilemma of the Spanish succession—to accept or to reject it—Louis XIV was damned if he did, damned if he didn't.

Now, in 1709, with French troops everywhere defeated, demoralized, straggling, starving; with the French populace "dying like flies" of plague and famine; with the nation on the brink of disaster (financial and economic as well as military), Louis XIV swallowed his colossal pride and sued for peace at any price: even the abandonment of prized Strasbourg, watchtower on the Rhine; even the abandonment of his grandson and his grandson's cause in Spain were not prices too high for Louis to pay in this crisis. The only condition at which the French monarch balked was that it should be a French army sent to Spain to expel his grandson from the throne and deliver it over to the Austrian Archduke Charles. "If there must be a war," came the refusal in Louis's usual well-chosen words, "I prefer to wage it against my enemies rather than against my children."

The people of France, in even such dire straits as they then found themselves, backed their King in his decision to fight on for "an honorable and lasting peace," as he had explained to them (an unprecedented condescension) in an open letter circulated throughout the realm.

If the nation's honor and security were at stake, these must depend upon the fortunes of war; only fate could decide the issue. But in the issue concerning the monarch's own personal honor and reputation, he could take action into his own hand, anticipating and circumventing the hand of fate. A question ever present in his mind was that of how he would come to be regarded by posterity

---

would have claimed it as the contingent heir. And if all Europe was leagued with Austria against France to prevent the Bourbon heir from coming into his vast Spanish inheritance, then just as surely France would have had to league herself with Europe, against Austria, to thwart the Habsburg heir. Either way, the European balance of power had been seriously impaired.

and history ("All the universe, all the centuries," being his words for it). Where he could bring influence to bear in that direction, he would not hesitate to do so.

His personal honor and reputation—his Glory!—were compromised by the contents of the black leather coffer, the *cassette noire*, deposited by Chancellor Pontchartrain and now reposing upon the broad marble hearth of the Council Chamber.

Only three men beside himself, and all as secretive as he, had known the contents of the *cassette noire*, and now he had seen all three—safe and silent—into the grave.

The first of the three had been lowered into his grave in 1683, only three years after the trial documents from the Arsenal Chamber had been secreted in this chest: the first man to die had been Colbert, Secretary of the Interior, Exterior, and Exchequer; the portfolios of Navy, Colonial, and even Cultural Affairs all under his arm.

The next to die, in the year 1691, was the second genius in the King's Council (the King's "Evil genius," in some opinion), Minister of War Louvois, who had transformed a medieval into a modern army, into the most effective fighting force since the Roman legions (and then, inevitably, on the lookout for the opportunity to use it). Although the rumor spread that Louvois had been poisoned (some said "at the King's command"; others, "at that of the King's mistress, Madame de Maintenon"), the rumormongers were reckless and the accusations unsubstantiated; and certainly there was never a question of Louvois's having betrayed the King's confidence in the matter of the black coffer documents, or any other. (It was simply that the court of Versailles was jumpy about sudden death; all Paris, all France was in the grip of a poison psychosis since the Chamber of the Arsenal trials in the late 1670's.) No, Louvois's fall from favor in 1689 stemmed from an entirely unrelated source: when the King attacked his Minister of War with a pair of fire tongs (from the very hearth where the black coffer was now reposing), it was because Louvois had presumed to authorize the sack of the Palatinate and the devastation of the

German Rhineland without first consulting His Majesty who, jealous of every iota of his limitless authority, acted as his own chief of staff as well as his own Prime Minister.

Of that trio of the King's confidants, the third and last had died on June 14, 1709, one month ago almost to the day, and his was the death which apparently spurred the King to the action that engaged him in his Council Chamber, presently, in mid-July.

The name of the deceased: Nicolas de La Reynie, credited with the creation of the Paris police, with the cleanup of the capital, in the literal sense as well as the figurative. Thanks to La Reynie, mud and ordure were swept from the streets, five thousand lanterns lit, and regular patrols inaugurated. Thanks to La Reynie, Paris's half million citizens felt safer in venturing out upon the streets, especially after dark, than ever before in the city's long history. The King deserved credit, too, for having chosen the one man in all the kingdom—a notable talent of Louis XIV's—best suited to fill the newly created post of Lieutenant-General of Police in His Majesty's "good city" on the Seine.

It was in another role, however, that La Reynie assumes importance to this story, as *Rapporteur-Commissaire* (for a translation of which the *Ancien Régime* legal term, our American court-martial title of Judge Advocate comes closest) in the Poisons Affair trial. As the King's chief investigator and coordinator for the tribunal appointed by the King to sit in judgment in the Chamber of the Arsenal in 1679, La Reynie had been entrusted—throughout the course of the previous quarter century—with the key to this cache of special material, sequestered from the official trial dossier, and secreted in the black leather chest. With La Reynie's death, the King was confronted with the necessity of making other disposition of these very secret documents. At this late date (with the King in his seventy-first year, it was late indeed considering the average life span of an eighteenth-century man), it seemed an unnecessary risk to take a fourth person into his confidence; to entrust his name, his fame—his Glory!—to the discretion of any other living creature.

For the mystery of the black leather coffer was the mystery of the Poisons Affair; along with that of the Man in the Iron Mask, the two most tantalizing mysteries of the seventeenth century, the two best-kept secrets of the age, kept by a man uniquely talented at keeping a secret—Louis XIV.

Wrapped in his ineffable majesty, in his imperturbable dignity, he seemed impervious to the outrages of fortune which had turned outrageous only in his latter years. He was observed scarcely to flinch at the deaths of three Dauphins, three throne-heirs, within a twelvemonth. And yet the shameful business of the Poisons Affair seemed to embarrass him and touch him to the quick—to judge by the infinite pains he took to conceal it from the eye of history.

Pride was his Achilles' heel. The Poisons Affair cast discredit on his court, that paragon upon which all the other courts of Europe were modeled: elegant, polished, it was credited with being enlightened, too. The word "enlightenment"—as used in that dawn of the Age of Reason when the voices of Galileo, Newton, and Descartes were beginning to fill the air—implied a mental climate that was scientific, logical, and, above all, rational. And yet here was the elite of the French court shown up by the exposés of the Poisons Case trial as anything but rational; as irrationally, even criminally, superstitious.

The loftiest nobility of the land had been involved in that sordid scandal known as the Affair of the Poisons. The poison ring—a collection of the most vicious criminals of the Paris underworld—dredged up by La Reynie's dragnet and on trial for their lives, dared make charges against "high and puissant" lords and ladies, and made some of the charges stick. Court summonses were issued in the names of Counts and Countesses, Marquis and Marquises; a Duchess was haled before the bar of the Parlement of Paris; a Princess of the Blood Royal took fright and flight across the border; a Duke and peer of the realm, a maréchal of the French army submitted to months of questioning and incarceration.

Before it was over, the criminals in the dungeons of the Bastille and of the Fortress of Vincennes had dared to name a name more exalted still, a name linked inextricably with His Most Christian

Majesty's: Athénaïs, Marquise de Montespan, one of the chief glories of France—along with Notre Dame, the Louvre, Versailles. If these were the showplaces of the nation, Madame de Montespan was the showpiece, the brightest ornament of the court: "A triumphant beauty to be paraded" at state receptions, to adorn the steps of the silver throne, her jewels glittering more brightly than the Queen's. "*La Belle Madame*," "*La Belle Beauté*" constituted a sight to dazzle all eyes, "to impress all the Ambassadors" (to hear Madame de Sévigné tell it, and to hear her tell it was to hear it in the best French of a century renowned for the best French ever spoken).

The heinous charges made against Mme de Montespan, the King's then regnant mistress, were never allowed to reach the ears or eyes of the King's duly appointed judges in the King's Court of the Arsenal. The prisoners who made the charges, and La Reynie to whom the charges were made, were all now dead: La Reynie dead within the month, of old age, in his bed; the prisoners dead in 1682, at stake or gibbet; or in the course of the past thirty years, in their chains, in the remotest prisons of the realm. The transcripts of the interrogations and confessions in which these accusations had been made were sequestered by La Reynie, at the King's express command, and thus never formed part of the documentation of the trial proper. The official trial dossier—accumulated throughout the course of three long years and 210 court sessions—came eventually to fill "twenty-nine large packets and eight chests," according to an official inventory signed by the court clerk in 1682; this great batch of material was duly filed for record among the court archives where it belonged; preserved intact to this day, and available for examination in the Library of the Arsenal.

Having gone to such lengths to preserve the secret of the black coffer, the King was not likely to allow it now to escape those confines. The lid must be kept tight shut, sealed—or the contents destroyed.

The King's decision in the matter is recorded in the official minutes of the meeting of the council of state: dated July 13, 1709, neatly penned by the secretary of the council, still clearly legible, still preserved among the archives of the Quai d'Orsay:

"His Majesty" (the text reads), "presiding at a meeting of his State Council, having seen and having examined the minutes and the transcripts handed to him by Monsieur the Chancellor . . . has given orders that these documents be burned in his presence. . . ."

Chancellor Pontchartrain would have been obliged to leave his seat to take the black leather coffer from the King, and to direct the burning of the mass of papers it contained in the fireplace where giant logs were crackling: a necessarily lengthy procedure, feeding to the flames that sheaf of documents, one by one; allowing time for each yellowed sheet to catch fire, flare up, burn and glow, shrivel and disintegrate into ash—to make sure no scrap survived.

The councilors must have watched the proceedings with curiosity and discomfort, through a cloud of smoke which evidently did not discomfort the King. Warned by his celebrated architect Hardouin-Mansart that the palace fireplaces would smoke if the chimneys were not raised, Louis XIV was aesthete and Spartan enough to choose to endure the smoke rather than to mar the garden view with unsightly chimneys.

Even so, the air on this occasion may have seemed extraordinarily noxious, thick with abominations as well as with the acrid fumes seeping from the fireplace. For the names, the signatures scrawled on those yellowed sheets he had examined prior to consigning them to the flames could not have failed to stir His Majesty's memory. Hideous figures may have swirled out with the gray smoke from the hearth: the Abbé Guibourg, lewdly squinting renegade priest and chief of the Paris covens; La Voisin, Queen of the Witches, High Priestess of the black arts; Le Sage and Mariette, a sorcerer and his apprentice, all engaged in the Devil's business, with poison as a sideline. Impossible to descry the peerless beauty of a Madame de Montespan in so ugly and evil a company! Would it not be completely out of character for that proud, that superb creature to have stooped to such as this and these? What charges could they have brought against her? And what validity to their charges? More important still, how did the King find her? Innocent or guilty?

The truth of the Poisons Affair—his secret and hers—has been said to have gone up in the bonfire of the Council Chamber on July 13, 1709. Certainly Louis XIV himself was convinced that he had succeeded in destroying every shred of evidence, pro and con; in obliterating every trace of the squalid episode from the record; in protecting her name—and through hers, his—from the taint of scandal. But his carefully formulated design to draw a curtain over certain scenes of the Poisons Affair was foiled and frustrated by a man who never dreamed of challenging—much less thwarting— the will of his royal master. Like other loyal subjects of that seventeenth-century kingdom, this one owed and rendered worshipful, implicit obedience to his lawful, consecrated King, his sovereign and that of France, by divine right. Insubordination was an act he would not consider. Lieutenant-General of Police La Reynie, however, was a conscientious and a zealous magistrate; an honest, patient, dogged, and relentless investigator. La Reynie, furthermore, was a notetaker. Not satisfied with the official transcripts, the verbatim accounts of every interrogation, every confession and confrontation, every conference, meticulously written out in longhand by the police secretariat, La Reynie brought his own notebooks along to the courtroom, to the cell, to the interrogation hall and torture chamber; and before the three years of the trial were out, filled them with voluminous and detailed notes in his own cramped and careful hand, so precisely inscribed that it represents one of the rare examples of seventeenth-century script decipherable without the benefit of a paleologist-archivist; page after page of notes on his own personal impressions, his fears, his suspicions; summaries, analyses, even diagrams of his ratiocinations, deductions, and conclusions.

After the final session of the tribunal in the Chamber of the Arsenal, in 1682, La Reynie must have filed away these notes of his for possible future reference, either in his office at the Châtelet Court or at home, in his study or his library. He might have considered it unwise to do away with notes pertinent to the case as long as any of the convicts were known still to be alive. Or perhaps he had intended to make some final disposition of the notebooks before his own death came, but was surprised by its coming, even at the age of eighty-four.

However it was, the wonder is that his notes survived his death —and who knows what other vicissitudes in the years that followed. The wonder is that they are safe today and, it is to be hoped, for several centuries more; protected from careless hands, from mildew, dessication, and other ravages of time in the vaults of the Manuscript Room of the Bibliothèque Nationale in Paris, where they were deposited in 1862.

Otherwise, there would be no story.

PART ONE
The Magnificent Lovers

I

First Loves

THE HISTORY OF THE LIAISON between Louis XIV and the Marquise de Montespan—a ten-year alliance convulsed with passion and temper, a contest of wills within the very throes of love, less a love affair than an affair of state, a national and international scandal from first to last—the story of that attachment begins in the 1660's at the courts of Saint-Germain and Fontainebleau, when the Château de Versailles was still on the drawing boards of the royal architects.

The court taking form around Louis XIV in the early 1660's was as gallant and gay and youthful as the monarch, then in his early twenties; all those in the charmed, inner circle of his court, in their twenties too: elegant, refined, cultivated, sophisticated, and courtly, to a degree the courtiers of preceding reigns had not attained.

Louis XIV (fourteenth Louis in the long line of the dynasties of France, stretching back past the Bourbons, past the Valois, the Capetians, the Carolingians all the way to Charlemagne) was hailed at his birth in 1638 as *Dieudonné*, "God-given," "Gift of Heaven." There was actually something in the nature of a miracle in the fact that a child should have finally been born, after twenty-two years of bitter, barren wedlock, to the unhappy and estranged, the mutually mistrustful couple seated on the throne of France: Louis XIII (second in the line of the Bourbon dynasty; son of

» 17 «

Henri IV, the white-plumed founder of the dynasty) and Anne of
Austria (a misleading appelation for a typically Spanish Infanta,
sister of Philip IV, King of Spain). The birth of a throne-heir, a
Dauphin, the future Louis XIV, was the occasion for national rejoicing. (The birth of a second son, Philippe, to Louis XIII and
Anne of Austria, in 1640, furnished further guarantee of the succession in the Bourbon line.)

The Roman numeral XIII may have been an ill omen for this
Louis: he had neither the way nor the luck with women enjoyed by
his father and his son. But the state of the nation he bequeathed his
young son was sound, thanks to his own military prowess and to
the superb statesmanship of his two Prime Ministers, first Cardinal
Richelieu, then Cardinal Mazarin. Between them, they had under-
taken the work of creating national law and order out of the chaos
of the feudal states, out of the semi-independent duchies and principalities of which France had been comprised, unifying these into
a nation by imposing the central and royal authority upon the
feudal lords, formerly sovereign in their own dominions.

Upon the death of Louis XIII and during the minority of Louis
XIV, Mazarin acted as head of state; the Queen Mother as Regent.
The Cardinal preserved the integrity of the nation in the face of the
insurrections that broke out in Paris in 1648—the civil wars
known as the Fronde, the last convulsive struggles of the great
feudatories against the encroachment of the central, royal authority. The Parlement of Paris got in its word of protest, too,
against the growing absolutism of the monarchy, demanding rights,
reforms, even a constitution—new words and concepts blown in by
the winds of revolution from across the Channel where the English
Parliament had lately made just such a claim of King Charles I,
and won it—although over the King's dead body.

The privations and humiliations of those years of domestic
turmoil—the affronts and affrights, the intrusion of a Paris mob
into the boy-King's palace bedchamber, his flights from the city to
the safety of outlying fortresses—all marked young Louis XIV's
character and determined his policy throughout his life.

First Loves

If he was to make a national policy of grandeur, if he set out to dominate Europe, and then to dazzle it by the splendor and magnificence of his court at Versailles (setting it at a safe distance, twelve miles, from the tinderbox of Paris), all these actions may have had their motivation in the vicissitudes of those formative adolescent years.

With the surrender of the Parlement and of the Princes' party to the royal forces in 1652, it was time to plan for Louis's coronation, to be performed at Rheims Cathedral in 1654. But despite these elaborate and symbolic ceremonies, the reins of government remained in the clutch of Cardinal Mazarin until the day of his death in 1661. Perhaps, as charged, the crafty Italian did willfully retard the young King's education, but Louis XIV was perspicacious enough to perceive his own educational shortcomings, even to admit them; seeking to acquire more information in areas he considered important to his cherished craft of kingship.

There was no remissness evident in his sexual education, supervised presumably by his mother, as was then and as continued to be a Continental custom. Young Louis exhibited not only a precocious majesty but a precocious sexuality.

Contemporary gossip has it that to initiate her son into the rites of Venus, the Queen Mother had selected one of her confidential attendants, a certain Mme de Beauvais, in her forties, no aristocrat and certainly no Venus; but a hearty, healthy woman (free of the prevalent venereal diseases) with a hearty, healthy attitude toward sex. Whether she accommodated the Queen Mother or acted on her own initiative, whether she waylaid the "tall, strong, well-grown, handsome" young Prince on his way from the bath or in the attics of the Louvre, whether he was then fifteen, sixteen, or seventeen—the versions vary according to a variety of stories and street songs current at the time—"The old Circe," as the splenetic Duc de Saint-Simon calls her in his Memoirs, must have accomplished her mission with expertise and gusto, for the King thenceforward accorded her and her family a marked generosity and consideration; all her life, she enjoyed a peculiar prestige at his court. Thenceforward, love and glory—euphemisms for lust and pride, for ego and libido—were to constitute the dominant passions in the monarch's life.

"The King was gallant, often to the extreme, to the point of debauch," his sister-in-law, the second Duchesse d'Orléans, herself smitten with him, would say of him later. "Anyone at all would do, just so long as she was female . . . just so she gave the impression of loving him. . . ." (and what could be simpler than to fall in love when the young man in question was not only highly personable but King of France as well?) "It made no difference to him whether she was a lady of quality, a chamberwoman [a reference to Mme de Beauvais] or a gardener's daughter. . . ." (a reference to the one in the gardens of the Louvre, who had borne him, according to report, the first in the long, long list of his illegitimate children).

As for the reference to "a lady of quality," the first would be Olympe Mancini, the first to be singled out by His Majesty from among Cardinal Mazarin's quintette of fascinating Italian nieces, "the Mazarinettes," as they were called at court, sloe-eyed and fast-living, although all five—as if by some unanimously adopted family policy—contained their notoriously licentious proclivities until after they had pronounced their marriage vows. Olympe, coming into her full endowment of dark, opulent beauty and of coruscating, cynical wit at a mere eighteen, piqued the King's interest, diverted and delighted him—eighteen years old himself at the time, but light-years behind the cunning and subtle Italian girl, who seemed to have sprung into being, like Minerva, fully grown, fully armored, and worldly-wise.

Had a Mancini aspired as high as the throne of France, a horoscope cast at the Cardinal's orders and precisely at that conjuncture must have dashed Olympe's hopes. Her ardor never too hot to interfere with her cool calculations, she would yield to the King's advances only after a brilliant match had been arranged for her with a Prince of the French Blood Royal, a Prince of Savoy, Eugène Maurice, Comte de Soissons. Only then, as Comtesse de Soissons, would she open her arms to welcome, to attract the young monarch, into "the brilliant social whirl of which she was the vortex," the smartest of the smart young set of court and capital. By 1657, "with the King firmly fixed in her orbit . . . she disposed of tremendous power and influence" (according to Saint-Simon). "It was in the distinguished and gallant clique where the Comtesse de Soissons held sway . . . that the King acquired that air of courtesy and gallantry which he was to retain all his life and which he knew how to blend with vast dignity and majesty."

It was the Mancini girls—Olympe and Marie, between them, and in that order—who undoubtedly smartened, sharpened, and sophisticated the callow youth on the French throne. If Louis XIV, in 1657, "appeared half-enchanted" by the newly wed Olympe (to quote Mme de Motteville, Anne of Austria's lady in waiting and memorialist), by 1658 he had strayed away to her younger sister, going straight from Olympe's arms to Marie's (with only the briefest detour, briefest interlude of romantic interest in a Mlle de La Motte d'Argencourt*).

Where Olympe had failed to arouse a *"grande passion"* in Louis XIV's breast (in Mme de Motteville's analysis), Marie succeeded: he and she embarking tremulously upon a first love—rapturous, tender, touching—rudely terminated by Cardinal Mazarin at the pair's first intimation of serious intentions such as wedlock. It was, furthermore, a chaste love—a romance rather than an affair—if the pronouncement of Marie's groom, Prince Colonna, grand constable of the Kingdom of Naples, is to be credited.

Colonna greeted his bride-to-be ("the girl beloved by a King") with some misgivings when she arrived in Milan in 1661 for the final marriage rites. Ravishing her within moments of her arrival, in the cabin of the state barge in which she had traveled, he loudly

---

* Mlle de La Motte d'Argencourt—a blue-eyed French blonde as a change from brunette Italians—caused a heart flutter so faint as scarcely to deserve recording save for the fact that Mlle de La Motte paid for her half-hour in the sun by a lifetime in a convent. A vigilant Queen Mother ordered her immured there—the first of the King's Favorites to travel the road that led from palace to cloister.

and clearly expressed his astonishment at having found her a virgin. "The Constable, who was convinced that the loves of kings are never innocent" (according to the Memoirs of Marie's sister, Hortense Mancini), "was so thrilled to find himself mistaken in the case of his bride that he calmly accepted the fact that he had not been the first to possess her heart."

Neither the first nor the last. Although she made a spectacle of the fact that her heart had been broken along with the King's broken promises, it must have been the fragments—the bits and pieces—she tossed carelessly to lovers here and there along her route, before and after her frequent conventual retreats, up and down the Continent—her restless and tormented spirit finding surcease "in neither God nor the Devil," according to one contemporary. "The wildest and the best of the Mazarinettes" (in Saint-Simon's estimation), the Princess Colonna could never adjust herself to a world in which she had expected to be a Queen.

As for the King, it might be said that his attachment to Marie constituted the sentimental crisis of his life; here he appeared in his one moment of vulnerability, in his one human moment, before the curtain of impenetrable majesty was drawn across his private life. The fourteenth Louis of the royal house of France was familiar with the Corneillian concept of "glory" as conquest of will over self. Louis XIV's Valois and Bourbon forebears provided examples of this same royal code of honor, this supreme devotion to dynastic duty. Once and once only, in his youthful romantic involvement with Marie, did Louis show himself reluctant to sacrifice his sentiments as a man to his interests as a sovereign. Ever after, in all the subsequent, numerous passionate involvements of his long life, he would be seen to be in full command of the situation and of himself—in the analysis of the Comtesse de La Fayette, "The master of his mistresses and of his heart."

II

The Queen and Madame

Louis's INTERESTS AS A SOVEREIGN were supremely well served by marriage with his cousin once removed, the Infanta Maria Teresa, elder daughter of Philip IV, King of Spain.

The marriage contract formed part of complex military, economic, and territorial negotiations brought to a conclusion highly advantageous to France by that skilled negotiator, Cardinal Mazarin, in 1659. The Peace of the Pyrenees, as the treaty was called, was the ailing Cardinal's greatest triumph, and his last: France at peace, after forty-one years, with all her neighbors, and assured the hegemony of the Continent: Spain a crumbling colossus; Austria, disengaged from Europe temporarily, facing East to meet the menace of the Turk; England paralyzed by internal disorders, by the power struggles between the leaders of Cromwell's army, the proponents of republican government and the proponents of the restoration of the Stuart monarchy.

Mazarin "conjured" Louis (the very verb he used, the same in French as in English) to break off with his inamorata, Marie, and to go with good grace, good will, an open mind and heart to greet his Spanish bride at the border: "Get control of yourself for the sake of your glory and your honor. . . . You are endowed with the qualities to become a great King; make up your mind whether you wish to become one."

Above all things, Louis XIV wished "to become a great King";

accordingly, he bade goodbye to Marie Mancini, at the window of her carriage, as she drove out of the Louvre courtyard into exile. ("Ah, Sire, you love me; you are King; you weep—and yet I am forced to leave you!" Jean Racine borrowed her great last line eleven years later for his tragedy *Bérénice*.)

No less a genius than the Spanish court painter Velázquez was commissioned by Philip IV to decorate the stage and to stage-manage the preliminary marital ceremonies in Madrid. The talented hand of Le Brun, France's premier artist and coordinator of the decorative arts, was surely visible in the design of sets and costumes for the final act of the marriage, on June 9, 1660, in Saint-Jean-de-Luz, and for the gala entry of Louis XIV and his new Queen into their capital city on August 26, the most lavish public spectacle of the century. "Such magnificence as is to be seen in no other country in the world," was the boast of the *Grande Mademoiselle*, the King's own first cousin, proud to take her place in that splendorous cavalcade along with the royal family.

The young Queen Marie Thérèse constituted the main attraction, in a specially designed open golden chariot, gowned in pearl-stitched cloth of gold and adorned with all the crown jewels of France. Nature had been less lavish with her adornments—Velázquez's flattering portraits notwithstanding. Save for the bloom of youth on her fair skin and her silky golden hair, save for the aura of glamour investing a royal personage, Marie Thérèse could not have elicited such an adjective as Mme de La Fayette's or Voltaire's "beautiful."

As for the King, however, his "male and heroic beauty arrested every eye" (not that Voltaire beheld him with his own eyes, but he had the description firsthand from eyewitnesses). Dazzling as the sun which glittered on his ruby-studded raiment and which was shortly to be adopted as his own personal emblem (his official sign and symbol), he deftly reined in his caracoling Spanish steed before a house on the rue François Miron, and doffed his red and white plumed hat with a flourish and grace such as no gentleman in his kingdom could equal in a salute to the occupants of the balcony of the Hôtel de Beauvais—an imposing residence recently bestowed upon Mme de Beauvais, the Queen Mother's attendant, in token of the King's appreciation of her signal and peculiar services at his hour of puberty.

Seated beside the Queen Mother at the tapestry-draped, flower-decked balcony rail was Cardinal Mazarin, architect of the peace and of the alliance between France and Spain; too weak and sick to ride in the triumphal procession; within six months, now, of his death.

Louis XIV, ready and eager to gather up all the reins of government from Mazarin's failing hands, was already to be seen as the apotheosis of supreme power, incarnation of absolute monarchy. So Mme de Motteville saw him, that day, from the same balcony, happily on hand to record his appearance: "Such a one as poets hymn and divinize!"

Another lady in that same balcony, though far to the rear in rank and seating arrangement, was Mme Scarron, indigent but beautiful and resourceful widow of the second-rate poet Paul Scarron, making a career of making herself useful and agreeable to all her powerful, highly placed relatives and acquaintances. The next day, in a letter addressed to a provincial correspondent, Mme Scarron described the magnificent cortège of the royal newlyweds: "I was all eyes for ten or twelve hours without interruption. . . . Nothing more beautiful could be imagined, and the Queen must have gone to bed, last night, well pleased with the husband she had chosen." (Mme Scarron, under another and more high-sounding name, that of Marquise de Maintenon, would eventually take her turn in the King's bed; the last but not the least in a long line of ladies vying for the honor.)

To say, as Mme Scarron did, that the Queen was "well pleased with the husband she had chosen" was an understatement. Marie Thérèse had "conceived a violent passion for the King," as all the court, including Mme de La Fayette, could plainly see: an inordinate, an indecorous amorousness, embarrassing to the King, and the very last thing to have been expected of a member of the royal family of Spain, all embalmed in protocol and ritual, all frozen stiff in their majesty.

The King, at first, during the days of the honeymoon, seemed well pleased himself: "In the best humor in the world," his cousin-german, the *Grande Mademoiselle*, remarked in her Memoirs. "He laughed and capered and sought out the Queen's company with such marks of tenderness and cordiality as pleased us all to see."

Had the Queen only spoken French! Had the King only spoken a more fluent Spanish! Marie Thérèse (easier to Frenchify her name than her person) would eventually learn to speak her husband's tongue, but never with style, never with elegance; her Spanish accent grating to French ears. Equally grating to French tastes was her stubborn display of morbid Spanish piety, encouraged by her Spanish confessor, whom the King probably resented more than he did her troupe of grotesque Spanish dwarfs. The Queen herself stood little taller than those buffoons of hers with pet names such as "Poor Lad," "My Boy," "Dear Heart." She was not misshapen like them, but she was squat, dumpy, without grace as without wit—all cardinal sins, like her accent, by French standards.

The Dauphin, the throne-heir of France, born to Marie Thérèse and Louis XIV in 1661, was the first of the six Children of France to be begotten by that pair, and the only one to survive beyond childhood.

Marie Thérèse mistook Louis's assiduities for tokens of uxoriousness; whereas it was, instead, in conscientious fulfillment of his dynastic duties that he came nightly to the marital bed.

When he began to stray, as he shortly would, it had to be remembered, in all fairness, that it was the monarch for whom a Queen had been selected, not the man who had chosen a mate.

If, during the first year of the marriage, the King did not stray, one reason was his absorption in affairs of state, "upon which he concentrated all his efforts so as thoroughly to familiarize himself therein."

Upon the death of Mazarin in early 1661, Louis resolved never to appoint another Prime Minister, but to reserve supreme authority unto himself and to head his council table. Like every successful executive, he had a talent for organization, for selecting and impressing the most capable men in his kingdom into his service. "The exercise of royal duties" (a king's job, to translate his own word, *métier de roi*, into the vernacular) "is great and noble and delicious" (his very word, *délicieux*) ". . . no other calling in the world so gratifying!" he exulted in his Memoirs. "To this occupation," Mme de La Fayette declared, "he devoted the major portion of his time; the rest he shared with his wife, the Queen."

Until mid-year of 1661, that is; until Mme de La Fayette's pet Princess, Henrietta of England, took center stage after her marriage in March to the King's brother, Philippe, Duc d'Orléans. Henrietta, daughter of that unfortunate Stuart King Charles I, who had lost throne and head in Cromwell's *coup d'état* in 1649, had fled with her mother (a daughter of the French King Henri IV) to the court of France, and grown up under the young Louis XIV's eye, spurned by him as a possible bride (no "little girls" for him, thank you! until much later in his life), dismissed by him as too young and skinny: "A bag of bones from the Holy Innocents Cemetery!" he had jeered at news of his brother's engagement to this little cousin. When he eventually looked up at his brother's bride, he discovered that she had suddenly blossomed into delicious womanhood, an ethereal, enchanting, adorable creature—utterly wasted on her pederast of a husband.

Her husband, known to the court by the grandly simple title of "*Monsieur*," was a handsome—or, rather, a pretty—youth. The cultivation of his homosexual tendencies had been the deliberate handiwork of his mother: she had encouraged his "playing lady, in skirts, with pierced ears, diamonds and beauty spots," with perverts as playmates (as one such, the Abbé de Choisy, that tonsured transvestite, recounted in his Memoirs). This was a pattern which the Duke, like the Abbé, would find "difficult to break away from." No one knew better than the Queen Mother the threat posed to the throne in the person of the monarch's younger brother: she had shuddered through conspiracy after conspiracy concocted by Gaston d'Orléans against his brother (her husband) Louis XIII. Now she purposely vitiated the will and character of her younger son in order to protect the crown of the elder, Louis XIV.

Monsieur managed, with the aid of sacred medals clanking on his private parts, to rise to the occasion and to sire six children by his two wives. Three were by Henrietta, his first *Madame*, who was "born with all the graces and with an infinite power to please." To please all, that is, save her husband. But then, as her friend Mme de La Fayette well knew, "The miracle of inflaming the heart of that Prince was beyond the power of any woman in this world!"

Frail as she was, and proud and intelligent and cultivated, she was a reckless flirt, an intrepid coquette, a gentle Princess with a wild streak. She lived dangerously when she antagonized *Monsieur* and his vicious male favorites, and may have paid for it with her young life. Fey as she was, did she have a premonition of impending tragedy—and a yearning for immortality—when she asked her lady in waiting, the Comtesse de La Fayette: "Don't you think that the story of my life would make interesting reading? You write well. You do the writing, and I will furnish you with material for good memoirs."*

In the radiant spring of 1661, according to Mme de La Fayette's *History of Henrietta of England, Monsieur* and *Madame* joined the King and the two Queens and the nomadic court at the woodland Château of Fontainebleau, "*Madame* bringing joy and pleasure in her train. The King, seeing her close up, realized what a mistake he had made in not recognizing her earlier as the loveliest person in the world. He developed a strong attachment for her and showed her a pronounced complaisance. . . . All the parties, all the divertissements centered round her; they were all planned in her honor; and it seemed that the King's sole pleasure consisted in the pleasure afforded her. . . . It was midsummer and, every day, *Madame* went bathing . . ." (in the Seine, decorously swathed in voluminous linen shifts). "She set out by coach because of the

* Mme de La Fayette's *Princesse de Clèves* (1678) was the prototype of the French psychological novel, still a valid one; the only novel of that golden age of French literature to survive and hold interest in this age.

heat, but returned on horseback, followed by all the ladies of her court" (Mme de La Fayette among them), "dashingly costumed, with a thousand plumes fluttering on their hats, and accompanied by the King and all his youthful band of courtiers. After supper all set out again in light open carriages for a promenade about the canal, lasting until all hours of the night, and to the accompaniment of violins" (always the violins, the King's twenty-four violinists accompanying him everywhere, on campaign as on promenade, playing nightly at supper in his antechamber until the last days of his last illness—mood music for dying as for romancing).

"The King's attachment to *Madame* soon began to stir and to occasion a variety of interpretations." Mme de La Fayette's interpretation is subtly stated: "I believe that she [*Madame*] pleased the King in a way other than as a sister-in-law. I believe, furthermore, that whereas she thought he pleased her only as a brother-in-law, he pleased her in, perhaps, another way. But, after all, since they were both infinitely attractive individuals and both born with a disposition to gallantry, and since they were thrown together daily in the midst of pleasuring and entertainments, it appeared to everyone that they were in that state of intense emotional involvement which is the forerunner of a grand passion. . . . The King and *Madame*, however—without seeking to explain, one to the other, the state of his or her affections—continued to conduct themselves in such a manner as to leave no doubt in anyone's mind that there was far more between them than mere friendship."

No doubt in the minds of the King's mother, his wife, and his brother; all of them seethed with indignation. The King bridled at constraint; if his wife or mother sulked, she would be denied the light of his countenance. The young Queen would apply herself to the lesson—the first in a twenty-two-year course—in submission and resignation to a willful and lustful King.

III

La Vallière

IN MIDSUMMER, in June or July of 1661, the King and *Madame* applied themselves to devising a plot designed to dupe the royal family into believing that it was not *Madame* but one of her fair maids of honor who drew the King so often to *Madame*'s circle.

The choice, probably *Madame*'s—an accomplished *intrigante* —fell upon Louise de La Vallière, "Not a flawless beauty . . . but an infinitely appealing one," according to the Abbé de Choisy, who could boast exalted playmates, Louise as well as *Monsieur*.* "She had an exquisite complexion, blond hair, blue eyes, a sweet smile . . . an expression at once tender and modest . . ."

"Sweet" was evidently the word for her, Madame de La Fayette using it, too, though in a faintly deprecatory tone: "Very sweet, very pretty, very naïve," as if to say that Louise had been chosen for the very reason that she was innocuous, bland, even insipid in comparison to a sprightly, spirited, scintillating *Madame*; and humble in origin in comparison to a Princess of the Stuart-Bourbon line (the de La Baume Le Blanc de La Vallières, of minor provincial nobility, owing their modest place at court to the grace and favor of the Orléans family).

*The Abbé de Choisy claimed to have played at innocent "games of Colin-Maillard and Cligne-Musette" with Louise at the Château de Blois; and to have "played bare-assed on secret stairways" of the Louvre with the Duc d'Orléans.

But in comparison to all the egotistical, importunate, imperious personages about him, Louise de La Vallière's self-effacing nature and her mild, tender, gentle soul must have touched the King like a balm. And before that summer of 1661 was out, the King had discovered that the shy La Vallière had charms of her own, and had succumbed to them—although *Madame* must be prevented, at all costs, from making this discovery. Were she to realize that her maid of honor was truly the object of His Majesty's attentions—rather than a blind for his attentions to *Madame*—then *Madame* could no longer be expected to provide opportunity for the lovers' encounters.

Instead, *Madame*—tripped up in her own toils—had now to be deceived along with the two Queens, along with Louis XIV's first affinity, Olympe Mancini, Comtesse de Soissons, ever hopeful of recapturing the King's fancy. Thus "the King had to proceed covertly, warily" to his wooing of the maid of honor, as Mme de La Fayette saw it: "He did not approach La Vallière in *Madame's* apartments or during the daytime promenades; but during the evening promenades, he would step out of *Madame's* carriage to go to La Vallière's, the door of which had been left open; and there, in the darkness, to talk with her, undisturbed."

The official horoscope of Louis XIV, cast by court astrologer Morin, must have shown the aspect of the planets as benign and the stars beaming propitiously at this Prince's nativity. Fortune indulged Louis XIV in even the matter of his first adult love affair, which was idyllic; in even the person of his first officially acknowledged mistress, who loved him—as few Kings could claim to be loved—for himself alone; who "would have loved him as much had he been a simple squire." She had been heard by Bussy to wish that her lover's "rank had been less exalted!" "He would have been a happy man had only all his mistresses been like Mme de La Vallière!," in the words of the Duc de Saint-Simon, who had few kind words for anyone.

"Lovable, young, gallant, magnificent," "A young Apollo!," a young Mars!—handsome as a Greek god Louis XIV may have been, if the words of the Abbé de Choisy, of diarist John Evelyn, and the sculpture of Antoine Coysevox are to be believed—even so, the young monarch was lucky in love in this first *grande passion* of his early manhood.

Modest "Little violet" that she was, in Mme de Sévigné's metaphor, "shrinking into the grass to hide," Louise de La Vallière shrank from fortune, honors, prominence—all the perquisites of a royal Favorite; the last ("Never another in her mold") to consent to a furtive liaison: "It was an affair to be spoken of only in whispers, though known to one and all," the speaker being the King's cousin, the *Grande Mademoiselle*. La Vallière would be the last royal mistress to blush unseen, the last to suffer the indignities of a hole-and-corner love life, in hideaway rooms and borrowed beds, in isolated suites of the Tuileries or Palais Royal—"All the doors left conspicuously ajar, although one would no more have thought of entering than if they had been sealed shut and forged of bronze!" in Mme de La Fayette's reportage, and surely a constant humiliation to a shy and essentially virtuous young woman, even though her assignations were with the premier King of Christendom..

For the very reason that Louise was so humble, so long-suffering, she was allowed by Louis to suffer long years through—the taunts of her patroness, *Madame*, for example, who gibed that she permitted "the King's strumpet" to stay on in her household only as an accommodation to the King. Not until 1663, just in time for the birth of their first child, was Louise provided with appropriate quarters of her own, a small pavilion close by the gardens of the Palais Royal, in Paris, and an apartment in the new wing of the old château at Saint-Germain.

Guilt-ridden from the beginning by the enormity of her offense against God and Marie Thérèse, Louise de La Vallière was not cut out for the career of royal Favorite, who occupied a quasi-political position at the French court; inevitably an enemy or an ally of the courtiers in their solicitation of the King, from whom all blessings flowed. Refusing to solicit for others the favors she would not seek for herself, Louise became unpopular. She was too good to be true: Mme de La Fayette attributed Louise's incredible disinterest to "a lack of intelligence. . . . Her only thought to love and to be loved by the King!"

Motherhood would provide Louise with no joys, only torments: the four children she bore the King between 1663 and 1667, snatched from the surgeon-midwife by Colbert, the most powerful man in the Cabinet, but not too proud to double as guardian of the royal bastards; her bed of labor, once, in an antechamber of *Madame*'s, the labor accomplished during the hour of Mass, the new mother on her feet and in full court regalia in time for the night's festivities. Of the stuff of which martyrs—not mistresses—are made, La Vallière made, and allowed the King to make, the worst rather than the best of her lot.

He was, to be sure, still young and inexperienced; still testing out the limits of limitless authority; just beginning to get the feel of absolute power, just beginning to stand up against his mother's moral preachments: "I can no longer resist the violence . . . of my passions," he admitted to her, "nor do I even feel the desire to do so."

He would not resist his passion for La Vallière, not even if it brought him and his mother to an estrangement. When Anne of Austria threatened to retire to a convent as a sign of her displeasure, he made little effort to dissuade her. At which point, the Queen Mother deemed it expedient to relent in her opposition, to admit La Vallière to her presence, even to a seat at her gaming table.

The young Queen, Marie Thérèse, always one step behind in the course of the King's love affairs, came slowly to the realization that it was no longer *Madame* of whom she had cause to be jealous, but "*Esta doncella*" (speaking still in Spanish), "that young girl with the diamond earrings" (pointing out La Vallière to Mme de Motteville) "is the one the King's in love with." It was ironic that Marie Thérèse's most bitter resentment should have been vented on La Vallière, the most considerate and retiring of her husband's Favorites; perhaps it was because Louise was the first. The time would come when the Queen would have acquired a standard of comparison, and wish her back. Meanwhile, she made the King a terrible scene. He cut off her reproaches with the word that so long as he came nightly to her apartments, she had no right to question the hour. Sometime during the early 1660's he was heard, by Mme de Motteville, to promise his wife "to reform and become a model husband by the time he reached the age of thirty," which seemed an eternity away to a man in his early twenties.

In his early twenties, and well beyond, Louis XIV evidenced a capacity for work as prodigious as his capacity for play—loving, hunting, dancing, gaming, fencing, jousting; in just about that order of preference, and with style and aptitude in all—and thus was justified in feeling that affairs of state never suffered neglect because of his love affairs or his love of sport.

In 1661, he and Colbert were already poised for the mighty leap forward they would make with France in mid-seventeenth century, out of medieval into modern times. The feat was to transform a complex of heterogeneous, factious, unruly feudal states into a single, orderly, centralized modern nation. Colbert, an efficiency expert and modern political economist, effected a reorganization of the national fiscal and administrative systems—"To put France in a position to be able to finance Louis XIV's glory," as he boasted. Industry and public works received their first great impetus.

Not only the economy but the arts and crafts were to come under government regulation, beginning with a great rash of national academies (an Academy of Science, of Music, of the Dance, of Painting, and of Architecture), all modeled upon Richelieu's prestigious, literarily oriented Académie Française. Artists were enlisted, subsidized, commissioned, impressed into the service of Louis the Great, a title officially bestowed by the Council of Paris in 1678.*

It was another stroke of luck for Louis XIV that his patronage reaped (it could not sow) so rich and brilliant a harvest of artistic achievement in every field: none like it since the Italian Renais-

---

* The title was commemorated by a gold medallion presented to the King by the newly founded Academy of Inscriptions and Medallions.

sance, none since the Augustan Age in Rome or the Periclean in Athens, with Louis's "The greatest age of the four," in Voltaire's chauvinistic estimate. "Fortune smiled on him," Voltaire proclaimed, for there was a rash of genius in seventeenth-century France, not only artists but generals, statesmen, and administrators of extraordinary talent.

Order assured within the borders of France, Louis XIV could look beyond them, especially to the north and east. With the great French feudatories transformed into courtiers, and cooling their high red heels in Louis's antechamber, he could turn his attention to an extension of the French hegemony across the Continent. If Louis, like Napoleon, was frankly aggressive, forthrightly imperialistic (the word not yet one of opprobrium in their day), the characteristic appeared to be a national rather than a personal one. Between the two of them, France was confirmed in her addiction to glory.

Where Colbert wondrously modernized the navy, Minister of Defense Louvois did as much with the army. The French army's arsenal of new weapons (including flintlock and bayonet) and its new techniques of warfare (including startling innovations in siege tactics and trench warfare) burst as stunningly upon Europe in the seventeenth century as would Nazi Germany's mechanized units, its Panzer divisions, its *Blitzkrieg*, in the twentieth.

From the top of the world where he stood, Louis XIV sent his bravadoes thundering around it. Once-proud Spain dispatched an Ambassador Extraordinary to the Louvre to ask the Sun King's pardon for an affront committed by the Spanish Ambassador against the French one in London. A public apology borne to His Majesty at Fontainebleau by a papal envoy from His Holiness, in 1664, was deemed insufficient expiation for a discourtesy to a French Ambassador at the Vatican. Louis issued an ultimatum to his cousin Charles II, only recently restored to the shaky English throne: the French fleet would henceforward no longer acknowledge English naval supremacy by being the first to dip its flag in salute. So be it: Charles II, still in the subsidy of his cousin Louis, would order the English ships to give a wide berth to the French to avoid a confrontation.

Louis XIV's glory as great abroad as at home, the Sun King was the name for him, as he himself acknowledged: "Doubtless the most striking and finest symbol for a great monarch because of its singular radiance . . . because of the light which it provides for all the other planets which surround it like a kind of court . . . because it is a source of life and growth to all the universe. . . . The sun, then, shedding its beneficent rays upon the earth, was the emblem I was persuaded to adopt as my own, with NEC PLURIBUS IMPAR [Not Unequal to Many] as my motto; one not without effect upon my ambition—the implication being that since I was sufficient of myself to so many undertakings in my own kingdom, I was doubtless capable of ruling over other empires. . . ."

The seat of empire would be Versailles.

It has been suggested that La Vallière was the inspiration for that château. Certainly, His Majesty escaped from the confines of court and family life at the Louvre and Saint-Germain into the forests and gardens of Versailles for hunting and other bucolic delights with his young love and young, gay, gallant companions. But it is more likely that the resolve to erect a palace at Versailles, "One befitting my grandeur," as he said—a temple dedicated to the cult of monarchy—had already taken form in his mind: the resolve to rival the mighty builders of the ancient world.

The splendor and grandeur of Versailles would provide the scene for an epic rather than an idyll. Louise de La Vallière was not cut out to play the heroine of an epic.

Of all the three hundred ladies at Louis's court, there was one who clearly was: the most glorious and glamorous of all the royal entourage, just making her debut in the galleries of the Louvre and the Palais Royal, just flashing her radiant presence there, a striking and effulgent beauty; highborn and haughty—Athénaïs, Marquise de Montespan, moving superbly to her post as lady in waiting to the Queen, creating a ripple of admiration in her wake, a wave of desire and covetousness.

"One of the most beautiful people in the world!" according to the Comte de Bussy, ogling her like all the other randy courtiers. "Her beauty a magnet to the eyes and a stimulus to the lusts of all the gallants of the court"—an opulent and voluptuous beauty, to arouse the erotic imagination of the court, the capital, the Continent; resplendent sex symbol of the Splendid Century.

IV

Athénaïs

S HE WAS HIGHBORN, of stock as ancient and illustrious as any
in France—not excepting the Bourbons, as her sister, the
Marquise de Thianges, made so bold as to tell the King to his
face. The Mortemart-Rochechouarts, as warriors, leaders, and
suzerains of the old French provinces of Poitou, Saintonge, and
Limousin, could trace their lineage back to the Dukes of Aqui-
taine, back into the eleventh and twelfth centuries and beyond,
back into what the official genealogists referred to as "The Mists
of Time." ANTE MARE, ONDAE was the wording on their coat of
arms: BEFORE THE SEA, THE WAVES ("Before the sea was formed,
the Rochechouarts bore the waves . . ." "Older than the sea," or
some such ultimate expression of arrogance will do by way of
translation).

Françoise de Rochechouart, the ultimate flowering of that
ancient family tree, was baptized on October 5, 1640. Willful and
fanciful, she would adopt the classical name of Athénaïs later. Her
birth had taken place that year in the Château de Lussac, the
favorite among her father's several domains in west-central France.

Half fortress, half country seat in 1640, only the three massive
stone piers which once supported the drawbridge still remain standing today;* although even in Athènaïs' day, the fortifications were

* Scarcely "worth a detour," according to the Guide Michelin of 1968,
it is listed as Lussac-les-Châteaux, 347 kilometers from Paris, 36 from
Poitou.

already crumbling into desuetude (the reduction of the feudal strongholds had been an integral part of Richelieu's nationalization policy). The only gunfire came from the noble huntsmen, in the nearby forest, in pursuit of wild boar and stag. The portcullis rusted; water lilies bloomed, swans floated serenely on the waters of the moat; the Middle Ages were giving way to the modern, the *château-fort* to the château. The pond no longer served as a first line of defense; unruffled by any martial air, it was stocked with carp, and pleasure barks crossed from the pontlevis to the oratory on the other shore where Athénaïs' devout mother escorted her and her three sisters regularly to prayer, during those few months of the year she spent with the girls in the provinces.

Athénaïs' father was the Marquis de Lussac, Seigneur de Vivonne, Duc de Mortemart, Prince de Tonnay-Charente, First Gentleman of the King's bedchamber, Chevalier of the Order of the Holy Ghost, a councilor of state, an important figure in the court of Louis XIII; his wife a lady in waiting to the Queen, Anne of Austria. The Rochechouarts' only son, Louis, eldest of the five children, accompanied his parents to court as early as 1664; at the age of eight he had been named a *menin*, one of six little gentlemen in waiting to the little King, Louis XIV, aged six, who had succeeded to the throne at the death of his father the year before.

The way of life of the Rochechouarts, like the rest of the French nobility, was in a state of transition. As was the French court: under bluff, roistering Henri IV, it had been a bawdy barracks room; under gruff, melancholy Louis XIII, a crude military camp; under Louis XIV, it would be transformed into the fabled, resplendent, elegant, stately, ceremonious court of Versailles.

As part of the process, the fierce French feudal magnates were being transformed into not only docile but polished courtiers, a cultivated elite. Louis XIV would finish the work of nationalization and unification begun by Richelieu and Mazarin: under the new economic and social pressures brought to bear in the Splendid Century, the overlords would be compelled to abandon their basic feudal role as defenders and administrators of their territories— their *raison d'être*, their sole reason for privileged existence—to follow the King and to pay him court, first at the Louvre and Saint-Germain, eventually at Versailles.

The Rochechouart girls were left behind at Lussac; little is known of Athénaïs' childhood beyond the fact that she spent it there with her sisters. In her early teens she was sent, like them, to school at the Convent of Sainte-Marie at Saintes, the capital of Saintonge province, not far from the Bay of Biscay.

There she was designated Mlle de Tonnay-Charente, to distinguish her from her sisters (enough domains in the family, fortunately, to provide each of the four with a different title). There, too, it may have been that she changed her commonplace baptismal name of Françoise to the uncommon, highflown Attic one of Athénaïs, for this was just about the time that classic Greek and Roman names became the rage in France—a vogue for Athénaïses, Sapphos, Clélias, and Lavinias as the result of the publication (1649–53) of Madeleine de Scudéry's bestselling romance, *Le Grand Cyrus*.

Cyrus and *Clélia* and the dozens of subsequent volumes flowing from Mlle de Scudéry's extravagantly romantic pen would probably have been found by Athénaïs in the library of her father, a man with a catholic literary taste which he would pass on to all his children. It is unlikely that any such taste would have been acquired by his daughters at a provincial convent in the 1650's.

The curriculum at such institutions was notoriously skimpy, few nuns being qualified to instruct in anything beyond the Catechism. A young lady of quality would be taught how to scrawl a letter of condolence or of compliment; how to sew a fine seam; how to raise her voice in song, preferably religious; how to make a graceful entry to and exit from a salon; how to distinguish in the address of a Princess of the Blood or a Duchess, as compared to that of a mere Marquise or Countess. She might also receive some hints on the responsibilities of a châtelaine: notes on seigneurial rights and provincial customs, on household and estate management. But that was the extent of it.

The "grand manner," as it was referred to then, the Rochechouart sisters would have drunk in with their mother's milk—

grande dame that she was, and accomplished member of the Queen Mother's retinue (Anne of Austria herself constituting an exception among the great ladies of her time in that she knew how to read and write, and could give her ladies lessons on the guitar).

Mlle de Scudéry's novels—didactic, prolix, absurd, unreadable—constitute a curiosity rather than a contribution to French literature, but her exhortations did make an impact on the principles of female education, which she deplored: "Such gross ignorance as is displayed by so many ladies of quality is a dishonor to our sex! Why women should want to speak well but write poorly I cannot understand. . . . Their orthography is positively bizarre. . . . They lose all their wit the moment they pick up a pen; they make the most glaring errors in the written word, and yet mercilessly make mock of any poor stranger who misuses or mispronounces one in speaking. . . ."

She could have been talking about Athénaïs de Tonnay-Charente, undoubtedly the most celebrated and most scintillating conversationalist of her age—an age when conversation was regarded as one of the lively arts and reached its ultimate refinement—but who was totally undistinguished as a correspondent, and whose spelling was totally unorthodox (as, for that matter, was the King's).

"Seriously speaking," Mlle de Scudéry went on, "nothing is more bizarre than the educational system for females. . . . They are taught nothing to fortify their virtue or to occupy their mind. . . . Indeed, the only reproaches made them in their youth concern their not being cleanly enough about their persons, not showing style enough in their dress, not devoting themselves assiduously enough to their singing or dancing lessons. . . ."

The dancing master had had conspicuous success with Mlle de Tonnay-Charente, as Athénaïs would be known at court. She made her debut there, in 1662, in a nine-scene ballet programmed as *Hercules in Love*, a lavish production for which *Madame*, the Duchesse d'Orléans, had commissioned the poet Benserade to write the libretto, and in which the King danced two leading roles, that of Apollo, God of the Sun, and that of Mars, God of War (ballet in that century being considered a manly, even a kingly exercise; and one much favored by Louis XIV, as it had been by his father).

Athénaïs de Tonnay-Charente had been summoned to Paris in 1661 and named, by her mother's patroness, Queen Anne of Austria, as a maid of honor to *Madame*, recently wed to *Monsieur*, the Duc d'Orléans.

At court, Athénaïs found not only her parents but her *bon vivant* of a brother Louis, Duc de Vivonne, childhood playmate of the King's and now his boon companion, a member of that gallant and frivolous inner royal circle, despite the fact that he was prone to things intellectual.

There was a reunion, too, for Athénaïs and her sister Gabrielle, eldest of the girls, a bride at the age of seventeen and now the Marquise de Thianges, a great friend and favorite of the King's brother, *Monsieur*; less because of her feminine charms, to which *Monsieur* was impervious, than because of her sparkling, bubbling, coruscating wit and humor; her spicy, racy, risqué repartee. She enlivened all his parties, tossing off *bons mots* so prodigally that he could later pass off some as his own. The only thing to be expected from Gabrielle was the unexpected. She was an original, like all her family. If Athénaïs was "one of those people who light up the places where they appear," Gabrielle was one of those who spark any company they join. She was a great beauty, as were all the Rochechouart girls: "Beautiful as an angel!" the poet La Fontaine rhapsodized, rhyming "Thianges" with "*ange.*"

Athénaïs' sovereign beauty was remarked, although with some reservations, by Mme de La Fayette, a fellow member of *Madame*'s retinue: "A consummate beauty and yet, somehow, for some reason, not entirely appealing" (the reason, probably, the hauteur, the arrogance of Athénaïs' expression, that challenging glance and imperious air of hers).

There are fewer reservations in the praises of her beauty as sung by Primi Visconti (the Comte de Saint-Mayol), fascinating Italian mystagogue and adventurer, who made note of Athénaïs in his Memoirs: "She was of medium height and well proportioned.

. . . Her hair was blond,* and her eyes were azure blue. Her nose aquiline but exquisitely formed, her mouth small and vermilion red; her teeth exceedingly beautiful—in sum, her face was sheer perfection!"

If the King was too deeply engrossed in his love for Louise de La Vallière to focus on Athénaïs' glowing beauty, she had beheld him in all his glory from the day of her arrival at court, had gazed straight up into his handsome face the day of her presentation, from the depth of the three prescribed obeisances she had gracefully executed before him. He had been the first and foremost object of her attention, as he was of all the thousand or more members of his court.† He was the Sun King, and like the sun, the center of his universe; a sight so dazzling that the courtiers had to shade their eyes before his splendor.

He was, in the early 1660's, when Athénaïs first raised her eyes to him, an exceedingly attractive man, head and shoulders above all other men, as can be seen in Bernini's magnificent, spirited marble bust of him, modeled from life.

Louis XIV was in his early twenties when Athénaïs joined the court: a monarch so youthful, so ardent, and so agile as to venture out on the rooftops of Saint-Germain, to clamber about the chimneys, along the gutters, and into the window of one of the Queen's giddiest maids of honor, Mlle de La Motte-Houdancourt, who had been coached by the Comtesse de Soissons in the role of rival to La Vallière. (When news of the King's escapade reached the ears of *Madame*'s maids of honor—Athénaïs among them—they only wished that it had been their preserve which His Most Christian Majesty of France had chosen to go poaching!) The Duchesse de Navailles, Supervisor of the Queen's Maids and jealous of their "honor," ordered the windows barred to preclude further royal

---

* Whether she was a natural blonde or whether her hair was dyed was as difficult to determine then as now; dyes were in general use, and there was a vogue for blondes—the King's preference for blondes an established fact.

† The court of France was growing: numbering only some few hundreds in the days of Louis XIII, it would attain a maximum of several thousand by 1682.

prowling. "She came in for a great deal of chaffing and banter from the King," according to the *Grande Mademoiselle*, but it developed that His Majesty was less amused than had, at first, appeared to be the case; not long thereafter, he dismissed the stern Duchess from her palace post, relegating her and her husband, the Maréchal de Navailles, to the limbo of their great estates and châteaux; a fate, in those days, as dread as death.

A fate worse than death it seemed to the Comtesse de Soissons, to be parted from her lover and sent with her husband to the province of Champagne of which he was the governor—into exile for her role as ringleader in a scheme designed to exacerbate the Queen's relations with La Vallière. (The wicked Comtesse de Soissons might not have been allowed to return so soon to court had her connection with characters of the Paris underworld come to the King's knowledge in the early 1660's instead of later in the decade.)

The court was a labyrinth of intrigue to which a clever Athénaïs soon discovered all the clues: the principal *intrigantes* were the Comtesse de Soissons and *Madame*, both eternally conniving to recover former favor—their day as King's Favorite over, their only hope was to select the King's next Favorite for him and to use her as a pawn. To counter such strategems, the Queen and the Queen Mother offered feeble opposition, both jealous and suspicious of every attractive woman to enter His Majesty's vicinity.

The court, however, teemed with attractive women, and "Every woman in the realm was born with the ambition to become the King's mistress!" (as Athénaïs would have been the first to recognize, although the quotation is Visconti's). Mademoiselle de Sévigné would have been no exception to Visconti's rule. Among a dozen others—she caused a brief flurry of excitement at the court and the King's eye was momentarily attracted by her beauty, according to Comte de Bussy, her overly optimistic cousin.*

* Comte de Bussy had hoped to see his cousin installed as Favorite, but nothing came of it; Mlle de Sévigné finally married the Comte de Grignan and went with him to Provence, where he had been appointed governor by the King.

Bussy, with a tinge of sour grapes in his ink, penned a malicious comment on Athénaïs: "She had designs on the King's heart, and started laying her plans from the day she came to court."

If so, she must have come to the conclusion, in 1663, that her chances were not bright, the auspices not favorable. The King broke away for an occasional dalliance with a Mlle de Sévigné or a Mlle de La Motte-Houdancourt, but he invariably turned back to resume his idyll with La Vallière. Her position as Favorite had never seemed more solidly established.

Or so it must have seemed to Athénaïs de Tonnay-Charente when, at the relatively advanced age of twenty-three, she allowed herself to be swept off her feet by a handsome, swarthy, swaggering, swashbuckling Gascon with a moldering château high in the Pyrenees and a lineage equally lofty.

V

The Marquis de Montespan

Athénaïs' first, true love (Mme de La Fayette insists) came
to a tragic ending: "Mlle de Tonnay-Charente, who loved
the Marquis de Noirmoutier and who ardently hoped to marry
him,"* must have suffered shock and heartbreak at the news
that he had been involved with seven other young hotbloods in
a duel in 1662, in defiance of the royal edict against dueling—
so long a law unto themselves, the French noblemen would not
readily submit to the law of the King. One of the combatants
run through, the rest made a dash for the border. Athénaïs' fiancé,
wounded, crossed the Pyrenees and took up service with the
King of Portugal. She must have given up hope of his return
when the Parlement of Paris condemned all seven survivors, *in
absentia*, to death on the headsman's block.

The sole fatal casualty of that eight-blade fracas had been the
Marquis d'Antin. It was his younger brother, Louis Henri de
Pardaillan de Gondrin, Marquis de Montespan, to whom Athénaïs
de Tonnay-Charente was wed, one year later.

She was wed on January 28, 1663—between ballets: on January 20, the bride-to-be had danced a leading role in the *Ballet des
Arts*; on February 24, she danced again in another of those lavish

* The Marquis de Noirmoutier was a member of the de La Trémoille
family, renowned in the annals of France and an eminently suitable match
for a Rochechouart.

and popular court theatricals which served as perfect showcase for her grace and glamour.

It must have been a love match since the groom could offer the bride neither fortune nor prestige, for the Rochechouarts-Mortemarts were of themselves so prestigious that only an alliance with a Prince of the Blood or a sovereign could be considered to do them honor. The Montespans were an ancient and noble line of Guyenne and Gascony* but, having chosen the wrong side—the antiroyalist Princes' Party—during the Wars of the Fronde, they had no standing at court, no share in the golden shower of largesse that emanated from the throne. They could count numerous domains and châteaux throughout the border provinces, but they were typical of the seventeenth-century French nobility in that the revenues from those lands—the sale of produce, and feudal dues such as tithes, tolls, imposts, quit rent—were constantly diminishing, and could no longer suffice to maintain their ruinously extravagant way of life. If this extravagance seemed purposely encouraged by the example of magnificence set by the King, so it was. It was his policy to detach the *noblesse* from the land, to attract it to his court, to foster total dependence on his bounty as on his central authority.

The terms of the marriage contract reveal the lack of ready money on both sword and distaff side. Little of the bride's dowry was paid in cash; the groom's family put up no cash whatsoever, but did promise to pay all his outstanding debts.

New ones were incurred all too soon: the history of the early years of the marriage is to be found at the moneylender's, in a string of promissory notes and mortgages bearing the young Montespans' signatures. As early as August 21 of 1663, within seven months of their wedding, the Marquis and Marquise had signed a note for 7,750 livres, "For the purpose of outfitting the aforesaid seigneur Marquis de Montespan to follow the King to

* The village of Montespan is near Saint-Gaudens, close to the Spanish border in the Haute-Garonne. The family name was originally Mont-Espagne, spelled Mont-Espaign, corrupted eventually into Montespan. They claimed relation with the ancient noble houses of Comminges and Foix, who had supplied wives to the Princes of Béarn, from whom the Kings of Navarre traced their descent.

Lorraine. . . ." By the end of August, the Marquis's borrowings had risen to a total of 13,000 livres. The trail of the newlyweds through the years 1663–6 is blazed by a flutter of unpaid tradesmen's bills for lamés and lances, silver and saddles, *panniers* and *panaches*. By 1665, suits had been instituted and judgments rendered against the pair. By 1666, the Marquise's "diamond-studded chandelier earrings" were pledged as collateral for another substantial loan, at exorbitant rates of interest.

Early in 1664—or it may have been late 1663; the dates and facts are hazy—a child had been born to the Montespans: a girl, who was considered no blessing, in that day and time, to a noble family in straitened circumstances. (Where the marriage dowry was too great a drain on the family fortunes, the only alternative for a young lady of quality was to take the veil—to the glory of God and the easement of the family budget. The next to youngest of Mme de Montespan's three sisters had disappeared at an early age into the Convent of the Sisters of Sainte-Marie at Chaillot, and Mme de Sévigné's "plump, adorable . . . doll" of a granddaughter vanished from the family hearth and heart, at the tender age of five, into the Convent of Sainte-Marie at Aix-en-Provence.)

The birth of a male child to the Montespans in 1665—the Marquis, future Duke, d'Antin—should have been cause for rejoicing, although the marriage seemed already foundering on the rocks of bankruptcy, incompatability, and lengthy separations. The Marquis was off for months at a time on campaign; a rakehell, a roisterer, a wastrel; military prowess apparently his sole virtue; courage, his sole noble characteristic (the lack of which constituted the sole unforgivable sin in the eyes of the nobility).

For the Marquise, the center of her universe was the court, and she may already have recognized that her husband was too unstable, too boorish, and too brawling to make a success of a career there. Clearly, he lacked the sustained drive, the ambition, the finesse, and the acumen to attain to the heights she had in view.

By 1665, she had tried her skill at the court game of intrigue, stepping into the feud between the Duc and Duchesse d'Orléans, *Monsieur* and *Madame*, on the side of the former, in a machination too complex and too petty to merit analysis. "Mme de Montespan . . . perpetrated the blackest treachery imaginable against *Madame*," the Comtesse de La Fayette complained, ". . . and was thenceforward excluded from *Madame*'s presence. . . ." To the distress of *Monsieur*, whose favorite she had become, along with her sister, the Marquise de Thianges: "No question of a flirtation between them" (if we accept Madame de La Fayette's word for it); "but rather they were participants in a libertine confidence." *Monsieur* made such concessions as were necessary to secure Athénaïs' "readmission to his wife's pleasure parties . . . although she was never restored to *Madame*'s good graces. . . ."

She could afford to forego them, however, when she was named by the King, in 1665, along with two Duchesses and two Princesses, as one of the ladies in waiting to Queen Marie Thérèse. Presumably influence had been brought to bear by *Monsieur*, the King's brother, and by Athénaïs' brother, the rotund, rosy-cheeked, and genial Duc de Vivonne, in high favor with the monarch. Or it may have been that Louis XIV acted on his own initiative, his interest aroused, his attention finally arrested by Athénaïs' flamboyant beauty and personality. She was not one to pass unnoticed: with her exquisite, mobile face and voluptuous body, her vivacity and mordant wit, her inimitable (unfortunately unrecorded and sometimes unprintable) line of conversation, she dominated every company, she charged the atmosphere.

Had she struck the young monarch as too flashy a personality, too much of an intellectual, too forceful, too vital, too vivid, too sure of herself and her myriad attractions? There are reports from firsthand observers in support of this theory; from Primi Visconti, first of all, who apparently read minds and lips as well as Tarot cards and horoscopes, and who reported that: "Beautiful as she was, and witty, quick at repartee and banter, she had not at first appealed to the King. He even went so far, one day, at table with *Monsieur* his brother, as to jest about her efforts to attract him. 'She tries hard,' he is supposed to have said, 'but I'm not interested.'"

Then, the second *Madame* (overly fond, like the first, of her brother-in-law the King) wrote the story as she heard it, years later, in a letter to one of her inquisitive German kinsmen: "The King couldn't stand Mme de Montespan, at first, and reproached *Monsieur* and the Queen for keeping her constantly in their company, although later on he fell madly in love with the lady."

The Abbé de Choisy, that inveterate and effeminate court gossip, is another who repeats this rumor in his Memoirs: "During the time the King was so passionately in love with Mlle de La Vallière, he appeared to be amused by Mme de Montespan's obvious coquetries in his direction. 'She would very much like to make me fall in love with her,' he said, laughing. And that was true. She was clearly laying siege to his heart."

Not too surprising, really, in view of her limitless ambition, their daily proximity, and his manifold attractions as a man as well as a monarch. "He was attractive as a man," Comte de Bussy makes the point: "A man born to conquer female hearts—even without his crown, without his scepter! . . . The brightest flame of his spirit and flesh, body and soul were reserved, it might be said . . . for the objects of his passions."

"Even had he been born a private individual," the testy Duc de Saint-Simon acknowledged, giving the royal devil his due,* "he would have been fated to wreak havoc in female hearts. Beyond any of his subjects, he was a man—especially in his youth—cut out for love."

It could not have been otherwise. The outcome was inevitable in the coming together of these two most superb specimens of their sex and species in their time. Once each had taken the measure of the other, each had recognized his or her own true mate in magnificence, and would have settled for no lesser.

. . .

---

* The Duc de Saint-Simon begrudged every word of praise he was forced to pay the monarch who, throughout the quarter century of their daily association, ill concealed his disdain for the acidulous, assiduous little courtier.

The Marquis de Montespan

In early 1665, after the birth of her second child, Louise de La Vallière may have looked wan and lackluster, but the King threw Comte de Bussy into the Bastille for poking fun in rhyme at her:*

> *How happy is King Louis's lot*
> *To kiss those amorous lips, that slot*
> *That goes from one ear to the other.*
> *Alleluia!*

The Marquise de Montespan is likewise credited with a poem lampooning La Vallière, although the attribution can no more be proven in her case than in Bussy's. Since she was known to have tried her hand at verse; known, too, for her wit and malice, it may be that she began to sharpen her pen on Louise, with these lines:

> *Walk with a limp; be gauche, fifteen,*
> *Be flat of chest and blank of brain;*
> *Your parents—God knows who!*
> *Then, like a raw girl of your sort,*
> *Bear bastards in the outer court,*
> *And what becomes of you?*
> *Why, by my faith, between the covers,*
> *You sleep beside the Prince of Lovers!*
> *La Vallière proves it true.*

If Mme de Montespan was actually the author of this cruel stanza, she was neither "embastilled" (there was actually a verb for

---

* "He forfeited the Splendid Century," Sainte-Beuve said of the Comte de Bussy-Rabutin, "for the sake of a few lines of paltry verse." The lampoon against La Vallière brought the King's wrath down upon his head, as did the publication also in 1665 of *The Amorous History of the Gauls* (*Histoire amoureuse des Gaules*), a scandalous chronicle which had nothing to do with ancient Gauls but with the lords and ladies of Louis's court, flimsily disguised under fictitious names. After thirteen months in the Bastille, Bussy was ordered to depart the court and the army to retire to his Burgundian estates. Carried away as he was by his own mordant wit and humor, one could wish that he had stood up to the King's displeasure with the same bravado by which he had incurred it, instead of whimpering through his lifelong exile, petitioning His Majesty's pardon to the end of his days, which came in 1693.

it, *embastiller*) nor exiled, as Comte de Bussy had been for his versifying. Instead, the guileless La Vallière, pregnant again in 1666, pressed invitations on her charming friend to visit and enliven the salon of the elegant little pavilion at Versailles in which the King had, by then, installed the Favorite.*

"Madame de Montespan's greatest charms" (as Visconti appraised them) "consisted of a grace, a wit, a talent for persiflage and pleasantry which so delighted La Vallière that she could not do without her and constantly extolled her to the King. Hearing so much about her and so much lavish praise, the King quite naturally developed a strong curiosity to know her better and, before long, came to prefer her [Mme de Montespan] to the former Favorite. La Vallière later complained about the treachery, but had only herself to blame for what happened."

By the spring of 1666, the Queen was pregnant, too; and she, too, needing "assistance to keep the King amused" (as the *Grande Mademoiselle* observed), turned to Mme de Montespan, her scintillating lady in waiting. The King's wife joined the King's mistress in conspiring to throw him into daily contact with the seductive Marquise.

There was talk at the court to the effect that if La Vallière's hold was weakening, it was the beautiful Princesse de Monaco who was most likely to succeed her in the King's affections. There was talk (overheard by the Abbé de Choisy, one ear always at the keyhole†) of an assignation arranged by the King in the Princess's apartment—only to be frustrated by her jealous and intrepid lover, the Duc de Lauzun, who removed the key left purposely in the

---

* The little pavilion on the rue de la Pompe in Versailles still stands today, full of a curious history. The onetime royal love nest served as a Revolutionary prison and was the scene, in 1792, of a bloody massacre of "*aristo*" prisoners.

† The account below is the Abbé de Choisy's. In the Duc de Saint-Simon's version, the assignation was to have taken place in the King's rendezvous rooms—a far more likely story; and it is the Princess who waits with Alexandre Bontemps, the King's valet, in a secret passage—the palace was a rabbit warren of secret passageways, secret staircases, secret doors—while the King, within his apartment, tries vainly to open the door which Lauzun has locked from the outside.

outside lock, and took it with him into the privy across the hall, where he hid to wait, and to watch the King furiously rattling the door he could not open.

Whatever truth there may have been to the rumors, the King granted a request from the Prince de Monaco for an audience; then presumably granted another: permission for the Princess to retire to her husband's principality, on the Mediterranean, in sanctuary from further advances by His Majesty.

The Marquis de La Fare, yet another courtier who considered his memoirs worthy of posterity, thought that it was at this very juncture that Mme de Montespan made her opening gambit:

"While the King was thinking about Mme de Monaco, Mme de Montespan had begun to think about him and was shrewd enough to do two things at the same time: first, she gave the Queen an extraordinary impression of her virtuousness by taking Communion in her company every week; secondly, she insinuated herself so successfully into the good graces of La Vallière that she was constantly to be seen in her company. By these means, she contrived to be constantly in the King's immediate entourage, and she exerted every effort to please him, in which she succeeded very well, being bountifully endowed with wit and charm, in contrast to La Vallière, who was sadly lacking in these qualities."

By November 1, 1666, the Duc d'Enghien (a Prince of the Condé family) could flash the first written report, by letter to the Queen of Poland, of a significant development in the King's love life: "He has apparently taken a fancy to her [Mme de Montespan] and, to tell the truth, she would well merit such an interest, for it is impossible to have more wit and beauty than she! Not that there is as yet, however, anything definite to point to . . ."

A second development, in that autumn of 1666, of significance to the rumormongers of the court, was the departure of the Marquis de Montespan for a six-month sojourn in his remote domains in Guyenne and Gascony, on the Spanish border,* leaving his Marquise at the court for the festive winter season, and to the

* The ancient provinces of Guyenne and Gascony lie within France's present-day Département des Hautes-Pyrénées.

attentions of the King. If the Duc d'Enghien had espied the signs of a burgeoning romance, could the Marquise's husband have missed the danger signals? Such a reliable reporter as the Duc de Saint-Simon insists this was not a case of the husband's being the last to know; that he knew because his wife, herself, had warned him: "The blame for the scandal must be laid on Mme de Montespan's husband rather than on her. She had warned him of her suspicion of the King's amorous inclinations, she had made it clear to her husband that she could no longer doubt the way things stood, and pointed out that a fête which the King was then arranging was intended as a compliment to her. She urged him, insisting as strongly as she could; she entreated him to take her away to his lands of Guyenne and to leave her there until such time as the King had forgotten her, and his fancy was elsewhere engaged. Nothing she said could influence Montespan. . . ."

Did she really mean it? "To take her away to his lands of Guyenne and to leave her there"! It taxes the imagination to think of that brightest ornament of the court in isolation in the grim and gloomy medieval stronghold of the Montespans at Bonnefont, on a craggy eyrie in the Pyrenees! It seems out of character for her to have pleaded to be removed from the danger of the King's advances which she has been unanimously described as encouraging. Unless she sought to absolve her conscience by shifting the responsibility for the momentous decision onto her husband? Unless it was a dodge of hers in that she knew him well enough to know that he would be rent and torn and overcome by the struggle between his necessitousness and his pride, between his greed and his honor.

The fête which the King was arranging in her honor was probably the *Ballet des Muses*, a Benserade-Molière triumph, the première at the Château de Saint-Germain on December 2, 1666. The Marquise de Montespan danced, in a shepherdess's costume, with the King in the dress of a shepherd. The lines of Benserade's libretto describing the Marquise's entrance are bold in their implication:

The Marquis de Montespan

She is prompt to flight
At the first danger signal.
Her conduct astonishingly discreet,
Though we have seen others equally wary
Overtaken by surprise!
The pinnacle of delight
Might already have been attained
Were it not for the Watchdog—Honor,
On guard over shepherdess and sheep.
If the name sounds impertinent,
What other can we give it?

If the "Watchdog—Honor" referred to the shepherdess's husband, was he not hundreds of leagues distant, drinking, gambling, debauching, hunting the fox and wolf and boar in their Pyrenean lairs?

The ballet was repeated at the Louvre on January 2, 1667, at which time the shepherdess was apparently still wary; at any rate, it was La Vallière beside whom the King took his seat after the performance.

Sometime that January, if not that night, His Majesty bestowed on Louise a final souvenir of his affections—their last child, to be born in the autumn. (Not that night, for the reason that the King was called away from the theater, still in costume, to attend the Queen's accouchement—another Child of France that would never reach maturity.)

The death of the Queen Mother, Anne of Austria, in early 1666, had pointed up La Vallière's deficiencies as a public figure, as an official mistress (*maîtresse en titre*, a word essential to the French vocabulary, since the position of "official mistress" was peculiar to the French scene). Louise simply could not rise to the occasion, could not assume her place as a prominent figure in the court hierarchy, as Louis XIV sought to have her do after his mother's death. Louis had evidenced a deep attachment, respect, and admiration for his imposingly regal and handsome mother, but he had chafed under her religious and moral strictures and, after her death, "he threw off all restraint," as his cousin, the *Grande Mademoiselle*, has pointed out. His mother's had been the last rein on his absolute power; Louis XIV would brook no further interference in either his passion for the flesh or that for glory; with no further check on ego or libido, his license and his bellicosity were to flourish.

VI

The New Favorite

THE FIRST EVIDENCE of Louis XIV's bellicosity was occasioned by the death of his father-in-law and uncle, King Philip IV of Spain, in late 1665. Philip's sole male heir and successor to the throne—the cretinous four-year-old Charles II—was not expected to survive; the Spanish Habsburg house doomed to expire with him.* Louis XIV would seize his wife's rightful share of the inheritance—first of all, the Spanish Netherlands—before the Austrian Habsburg Emperor Leopold should seize it in the name of his Empress, the younger half sister of the Queen of France.†

---

* If Maria Theresa was not bright, still Louis XIV could congratulate himself that she was sane—she and her half sister, Margarita Theresa, Empress of Austria, the last two sane members of the Spanish royal family after generations of inbreeding, of repeated royal intermarriage. The Bourbons, taking their last two Queens from that tainted Spanish stock—Louis XIII's Anne and Louis XIV's Marie Thérèse—were lucky to escape with only a scattering of eccentrics and dullards.

† By the terms of their marriage contract, Louis XIV and Marie Thérèse had specifically renounced all claims she might have on the Spanish succession, but because of the fact that the bride's dowry—specifically promised in that same contract—had never been paid by Spain, Louis XIV based his wife's claim to those northern borderlands on the ancient and hazy *Ius Devolutionis*, Law of Devolution or Transmission, whereby the children of a first marriage (as was Marie Thérèse) inherited in preference to those of a second marriage (as was the Austrian Empress).

The War of the Spanish Devolution was launched without warning in 1667. Feats of arms constituted the traditional proof of valor for a young and glory-minded king: this one saw the wars "as a vast field where great occasions might arise for distinguishing myself." Above all, the imperialistic instinct was asserting itself in the young monarch. If Henri IV, founder of the Bourbon line, had begun the work of welding together the nation out of feudal bits and pieces, duchies and principalities and counties; if Louis XIII, along with Richelieu and Mazarin, had continued it; then Louis XIV considered himself destined to complete it and, furthermore, to round out—or square off—the jagged edges and vulnerable indentations that showed up on the map of the French hexagon. Destiny had placed him on the throne of the nation with the largest population on the Continent, the greatest in manpower reserves; the French army was likewise the largest and the greatest on the Continent, as were the national revenues—save for those of that upstart mercantile and maritime republic, the United Provinces of Holland.

En avant, then! Forward March! Into Flanders, into the Low Countries, the Spanish Netherlands (the area today of Belgium). The campaign of Flanders (as the King referred to it) began in May, shortly after Louise de La Vallière had been created Duchesse de Vaujours (a rich domain on the Loire) and her eight-month-old daughter, Marie-Anne (Mlle de Blois) legitimized by edict of the Parlement of Paris, on May 13, 1667.

It was the first such edict in some half century, but legitimization of his bastards by a monarch was in the royal tradition of France. Henri IV, "The Great Legitimizer," had issued such directives to the Parlement, peremptorily and boldly. Louis XIV did not yet choose to challenge public opinion, which was less indulgent in such matters than in the old days, and he commissioned Paul Pellisson,* a prominent literary hack, to couch the command delicately and gracefully:

* Pellisson, a literary light not quite so bright as his Platonic lady fair, novelist Madeleine de Scudéry.

The New Favorite

"... Although her modesty has consistently opposed us in our intention to elevate her [Louise de La Vallière] to a rank proportionate to our esteem, the time has come when we can no longer postpone this public expression . . . of our singular affection . . . and recognition of her merit . . . nor can we longer put off this evidence of our tenderness for our natural daughter, Marie-Anne. . . ."

"Recognition of her merit." To some ears, those words sounded suspiciously like a grandee's dismissal of an old and faithful servitor. The *Grande Mademoiselle* was ready to wager "that there would be no more children born of that liaison."

No more, that is to say, after the birth of the child with which La Vallière was already pregnant: five months pregnant in May, haggard and apprehensive, little comforted by the prerogatives of a Duchess (the right to blazon her ducal coat of arms on the door of her coach, to drape its interior in scarlet cloth, and to drive it into the Marble Courtyard of Versailles or into the great square courtyard of the Louvre; the right to wear a train three yards long, and to sit in the Queen's presence on a *tabouret*,* a folding stool made of gilded wood, tasseled, and tapestry-upholstered).

Louise's apprehensions were justified when she received the King's orders to betake herself to her pavilion at Versailles at the very hour he was to set out for Flanders, accompanied by a goodly number of courtiers, by the Queen and the Queen's ladies—foremost among them, Mme de Montespan.

The French troops invaded the Spanish Netherlands on May 24, a splendid date to open a campaign; spring the ideal season, fine weather to begin a war. (Hopefully to end it before the bad weather set in, in autumn, when troops would go back into winter quarters, and the King and courtiers back to court and capital for the festivities of the winter season. Such was the seventeenth-century way of life.)

---

* Seats were the main status symbols of the Ancien Régime: the *tabouret* reserved for Duchesses, while other ladies sat on cushions or ottomans. As for the *fauteuil*, or armchair, only the King's wife or another monarch might sit in one in the King's presence.

The army and the court, and often the Cabinet, all jogged and jounced along together over the rough roads to the front, the army's general staff trailed by the King's household staff, infinitely complicating the logistical problem. In effect, the court of France went on tour, like a theatrical company, through the provinces, into neighboring and conquered territories which could not but be impressed by the radiant Sun King, "the great beauties of his kingdom," and his cultivated, aristocratic elite. As propaganda, it was highly effective: to be Frenchified seemed no dreadful fate. Europe was ready to succumb—if not to French arms—to French charms and blandishments; to the lyrical, lucid, logical French language, to French literature and art, to French manners and French fashions.

This War of the Spanish Devolution was one long triumphal procession for the King of France. In a mere nine days, Lille capitulated; the walls of Charleroi, Arras, Armentières, and Courtrai all came tumbling down like Jericho's, at the blare of his trumpets. In June, he sent for the Queen and her ladies—notably Mme de Montespan—to join him, to enjoy the spectacle and to see him in action, sword in hand, in the open trenches.

At La Fère, en route to the north, the *Grande Mademoiselle*—always included as a member of the royal family—found the Queen "in a state of acute distress" at the news that La Vallière was on her way, unbidden, to the front. Next day, the *Grande Mademoiselle* came upon the unhappy Favorite and her two ladies, "in the Queen's antechamber, sitting on their trunks, too weary to stand, without so much as a wink of sleep the night before. . . . When I entered the Queen's room, I found her dissolved in tears. She told me that she had just vomited, that she could bear no more. Whereupon Mme de Montausier shrugged, saying over and over: 'You can see what a state the Queen is in!' Mme de Montespan was even louder in her indignation than the Queen, explaining to me how great a sympathy she felt for Her Majesty, how justifiable she considered Her Majesty's complaint." The Queen snubbed La Vallière at every turn; at the church, at the carriage door, even ordering that she be excluded from the dinner, although the *maître d'hôtel* took pity on the wilting, six-month-pregnant woman in disregard of Marie Thérèse's order.

The Queen set off for Avesnes the next morning, in her great glittering gold coach drawn by six spanking white horses (drawn, on canvas, by the Flemish painter Van der Meulen, who had been brought along expressly to record the expedition). The *Grande Mademoiselle*, riding with the Queen, recalls that "all the conversation centered on La Vallière. Mme de Montespan kept saying that she could not get over that person's effrontery in daring to present herself before the Queen. 'It is clear,' she said, 'that the King did not send for her, and that when she set out, she must have foreseen not only His Majesty's displeasure but also that of the Queen.' Mme de Montausier and Mme de Bade elaborated on the theme to make clear their sympathies. Mme de Montespan resumed, saying: 'Heaven preserve me from ever becoming the King's mistress, but were such a fate to befall me, I would never be so brazen as to face the Queen!' So it went, throughout all the trip, all tears and laments. . . . The Queen gave orders to all the officers of the troops of her escort that no one, no matter who, be allowed to set out ahead of her, the next morning, so that she herself could be sure to be the first to greet the King. But when Mme de La Vallière, from an eminence, caught sight of the army in the distance . . . she sped ahead in her carriage, at full gallop, across the fields. The Queen saw her and was tempted to have her stopped. She went into a frightful rage. Everyone begged her to take no action, but simply to tell the King how she had been defied . . ." (a defiance on the part of the meek and mild, the tremulous La Vallière that would seem inexplicable except in her own words, years later, in her *Reflections on the Mercy of God*, where she wrote that it sometimes seemed to her that she had been "dragged along" by her desperate love for the King, in spite of herself, "as if by wild horses").

"When the King reached the Queen's carriage" (as the *Grande Mademoiselle* resumes the narrative in her Memoirs) ". . . they conversed a few moments. Then the King went over to the carriage of Mme de La Vallière, who did not put in another appearance in public that day. On the morrow, however, she rode to Mass in the Queen's coach, although it was already crowded, and we had to squeeze ourselves in to make a place for her. Later, she dined, as was her wont, with the Queen and the other ladies. . . ."

The Queen had had to swallow her indignation at that meal, but La Vallière could not have enjoyed her dinner either. Heavy with his child, she had not been publicly humiliated by her royal lover, but it was clear that the Favorite's favor was fast waning.

The *Grande Mademoiselle* describes the rise of the new star on the horizon: "We spent three days . . . [at Avesnes] during which time Mme de Montespan came and asked me to take her place at the Queen's gaming table. She spent all her time in her chamber, which was in Mme de Montausier's apartment, close beside that of the King, and it was duly noted that the sentinel, who had originally been stationed on a staircase leading from the King's apartment to Mme de Montausier's, had been transferred from that post to one at the bottom of the flight of stairs, in order to prevent anyone's ascending them. The King, too, remained in his chambers almost all the day, the doors all closed behind him. Mme de Montespan was conspicuous by her absence at the card games which she usually attended;* nor did she accompany the Queen on her promenades, as she did customarily. After three days had passed, the King went off with his army, in one direction; we in another. The first night of our journey we slept at Vervins; the second, at Notre-Dame de Liesse. There Mme de La Vallière, who was traveling back with our party, went to confession; and Mme de Montespan, along with her . . ."

There may have been a worldly cynicism in Mme de Montespan's visit to the confessional in the company of her vanquished rival, but it was in character for her—a practicing Catholic, a product of her mother's pious training—to have taken the first opportunity to confess her adultery: a double adultery, at that— between a married man and a married woman; holy wedlock twice

---

* A seat at the Queen's card table was as good as an extra pension; the simplest gambling games such as *Hoca* and *Brelan* were beyond Marie Thérèse's comprehension.

defiled—which was to compound the sin and exacerbate all the attendant circumstances.

If, in fact, the first carnal encounter between Louis XIV and the Marquise de Montespan had taken place in Flanders, if the famous affair had actually had its beginning there. A second contemporary source confirms it: "The first time the King saw her in private, he took her by surprise. She had been sharing a room with Mme d'Heudicourt but, one night, after Mme de Montespan had retired to her bed, Mme d'Heudicourt—who was in the confidence of the King—left the room, whereupon His Majesty came in, disguised in the uniform of one of Monsieur de Montausier's Swiss guards . . ."

Fresh from his latest victories at Douai and Tournai, the King rejoined the court and the ladies at the Château de Compiègne in July: "He visited Mme de Montespan, every day . . . in private," as the *Grande Mademoiselle* resumes the report, "going to see her in her room which was located directly above the Queen's. One day, at table, she [the Queen] told me that the King had not come to bed until four o'clock in the morning. In answer to her questions, he had told her that he had been busy till then reading letters and writing his replies. When the Queen asked him whether he could not find another hour for that work, he turned his head away from her, lest she see him laugh. Lest she see me doing likewise, I kept my eyes down, fastened on my plate." (For once, the *Grande Mademoiselle*'s account is not straightfaced; its motto usually, like Talleyrand's, "neither to condemn nor to approve, but merely to relate.")

The Queen's confusion as to the identity of her husband's latest light of love was "a court joke," the *Grande Mademoiselle* reminds us: "People laughed about it with the King."

"The King continues to encourage the Queen's jealousy of La Vallière," the Savoyard Ambassador reported, whereas there had never been less reason for it: the Favorite had scarcely laid eyes on His Majesty throughout the last months of her pregnancy. Their fourth child, a boy, the Comte de Vermandois, was born in October; another secret accouchement: the infant whisked away, as usual, within hours after birth, by Colbert.

Meanwhile, "the King continued his visits, in private, to Mme de Montespan. . . . He was in remarkably high spirits. . . . She was the gayest company imaginable when she went out driving with the royal pair . . . constantly bantering and laughing with the King."

The *Grande Mademoiselle* joined the royal party on a second expedition to the battlefields of Flanders, that autumn, sharing their hardships and a number of "great alarms"; sleepless nights upright in the royal coach, cannonballs rolling beneath its wheels. The King was having "such a wonderful time with Mme de Montespan" that he could laugh about their carriage turning turtle and hurtling over the garden wall of a Capuchin monastery at Orchies. The first night out, at Montdidier, the King spoke privately to the *Grande Mademoiselle*: "Mme de Montespan has quit the Queen's game of *Brelan* because the stakes have become too high for her. . . . Stakes twice that high would not dismay you, would they?" As the richest heiress in France, the King's cousin could well afford to accommodate him by taking the vacant seat at the Queen's table. During a three-day stay at Tournai, the wordly-wise spinster remarked that "Mme de Montespan no longer accompanied the Queen except to Mass; as for the promenades, she excused herself, saying that she was going to take a nap."

Madame de Montespan had, by then, supplanted La Vallière as the King's mistress, whether the Queen was as yet aware of it or not. She would be, shortly, for La Vallière was the last of the King's mistresses to blush at the title or to shrink from the limelight. Beginning with Mme de Montespan, the royal Favorites would publish their favor to the four corners of the earth.

And there were other differences: this was to be a grand passion rather than a great love; there was to be little evidence of tenderness in this new relation. But Mme de Montespan could rise to meet him in his stratosphere, soar with him in rarefied air as La Vallière could never have done. Marie Thérèse, daughter of Kings though she was, lacked the qualities to reign truly at the court of France, whereas Athénaïs de Rochechouart-Mortemart possessed them. Ironically, no Bourbon Queen would show herself so well endowed to play that role at Versailles as Athénaïs.*

The King, on the threshold of his thirties, was ready for a mistress such as this one. Tormented from the beginning by her sense of guilt, Louise could have shown little exuberance in her sex role. Athénaïs entered the King's embrace with both experience and abandon. He had outgrown his timid love, La Vallière.

He and Louise may have whispered sweet nothings into one another's ear, but neither had been sprightly at repartee or raillery. He had had amorous encounters aplenty, but little discourse with the ladies. He doffed his hat and bowed to them with a grace that was unsurpassed by any gentleman in his kingdom; he could manage a gallant rejoinder to a feminine sally, but he had not been remarkable for his conversational gambits. Recently, he had changed, matured; he was, "at that very moment" showing a new poise and sophistication *vis-à-vis* the fair sex, according to a letter written in September of 1667 by his glamorous and worldly cousin, the Duchesse de Longueville (a Princess of the Condé family): "Now, things are different," she observed. "He initiates a conversation and holds up his end of it, like any other gentleman"—like any other gentleman, she implied, of that highly cultivated, polished aristocratic French society which was to set the standard of elegance and culture for all of Europe, all the Western world, for centuries to come.

The campaign of Flanders at an end, with the end of summer, with the end of fair weather, the King would retire to his capital, there to celebrate his signal successes with the Spanish—as with Mme de Montespan!—in a round of festivities lasting all winter.

It appeared that the King had met with no more resistance from the Marquis de Montespan than with the Marquise—that gentleman presently off skirmishing against Spanish border raiders in the Pyrenean mountain passes. There were vague rumors of a

---

* Louis XV's Marie Leczinska was as inept and graceless as Louis XIV's Marie Thérèse. Decorative but frivolous, Louis XVI's Marie Antoinette lacked not the graces but the taste for such responsibility. Anne of Austria might have been the exception had her husband, Louis XIII, presided over a court such as his successors'.

scandal involving him at Perpignan: rumors of a bronzed Gascon peasant girl riding with him and his company of light cavalry, cramming her buxom charms into a trooper's uniform.

But it would be nothing to compare with the scandal in which the Marquis de Montespan would involve his wife and King, on his return to Paris, the following year.

The highlight of the gala spring season, the following year, that of 1668, was the première of Molière's *Amphitryon,* a ribald comedy with cuckoldry as its theme, to be construed as a veiled allusion to the Marquis de Montespan (unless to Molière himself, thought to be deceived by his wife as surely as the Marquis by his). The court was deliciously titillated by the analogy between the Father of the Gods and the King of France—a Gallicized version of the classic myth wherein the lustful Jupiter visits the fair and virtuous Alcmene in the form of her husband—a union of which the issue was the hero, Hercules.

Darling of the court though Molière was (legend has it that the King once deigned to share a supper with him to demonstrate to the supercilious courtiers that a man of letters was now to be treated as a social equal), even so, how did the playwright dare to present this allegory of the King's doubly adulterous amours before the King's own wife, before the court, before all the world? If it was bold to allude publicly to those amours, it was at the same time flattering to represent the adulterer as an Olympian, a divinity, above all mortal men as above their laws. How convenient for Louis XIV to have had France's greatest poet to condone his pagan ethic in immortal verse! As in these lines, in which Jupiter-Louis reassures Alcmene-Athénaïs:

> *To share with Jupiter*
> *Can carry no dishonor.*
> *Indeed, a man must take glory*
> *To see himself the rival*
> *Of the Sovereign of the Gods.*

The New Favorite

There were few men in the kingdom who would have disputed Molière's logic; not even a prince would deny his wife to his monarch . . . certainly not if the monarch were to manifest himself to her—as Jupiter did to Danaë—in a golden shower. The ancient feudal right known as the *droit du seigneur*—the seigneur's right to precede his vassal in the bed of the vassal's promised bride—had not been generally exercised in generations;* but the right of the lord paramount, the supreme liegelord of the land, was not contested in Louis XIV's century. As Restif de La Bretonne could write as late as the eighteenth century: "I did not question the King's legal right to demand of any man in the realm that he give him his wife or daughter, and my whole village believed as I did. . . ."

The Marquis de Montespan's father is reported to have exclaimed in delight at the news that his daughter-in-law had become the mistress of the King: "Praise be to God! Here is a stroke of great good fortune for our house!"†

It appeared, at first, that the new Favorite's husband agreed with his father. In the summer and autumn of 1667, when all the court and capital buzzed with the scandal, the Marquis fought on in mountain skirmishes along the southern border, in the King's service and on the King's subsidy. The Royal Intendant of the province of Roussillon wrote to Louvois, the Minister of War, to ask for authorization to equip and maintain Montespan's company of light cavalry, "Eighty-four men strong, well mounted and excellently outfitted. . . . He [Montespan] claims that he cannot afford the upkeep of this troop . . . so I recommend that subsistence funds be provided for his company. . . ." No sooner said than done. Indeed, Louvois went so far as to lead Montespan to hope for "a regiment of your own at the very first opportunity." Were not his letters extant, it would be difficult to credit that stern minister with

---

* Beaumarchais used the *droit du seigneur* as the hinge of the plot of his *Mariage de Figaro*.

† From the *Lettres Galantes*, a collection of letters written by Madame du Noyer, wife of the grand master of forests and waters in Languedoc, a close friend of the Marquis de Montespan in later years in Toulouse.

so cordial a correspondence, writing on October 14, 1667, to Montespan: "I rejoice at the splendid advantages His Majesty accords you"; and on November 22, following the action at Puigcerdá wherein the Marquis had distinguished himself: "The King has expressed his satisfaction with your valorous conduct in this encounter, and I can assure you that His Majesty will miss no opportunity to vouchsafe you proofs of his esteem." Louvois furthermore protected the Marquis when the bailiff of Perpignan complained of an attack by Montespan and his bravos on the town prison to recover the delinquent peasant girl who had been gallivanting up and down the countryside with him and his cavalrymen and who had been put behind bars at the request of her indignant parents.

The Marquis de Montespan had apparently adopted the advice offered by one of Molière's characters to Amphitryon at the hour of his wife's seduction by a divinity: "The wisest course is to say nothing."

Montespan said nothing until he arrived in Paris, in midsummer 1668, on leave from the southern front, with written permission from His Majesty in his pocket. He found the court and capital celebrating the birth of the fifth Child of France—the Queen still pale from childbed; Mme de Montespan radiant beside her, in a place of prominence at every gala.

What gadfly suddenly stung the complacent husband into such a fury? Was it the shock of finding his wife pregnant by another man, crowned head though that man might be? Was it because, as Bussy suggested, "Mme de Montespan, in acquiring a taste for the King's caresses, developed a distaste for her husband's, leading her to deny him his marital privileges, which caused him such despair that, despite his tender love for her, he slapped her in the face." If so, it was an inexplicably long-delayed reaction, according to the Marquise de Caylus,* another of the exceptional

---

* Madame de Caylus owed her exceptional education to her cousin, Mme de Maintenon, who served as the girl's guardian and preceptor. Mme de Caylus entitled her recollections of the court and reign of Louis XIV *Souvenirs* rather than *Mémoires*, which she considered "overly pretentious."

women of the court, and a voice of authority, since she had the story direct from her cousin, Mme de Maintenon, who would herself soon become intimately involved with the King and his inamorata: "I do not pretend to know all the details of the story as it concerned Monsieur de Montespan; all that I can say authoritatively is that he was generally held in disrepute, regarded as a madman. It had been up to him, in the beginning. He need only have taken his wife away, at that point; and the King, no matter how enamored he might have been, would not have pitted his authority against that of a husband. But Monsieur de Montespan, far from exercising such authority, was interested solely in the benefits to be derived; and his later actions stemmed from his resentment at not reaping the expected harvest of fortune and advancement. . . ."

He came into Paris in August, breathing fire. "He kicked up a frightful row," the *Grande Mademoiselle* declared. "An impulsive, unpredictable man, intelligent enough but lacking in judgment. . . . Monsieur de Montespan is presently on bad terms with his wife, and has been raving and ranting to everyone . . . about the rumors linking her name to the King's. . . . He came often to my house; and since he is my cousin, I felt free to scold him. One evening, he read me a harangue which he claimed to have delivered to the King, in which he quoted a thousand passages from Holy Scripture, several exhorting His Majesty to give up his [Montespan's] wife or fear the judgment of God. I said to him: 'You must be mad. You simply cannot go around making wild talk like that.' The next day, at Saint-Germain, walking on the terrace outside the Queen's window, I called Mme de Montespan aside to tell her that I had had a visit from her husband and that he was making a greater fool of himself than ever, so that I had had to rebuke him sharply. 'I am ashamed,' she answered, 'to discover that my husband is as much of a comic as my parrot; the two of them are furnishing entertainment for the rabble. . . . He is here, today, making dreadful charges against Mme de Montausier' [the Queen's lady of honor]. The words had scarcely left her lips when someone came to summon her to that lady's [Mme de Montausier's] apartment. . . . He

[Monsieur de Montespan] had just gone out the door, having spewed a thousand insults in her face, so outraging her that she lay shaking with anger on her bed. . . . She had felt obliged to inform the King, who was sending out after him with an order for his imprisonment."

The way Mme du Noyer heard the gossip in Toulouse, the Marquis had perpetrated horrors even more unspeakable: "He set out purposely to contract a disease so as to pass it on to his wife" (so that she might, in turn, pass it on to the King), "and would have succeeded in his scheme, had not precautions been taken to protect her from this peril. . . ." Saint-Simon embroiders on this theme by adding that "Monsieur de Montespan frequented the vilest brothels" to contract a venereal disease whereas, according to the references of contemporaries, he could have achieved the same result without going outside court circles.

Even the Marquis de Montespan's uncle, the Archbishop of Sens, became involved in the imbroglio by publicly denouncing, from his pulpit at Fontainebleau, a woman of that congregation guilty of the same sin as his niece, and by publishing throughout his diocese a series of the ancient canons against adultery. Mme de Montespan rushed furiously from Fontainebleau where the court was then in residence, and His Majesty ordered the Archbishop confined to the city limits of Sens.

The Marquis de Montespan's final folly was to drive up to the Château de Saint-Germain, his coach draped in black—in mourning for his wife, he proclaimed—and with four huge sets of antlers —stag horns, the classic symbol of the cuckold—decorating the four corners of the carriage roof in place of the hearse's customary funereal plumes.

The King's patience had run out by September 20, 1668, on which date he issued orders for Montespan's arrest and imprisonment at For l'Évêque. This proved a relatively short incarceration: October 4 saw his release, signed by Minister of War Louvois, "on condition that he depart Paris within twenty-four hours" and be on his way to exile in his father's estates in the far south, whence he was not to budge "on pain of death." The time had come, at last, when Jupiter-Louis would hurl his thunderbolts.

"The Seigneur Jupiter knows how to gild the pill," according to one of Molière's lines in *Amphitryon*. But did he? Was His Majesty not being niggardly in offering Montespan a mere "200,000 francs to console him for the loss of his wife"? That was the figure named by Bussy, but he must have had it at second hand, since he was in exile, withering away for the third year in Burgundy. The second *Madame* states flatly that "Monsieur de Montespan was an arrant opportunist. Had the King been willing to pay off more handsomely, he [Montespan] would have been reconciled. . . ."

Instead, the Marquis de Montespan multiplied the scandals, reports of which resounded all the way to the capital. Staging a macabre comedy, he summoned the remotest branches of his family tree to attend formal and elaborate funeral services for his wife. He accepted condolences from friends and relatives, standing at the central door of his ancestral Château of Bonnefont; to make the point, as the English Ambassador St. Albans points out, that "his horns—his cuckold's horns—were too high for him to pass through a lower, side door." The two Montespan children, the girl and boy aged respectively five and three, were dressed like their father in long, formal mourning garb.

There had apparently been no protest at his taking them into exile with him; neither from Mme de Montespan, never renowned for her maternal instincts; nor from the King—"A lover with delicate sensibilities" (according to Bussy), who could not have relished the sight of these living tokens of another man's possession of his paramour. It would have, furthermore, been awkward for Mme de Montespan's legitimate and illegitimate offspring to commingle. The first of these royal bastards, a girl, was reportedly born sometime in early 1669 and, reportedly dead in 1672, never brought into public view, her existence substantiated by only the sketchiest details.

If "Montespan's name was to become notorious through the fatal beauty of his wife," as Saint-Simon commiserated, the

Marquis himself contributed to some extent to the notoriety. Wild as a hare in the rutting season, he and his band of bullies terrorized the town of Illes-sur-Têt, raiding, raping, and looting, in the summer of 1669, finally storming a convent where a girl "of base and low estate"—less amenable than the damsel at Perpignan in 1667—had taken sanctuary from the Marquis's molestations. The girl, her mother, the Father Superior, and several peasants had all been injured in the affray before the prior could prevail upon the noble attackers to withdraw.

The Marquis de Montespan's latest escapade at Illes offered the King the ideal pretext to prosecute him: Minister of War Louvois wrote on September 21, 1669, to the Royal Intendant of the province of Roussillon "to use this misdemeanor as the occasion to break him [Montespan] . . . and to disband his company . . . all the while maintaining a show of justice. . . ." Convicted, along with several ruffians from his troop, Montespan dashed across the border to Spain to escape punishment—precisely the result the King had hoped for.*

The Marquis de Montespan's father died in 1670, so debt-ridden that his son had to renounce the personal estate, succeeding only to the title of family head and to a parcel of properties preserved intact in entail. Penniless, a refugee in a foreign land, the Marquis de Montespan was not long in petitioning the King for pardon and for permission to return to France. He must have feared the confiscation of his properties if he remained recalcitrant, an expatriate under indictment. A French officer, taking French

---

* The Montespans' young son, the Marquis d'Antin, accompanied his father into exile in Spain. The daughter, Marie Christine, was left in France in the care of the Marquis's mother. Upon the death of her grandmother, the girl was confided to the guardianship of the Archbishop of Sens, who placed this grand-niece of his in a convent at Charonne, where she died in the year 1675, at "approximately the age of ten," as the Toulouse Archives specify, and where her name is to be found recorded for the first and only time as "The Demoiselle Marie Christine de Gondrin de Montespan," probably the namesake of that younger sister of her mother's, who likewise disappeared at an early age into a convent.

leave of the King's army, could look for reprisals through the agency of the Royal Intendant, the administrator of provincial affairs.*

His Most Christian Majesty of France may have felt some embarrassment at the thought of his mistress's husband seeking refuge in Catholic Spain, complaining of persecution at the hands of his wife's lover.

On April 22, 1670, a royal pardon was forthcoming, removing the penalties imposed on Montespan and the other rowdies convicted with him, and clearing the way for their return to their native soil.

Chastened and subdued by his brush with absolute authority, Montespan scrupulously observed the boundary lines set him, hundreds of leagues from court and capital, leading the not unpleasant life of a provincial nobleman, supervising his estates, collecting feudal dues and tolls, exacting the prescribed *corveés* or forced labor from his vassals, improving fields and vineyards, replanting forests; pleasuring himself in hunting on his seigneurial preserves, fishing in his seigneurial waters, streams, and rivers; carousing, gaming, wenching.

His wife, the Marquise de Montespan, had moved in to share a magnificent apartment, at the Château de Saint-Germain, with Mme de La Vallière, the King's former mistress . . . If that is what La Vallière was? If not, then what?—The King's *other mistress?* Sexually insatiable as he was, it was conceded that he might need an alternate. No one outside the inner circle could say precisely what La Vallière was to the King, at this juncture, which was precisely the effect he had intended when he set up the extraordinary design for living that would be referred to as *Chez les dames*: "The King is visiting at the ladies' apartment," the courtiers tittered. It was a royal version of the *ménage à trois*, and the whispering galleries still echoed with it when the Duc de Saint-Simon

* The Duc de Saint-Simon considered himself relatively fortunate that, in resigning his commission in the army, he incurred no more concrete evidence of the royal displeasure than the King's personal disdain.

reached Versailles, a quarter of a century later: "It was Mme de Montespan's rare beauty that stirred him [the King] next, even during the reign of Mme de La Vallière. . . . Finally, the King took her [Mme de Montespan] away from her husband, causing such a disgraceful fracas as to resound across and horrify all the nations of Europe. The whole world was scandalized by the novel spectacle of two mistresses at one time!"

"The King needed a pretext for Mme de Montespan," was Comte de Bussy's interpretation of the situation, the togetherness of quondam and current official mistress. The King needed La Vallière's presence to cover up his liaison with Mme de Montespan: a child born *Chez les dames*, in "the ladies' apartment," could not be positively identified as the offspring of one or the other. Perhaps fear of the Marquis de Montespan still haunted his wife and her lover. One could put nothing past Montespan: a tale had made the rounds of a wild scheme the Marquis was hatching to abduct his wife and carry her off to Spain. "A madman capable of the wildest extravagances," as the King described Montespan in a letter to Louvois, might well try to abduct a child born to his wife and claim it as his own, the legally wedded husband's. And what court with any pretensions to justice could gainsay him?

VII

Chez les Dames

IN 1670, LOUIS XIV SET IN MOTION the first in a series of carefully laid plans to squash the United Provinces of Holland. "That Republic of cheese merchants!" he called them; their radical, democratic social and political experiments enough to outrage an autocratic soul such as his.*

Louis's first move against Holland was oblique: to secure the support of England. What better plenipotentiary could he have chosen than his winsome sister-in-law, *Madame*, to negotiate with her brother, Charles II of England; to pledge him French subsidy in return for his signature on the secret Treaty of Dover? Only *Madame*'s spiteful husband, the Duc d'Orléans, could object to her playing a role more important than any ever assigned to him: his resentment against his wife kindled by his male favorite, the Chevalier de Lorraine ("looking like the painting of an angel" but wicked as a fiend, as *Madame* was to discover too late).

* Louis XIV was outraged that the United Provinces should offer asylum to French Huguenot refugees, as to those of Protestant sects from all over Europe—asylum even to the Jews. Furthermore, a constant, contraband flow of insolent, pernicious, subversive books and newspapers from the free presses of Amsterdam and Leyden kept the French censors busy confiscating and burning. The French monarch was especially sensitive to the pornography, the scandal sheets dealing with his sexual exploits, or books such as Comte de Bussy's scandalous court chronicle, *The Amorous History of the Gauls.*

The entire court—with the exception of *Monsieur*, "who worked himself into a rage . . . and tried to prevent her going" —waved farewell to *Madame* as she set sail for Dover from Dunkirk on May 26, 1670.

When she sailed back on June 15, it was with treaty in hand and with her brother's signature and seal upon it, "with all the glory and honor [as Mme de La Fayette noted] attendant upon the successful accomplishment of such a mission."

"She returned looking so well and happy" that the *Grande Mademoiselle* thought she might also have "recovered her health in England. . . . The King received her with marks of high esteem. . . . Not so her husband . . . who often made most disagreeable remarks to her. . . . One day when the subject of astrology came up, *Monsieur* said that it had been predicted to him that he would have more than one wife and that, in view of *Madame*'s precarious state of health, he found reason to give credence to the prediction— which seemed to me an extremely horrid thing to say. . . . It was easy to see the grief *Monsieur*'s attitude caused her. . . . He spoke to me about *Madame* in tones so violent that I was shocked, and I realized that he would never come to a reconciliation with her. . . ."

Upon her return, *Madame* rejoined the King—together with his personal and household entourage as well as his full military establishment—and continued on with them in their royal progress through Flanders, which had begun in April and had proven to be "one continuous gala all the way from Saint-Germain to Lille. . . . All the conquered territories visited by the court in full panoply of pomp and splendor," according to Voltaire's *Century of Louis XIV*.

Voltaire deplored and derided all resort to war, but found at least one mitigating circumstance in the aggressions of this "enlightened" despot, Louis XIV, in that French enlightenment and culture were spread in the army's wake: "The King, who had made all his previous campaigns on horseback, rode for the first time, here, in a glass-windowed coach. . . . The Queen and her sister-in-law, *Madame*, and Mme de Montespan rode in this superb equipage, at the head of a train of others. . . . The Dauphin came next in line, with his retinue; then the *Grande Mademoiselle*, with hers.

"Madame de Montespan's triumph shone forth," Voltaire goes on to relate, "during the Flanders voyage of 1670. . . . At such times as she rode alone, she had four bodyguards posted at her carriage door. . . . It was to Mme de Montespan that all the court paid homage; all honors were for her save those reserved by tradition and protocol for the Queen. Her Majesty, however, was not privy to the secret; His Majesty knew how to keep affairs of state separate from affairs of the heart."

The Queen's disillusionment could not, however, be indefinitely postponed. "She had loved Mme de Montespan," the Marquise de Caylus says, "because she had believed her to be a respectable woman, loyal to her duties and her husband. Thus Her Majesty's surprise equaled her sorrow when she later found her to be unlike what she had imagined. The Queen's distress was made no easier by Mme de Montespan's lack of consideration. . . . Of all the King's mistresses, Mme de Montespan is the one who caused Her Majesty the greatest anguish; not only because that particular passion between Mme de Montespan and the King raged so long, not only because she took such few pains to spare pain to the Queen but, above all, because it was pain inflicted by a woman whom the Queen had trusted and vouchsafed a special friendship."

"How different from the unfailing consideration shown Her Majesty by La Vallière . . . ," the Duc de Saint-Simon draws the odious comparison, and then quotes the Queen's bitter and oft-repeated complaint against the new Favorite: " 'That whore will be the death of me!' . . . He [the King] paraded the two of them [La Vallière and La Montespan] in the carriage with the Queen, along the frontier, at the encampments . . . before the armies. Crowds came running everywhere along the route, pointing at the carriage and naïvely calling to one another to come and see the three Queens!"

"The three Queens" and the King and all the court made their way in late June back to Versailles—all save *Monsieur*, who, to spite *Madame* and deprive her of her hour of triumph, dragged her off to his château at Saint-Cloud on June 24.

For relief from the heat, *Madame* bathed in the Seine, strolled in the palace gardens and terraces above the river in the cool of the evening. By the end of June, she was suddenly and inexplicably stricken.

"Oh cruel night, tragic night, night of terror! when there rang out, as sudden as a clap of thunder, that shocking report: *Madame* is dying! *Madame* is dead"—these the words of Bishop Bossuet, presiding at the funeral ceremonies for the pale and lovely, frail and flighty Duchesse d'Orléans.

"Having uttered these lines, he [Bossuet] had to break off the funeral oration; sobs and sighs from the audience drowned out his majestic voice" (no mean feat, Voltaire implies, "to wring tears" from that cynical lot of courtiers, as Voltaire says he did, "in this the most stirring, most celebrated of his many elegiac triumphs").*

"*Madame* is dying! *Madame* is dead!" As quickly as that, it happened, on June 29, 1670: the fatal glass of chicory water; "the instant pain like fire in her entrails"; "the nine-hour agony"; the end—which came (said Voltaire) "in the flower of her youth and in the arms of Bossuet," who administered Extreme Unction.

"The sweetest Princess ever to walk this earth," lamented Mme de La Fayette, on the other side of the deathbed from the Bishop. She looked up and saw "Mme de La Vallière and Mme de Montespan come in together" (as usual!). Except for Voltaire's, all the accounts quoted here are by eyewitnesses. The *Grande Mademoiselle* stood weeping with the Queen inside the *ruelle* (the bed alcove, enclosed by an ornamental railing).

"The most embarrassing aspect of the whole affair," the *Grande Mademoiselle* quotes the Queen as saying, "is that Ma-

* The premier prelate of France, dedicated, incorruptible, rigid in his formalism, defender of the faith against the rising tide of doubt, Bossuet was furthermore "the greatest living manipulator of French prose"; alternately poet and prophet in the pulpit, it was primarily because of him that the funeral oration became an art form in France, a literary divertissement peculiarly French.

dame believes she has been poisoned!" "*Madame* asked for a counterpoison," Mme de La Fayette reveals, "and the physicians treated her accordingly, administering oil and other antidotes . . . including powder of viper."

The King of France, being "seriously disturbed"—and well he might be; his relations with the King of England gravely imperiled —ordered "a dissection to be performed by the principal physicians and surgeons of Paris." "Thus were allayed most of our suspicions," Lord Arlington, Secretary of State for England, noted by letter shortly thereafter.

Every contemporary memorialist comments on the ugly hostility that flared openly between *Monsieur* and *Madame*. *Madame* had lived dangerously up to the very end, "bathing in the Seine, strolling in the moonlight," although more dangerous still (in Mme de La Fayette's, in Voltaire's, and in the *Grande Mademoiselle's* opinion) had been her influence on the King in His Majesty's decision, in early 1670, to exile *Monsieur's* vicious darling, the Chevalier de Lorraine.

It was the Chevalier who sent the poison from Rome to confederates in the Orléans household, according to the inside story the Duc de Saint-Simon heard years later. Although Charles II of England "refused to accept a letter written him by *Monsieur*," whom he suspected of being *Madame's* murderer, Louis XIV of France satisfied himself, according to Saint-Simon, that his brother was technically innocent. Mme de La Fayette considered *Monsieur* "totally incapable of such a crime. . . . I observed him attentively as we stood side by side in *Madame's* bed alcove. . . . He showed no embarrassment whatsoever at *Madame's* insistence that she had been poisoned, and he favored testing the suspected chicory water by giving it to a dog. . . ."

Monsieur was to take a second wife, as the astrologer had predicted, just as soon as the protocol-specified court mourning had been complied with—the second *Madame*, a Princess from the Palatinate. Hefty, hale, and hearty Elizabeth-Charlotte of Bavaria reluctantly crossed the Rhine, reluctantly forfeited her claim to the English throne (which went to her Hanoverian cousin, George I), reluctantly entered into wedlock, in 1671, with the Duc d'Orléans, that sinister widower—rouged, bejeweled, simpering among his minions. An Amazon, the new Duchess's chief pleasures were hunting and letterwriting (interminable letters, twenty to twenty-five pages long, to her innumerable royal kinsmen). No Sévigné, the new *Madame*'s comical, malicious, often ribald correspondence may lack style but forms one of the best sources of information on daily life at Versailles. She not only spoke her mind, she wrote it. She could always laugh at herself, she said, and "That is fortunate because I find lots to laugh at . . . ugly as I am . . . squatty . . . square as a cube . . . red as a shrimp . . . pockmarked . . . teeth rotting. . . . Ah, well, a good conscience outlasts a good appearance!" Her heart would remain "true to Germany till the very last day." As would her stomach: just give her "beer soup . . . smoked sausage and sauerkraut!" She would "never get used to that detestable French cuisine!" Nor to French manners and morals. *Madame* would take to nothing French—except the King.

The King would respond to this new sister-in-law's unstinting adoration with an embarrassed, a self-conscious, a quizzical affection. Needless to say, however, he would never give his brother, *Monsieur*, cause for jealousy over this second *Madame*, as had been the case with the first.

Further complications were to be sedulously avoided: His Majesty was encountering difficulties enough, at that hour, with his ladies.

Louise de La Vallière had suddenly taken it into her head to disappear from the palace at dawn on Ash Wednesday, 1671. When she was finally tracked down, it was at the Convent of Sainte-Marie de Chaillot. Not that a conventual retreat had been a sudden decision on her part: she had been planning it ever since her bout with a grave, strange illness in the previous year. Regaining consciousness after three days, she had opened her eyes to see "Doctors on one side of my bed, priests on the other; the ones, despairing of my life; the others, of my soul," as she explained in her *Reflections on the Mercy of God,* the account she began to write three days after her miraculous recovery. "It did not seem too much," as Mme de Sévigné relates her thoughts, "to be allowed to dedicate the rest of her life to her salvation—having devoted all her youth to the King."

But the King thought otherwise, and ordered her back from Chaillot, before midnight, to Versailles (whither she returned as meekly as "a little ninny," in the *Grande Mademoiselle's* estimation).

"The King talked with her for an hour, weeping openly . . . with joy." (Mme de Sévigné informed her daughter as early as the next morning, Thursday, February 12.) "Mme de Montespan went out to meet her, wide-armed, teary-eyed. What kind of tears, you can well imagine! . . . Tender conversations ensued between Him and Her, between Him and the Other. . . . I dare not write more on the subject . . . but it is all very difficult to figure out. . . ."

Comte de Bussy figured it out without difficulty: "The King's purposes were purely selfish, dictated by personal interest." La Vallière was still needed *Chez les dames* as a front for his liaison with La Montespan.

In the spring of 1671, on a brief military promenade to Flanders, the King commanded the Queen to join the company as a sort of chaperone to his two ladies. "Without Her Majesty," the Italian Visconti snickered, "the presence of the two Favorites in the King's retinue would have caused a scandal." It was not, by any means, all one large, happy royal family. One night, in an emergency, all seven had to be accommodated in a single bedchamber; the one bed reserved for the Queen; mattresses were arranged on the floor for the others; in a row *Monsieur, Madame,* the King, the *Grande Mademoiselle* (who tells the story), La Vallière, La Montespan. " 'What?!' exclaimed the Queen, 'All of us here together?' —'If you leave your bed curtains open,' the King observed, not without some irony, 'you can keep an eye on us all!' "

Chez les dames, in the ladies' apartment at Saint-Germain, La Vallière was subjected to incredible indignities. Is the Abbé de Choisy to be believed when he reports that "the King, returning from the hunt, would go to Mme de La Vallière's apartment to remove his boots, change his clothes, and powder himself; then, after scarcely bidding her good day, he would pass into Mme de Montespan's suite and spend the entire evening there"? Could the King and Mme de Montespan have been as cruelly inconsiderate as Mme de Caylus indicates? "Mme de Montespan showed little delicacy in sharing the same roof, the same table with Mme de La Vallière. Mme de Montespan, taking cruel advantage of her, made a point of being waited on by La Vallière, declaring that she could never be satisfied with her costume unless the other gave the finishing touches . . . to her toilette. . . . Mme de La Vallière, on her part, comported herself with all the zeal of a personal maid whose fortune depended entirely upon her mistress's pleasure. . . . How many indignities she must have swallowed, how many affronts she must have suffered!" Could *Madame* have been exaggerating when she writes that "Mme de Montespan mocked Mme de La Vallière in public, treated her exceedingly ill, and influenced the King to do likewise. . . . The King had to go through La Vallière's rooms to reach La Montespan's. He had a fine spaniel called 'Malice'; at Mme de Montespan's instigation, he tossed that little dog into La Vallière's lap as he passed her, saying, 'Here, now, I'm leaving you in good company. . . . So, don't mope . . .' "?

Louise de La Vallière, addressing herself to God, in her *Reflections*, herself answers the question of why she endured the torment: "I stay on in this world of the flesh in order to expiate my sins upon that same scaffold upon which I offended Thee. Out of my sin shall come my penance . . . those whom I adored now act as my executioners. . . ."

One penance exacted of her was that she act as godmother to the progeny Mme de Montespan yearly bore the King.

"If Mme de Montespan had despaired at her first pregnancy, as I have earlier mentioned" (Mme de Caylus, who mentions it), "she consoled herself at the second, and as far as the rest were concerned . . . seven in all . . . she displayed a supreme insolence. Although the policy of secreting the children was adhered to, no further attempt was made to conceal the mother's pregnancies."

Not so, said *Madame*, the new Duchesse d'Orléans: "Mme de Montespan designed [and popularized, of course] a floating dress [designated on the fashion pages as 'The Innocent'] . . . beltless, loose hanging, to conceal the waistline, although when she put it on, it was as though she had written across her forehead the very thing she sought to conceal. At court, everyone said: Mme de Montespan is wearing her *robe battante*; she must be pregnant again!"

Mme de Montespan's first child by the King, the nameless girl born sometime in 1669, had been spirited away and entrusted to the care of a Mlle des Oeillets (a confidential maid of Mme de Montespan's) for its brief, secret three-year span of life.

The second child, Louis Auguste, the future Duc du Maine, "favorite of all the King's children" legitimate or illegitimate, was born on March 31, 1670. "And snatched up at the stroke of twelve the very night of his birth, by M. de Lauzun, who told me the tale" (says the *Grande Mademoiselle*, Lauzun's fiancée*). "With no time even to swaddle the infant, he [M. Lauzun] rolled it in a towel, wrapped it in his cloak, and rushed it to the carriage waiting at the small park of Saint-Germain, perishing with fear lest the little creature cry out. . . . The children [of Mme de Montespan and the King] were put in the charge of Mme Scarron, a highly intelligent woman and a pleasant one. . . ."

A cool and calculating one, as well, adept at machinations; latterly, if not originally, sanctimonious. Indigent widow though she was, at thirty-four, with no roof to call her own save that of a poor attic room in the Ursuline convent, dependent on the grace

---

* The *Grande Mademoiselle* was the Duc de Lauzun's fiancée but never officially his bride. Not even Lauzun—"the most insolent little fellow to be seen in many a century"—would have dared propose marriage to a Daughter of France. The *Grande Mademoiselle*, who had rejected offers of marriage from Kings and Princes, hopelessly enamored of the insolent, intrepid, bantam Duke, had done the proposing. The King reluctantly granted permission, but rescinded it when the royal family and Princes of the Blood protested the mésalliance. The Duke was imprisoned for ten years in the Fortress of Pignerol for his presumptuousness. It was thought that a secret marriage had been performed despite the King's injunction.

and favor of influential friends and relatives, still she did not jump at Mme de Montespan's offer to superintend the upbringing and education of the children born to that lady out of wedlock. "When Mme de Montespan made her the proposition . . . as the person of all her acquaintance best fitted for the post* . . . Mme Scarron replied," according to her protégée, Mme de Caylus, "that if the children in question were Mme de Montespan's, she would not be interested in such a duty, but if the children were the children of the King, and if His Majesty himself was to request her to undertake their care, then she would obey. The King made the request of her, and she acceded. . . . At this juncture, an extraordinary future opened up before Mme Scarron; there sounded forth the overture of fate. . . ." It was no freak of fate, however, but the product of a deliberate strategy on the part of a consummately artful and subtle woman. The assignment as governess of the royal bastards, sometime in 1669 or 1670, merely served her as an opening wedge.

Here, for once, the Sphinx speaks for herself: "I often went about on foot and in disguise, carrying meat or linen under my arm . . . checking on the various nurses. . . . Sometimes, if one of the children fell ill, I would spend the night, not returning to my own house until the dawn. There, I would enter by a small, rear door; change my clothes, and go out by the front door to take a carriage to the Hôtel d'Albret or the town house of the Richelieus" (Mme Scarron had met the Montespans through their cousins, the d'Albrets). "All these precautions were taken to ensure that my regular coterie of friends should notice nothing unusual nor ever suspect that I had a secret to hide. I resorted to frequent bleedings to reduce the likelihood of blushing at their questioning. . . ." (In view of the fact that Mme de Montespan bore the King a child almost yearly—pregnancies constituting the chief occupational

* Mme de Caylus refers throughout to Mme de Maintenon rather than Mme Scarron. The name Mme Scarron has been used in the translation of these passages from *Souvenirs* in order to avoid chronological confusion. For bestowal of the marquisate de Maintenon on Mme Scarron in 1674, see p. 89.

hazard of a King's mistress—it is clear that Mme Scarron's secret life was busy.)

"A strange life, indeed, she is leading," Mme de Coulanges wrote to her cousin, Mme de Sévigné. "Not a mortal soul now has any contact with her . . ." By 1671, the lot of them—Mme Scarron, the royal bastards, a staff of domestics and nurses—would be set up in a house hidden deep within extensive gardens on the rue de Vaugirard, "that large and handsome house to which no one has entrée," as Mme de Sévigné, Mme Scarron's close friend, wrote to her daughter in the provinces.

"The King did not take to me, in the beginning"; we have Mme Scarron's own word for it. "He found me too pedantic for his tastes."

Mme Scarron eventually brought him around, insinuated herself into his good graces; she was an expert at it, as at the waiting game. There was poetic justice in Mme de Montespan's falling into a trap so similar to the one she had herself set for La Vallière.

The children secreted and under guard, the King's next step was to regularize, insofar as possible, Mme de Montespan's highly irregular position. By July 11, 1670, separation proceedings were under way at the Châtelet Court of Paris: a petition entered there by Mme de Montespan for legal relief, to ask for "separate maintenance"; to throw off "the shackles of coverture," permission to domicile separately from her husband; to recover her dowry from out of community property holdings—on the grounds of cruelty and improvidence.

Despite the fact that the judges at the Châtelet must have been well aware of the King's intense personal interest in the Montespan *versus* Montespan Case, it would drag on—blind and stubborn judicial obstruction against despotism—over four long years.

The springtime of 1672 was a time not for love but for glory: in April, the French army (over 100,000 strong, odds of 4 to 1 over the Dutch) marched out toward Holland and the northeast frontier, which was still too close for comfort to Paris.

No ladies had been invited on this expedition: Mme de Montespan, wearing a *robe battante*, awaited the birth of the third of the royal bastards (the Comte de Vexin) at the Château de Livry, just outside the capital. Louis XIV considered it well worth a detour to stop to bid her one last fond farewell before he rode off to join his army.

Madame de Sévigné kept her daughter Mme de Grignan posted, as on May 4, 1672: "The lady whom you refer to as The Incomparable" (the mails notoriously susceptible to interception and censorship, mother and daughter wisely resorted to a code in reference to the royal ménage) "was visited by her lover. He stopped off to see her en route . . . spent two hours with her, and saw his children there, it is believed, for the first time. . . . The Fair One will stay on, there, for three or four months. . . . Guards have been posted, and one of her friends is keeping her company. . . ." Mme Scarron was the "friend."

A poem attributed to Mme de Montespan's pen (a lady's lament on the seventeenth-century way of life) may well have been addressed to her warrior-lover at this parting:

> *Already I hear the noise of arms,*
> *The drums call forth their King,*
> *Again I feel those wild alarms*
> *You cause me all my years.*
> *Must I forever shed such tears*
> *At each return of Spring?*

The foremost exponents of the various arts—and they were legion in this profuse blossoming of artistic genius—were enlisted to memorialize history, on the spot, as Louis made it; Pellisson with his pen and Van der Meulen with his brushes were on the banks of the Rhine on June 12, 1672, to ensure that its crossing, at Neuss, would go down in the annals of time along with Actium, Agincourt, Hastings, Poitiers. A splendid, bloody spectacle from which the Flemish artist censored every drop of blood: the only daub of crimson on his canvas for the plume of Louis's war bonnet. "The most magnificent, best-disciplined fighting force of the world"

(Voltaire a better chronicler than Pellisson): "An object of terror and admiration to all the countryside. . . . The King at the head of his personal guard corps . . . their uniforms glittering with gold and silver . . . the flower of the feudal aristocracy, radiant with youth and good looks. . . . The French . . . envisioned the Crossing of the Rhine as a greater prodigy than it really was. . . ." No Rubicon; the Dutch shore scarcely defended, the significance was primarily symbolic—the penetration of the frontier of Roman Gaul, a river to block Caesar's passage, but not Louis's.

On June 12, 1672, with "total victory in sight, Amsterdam ready to surrender its keys," why did Louis XIV disengage himself and his army? "For the sake of love!," by Saint-Simon's indictment. "The King yielded to his impatience . . . flew to Versailles to join his mistress." The Duke, who subscribed to the romantic theory of history, believing in the power of the individual to affect the course of it, insisted that, in this instance, the King's "love for Mme de Montespan proved fatal to his nation and his glory."

While Louis dallied in her arms at Versailles, late in June, Holland committed national suicide, opening her dikes and sluices, her main arteries; exposing her heartland to the sea; rendering it, at the same time, impassable to the invader.

The French were frustrated but the United Provinces, for all their "republican virtue," as Voltaire termed it, could not long survive, four feet under water. Louis XIV, ruthless in his peace terms, aroused the courage of despair, and raised up his own nemesis in the person of young William, Prince of Orange, to whom the Dutch turned, in this crisis, as their Stadholder. (Still Louis's implacable enemy, he would mount the throne of England, in 1689, with his wife, the English Princess Mary, daughter of James II.) William of Orange rallied the principal powers of Europe, aligned them in the first of the several coalitions he would organize to resist French domination of the Continent.

Voltaire, from his vantage point in the next century, concluded that the 1672 campaign against the United Provinces had constituted an "ephemeral triumph," celebrated by Louis XIV "too soon and too pridefully."

In 1673, another campaign was launched, and Mme de Montespan, Louise de La Vallière, and the Queen all joined the splendid court caravan that set out for the Dutch front to lay siege to Maestricht, which capitulated in eight days' time. (D'Artagnan along with one hundred and twenty of his musketeers perishing in the final frenzied assault.) But Maestricht proved another hollow victory: the conquest of Holland proper continued to elude French arms and French troops would shortly be evacuated.

Mme de Montespan stopped off at the citadel of Tournai with her hired companion and confidante, the Widow Scarron; when the Favorite put on her *robe battante*, the secret was out. The child born on June 1, 1673, was a girl, to be named Mlle de Nantes, to be legitimized by a special edict of Parlement, that winter, along with her brothers, the Duc du Maine and the Comte de Vexin.

By mid-July, Mme Scarron had returned to Paris with the infant, and Mme de Montespan had rejoined Marie Thérèse and La Vallière—"the three Queens" together again in the golden royal coach. La Vallière was soon to depart the circle: Bishop Bossuet had promised her his mighty support in winning the King's permission for her retreat to a cloister. La Vallière had humbly submitted to La Montespan's caprices; the new "inseparable," Mme Scarron, would not bow down before her. She would defy the Favorite on the subject—among others—of the childrens' education and upbringing, and she would win the King to her point of view, with the carefully implanted suggestion that Mme de Montespan was, at best, an indifferent mother. She showed no sign of pining for her legitimate son and daughter, off in Gascony with their father. Nor had she displayed great emotion, in 1672, at the death of her daughter by the King, their first child, born in 1669. "Mme de Maintenon was as touched as the tenderest mother" (Mme de Caylus says of her guardian); "far more, indeed, than the child's real mother, which inspired the King to remark, referring to Mme Scarron: 'She knows how to love. There would be delight in being loved by her. . . .' "

The King, as Mme de Caylus intimates, had begun to discover the governess's attractions, visiting her and the children more and more often in the rue de Vaugirard in Paris, expressing his disappointment when he failed to find the Widow Scarron in the company of his mistress.

A far more dignified title was shortly to be granted the poet's widow: the King, in bestowing on her the estate, the Château, and the marquisate of Maintenon, in 1674, would invest her with the name by which she goes down in history, that of Marquise de Maintenon.

VIII

The Age of Montespan

IN MAY OF 1674, with Vauban to guarantee the success of the sieges, Louis XIV conquered and annexed to France the province of the Franche-Comté (a region tucked away between the Alps and the ancient duchy of Burgundy; another Spanish property, a Spanish finger jabbing into the ribs of eastern France).* That same year, the Grand Condé piled up Pyrrhic victories in Flanders fields while Maréchal Turenne sacked and ravaged Alsace, Lorraine, and the Palatinate.

The newly conquered Franche-Comté was not to be edified by the spectacle of the King's "three Queens." On April 20, the day before the King's departure for the front, the heavy gates of the Carmelite convent had closed forever upon Louise de La Vallière. But the buzz of excitement on the subject had died down by the time the courtly caravan, jogging alongside the military, had left her and Paris ten leagues behind. "After all," the *Grande Mademoiselle* had shrugged, "she is not the first sinner to be converted."

"The Master," as La Vallière had come to call her former lover, had yielded at last to her "importunings." The "ladies' apartment" was no longer to Mme de Montespan's liking. If she had

* The Franche-Comté had fallen to French arms in 1668, but had been ceded back to Spain by the terms of the Treaty of Aix-la-Chapelle as a concession to the Triple Alliance.

accepted it originally, it had been, as Mme de Caylus suggests, as a necessary evil "whereby to deceive both her husband and the public." But a day had come when, "in a bad mood with the King, over some other matter—as she often was—she complained of that communal living. She claimed that it reflected a lack of delicacy on the part of the King. To appease her, the monarch replied with great tenderness and gentleness that it was an arrangement which had come about without his realizing it. . . . 'If you have failed to realize it,' Mme de Montespan snapped, 'you can be sure that such was not the case with me.' " ("Not even the King," says Saint-Simon, "was spared Mme de Montespan's ill humors.")

Bishop Bossuet, pleading La Vallière's cause, had originally encountered opposition and scathing sarcasm, he wrote, from Mme de Montespan. But she had finally "grown highly impatient," according to Comte de Bussy, "to see the Duchess off to the nunnery."

La Vallière could make her adieux without excessive anguish, she confessed, to her children, two beautiful little strangers, Mlle de Blois, now eight, and the Comte de Vermandois, aged six, both since birth in the care of the Colberts. They were to be left with a touching family portrait by Mignard—themselves and their mother —a sentimental study abounding with symbols: the rose, in La Vallière's graceful hand, drooping and dropping petals; at her feet, discarded, cases spilling jewels, spilling gold, likewise cast aside: a mask, a guitar, sheets of music, playing cards, a globe, the appropriate title engraved on the base of the column in the background of the painting: SIC TRANSIT GLORIA MUNDI.

La Vallière bade adieu to the Queen, throwing herself at Her Majesty's feet to beg Her Majesty's pardon. "Since my offenses were public," Comte de Bussy quotes her as saying, "it is fitting that my penitence be public, too." Her last supper she took in Mme de Montespan's magnificent new Versailles apartment. The next morning, the morning before the King's departure for the front, the Duchesse de La Vallière attended the King's Mass, there to bid him final adieu; at which he wept, according to witnesses, although in Sainte-Beuve's dictum the King would never—never in the next thirty-six years of La Vallière's cloistered existence—"forgive her for being able to tear herself from his presence, for preferring another to himself—even though that other be God."

By nightfall of the twentieth, the novice in the Carmelite convent was shorn of her greatest glory, her famous silver-blond hair; and by her own hand, as Bussy heard it. Yes, but! wrote Mme de Sévigné in a letter, next day, to the provinces: "But she spared the two fine curls on her forehead!" Despite Mme de Sévigné's cynicism, Louise de La Vallière had chosen the most austere of all the conventual orders, with the rule of silence prevailing; with the narrowest, barest cell and a wooden bed shaped as a coffin; with all personal property forbidden, save only a wooden spoon and earthen bowl in the refectory; with the manual work schedule long and arduous, from five in the morning to eleven at night. That "delicate, cherished, pampered flesh" of hers, as Bossuet referred to it in his sermon, would be mortified by a hair shirt, by crude heelless rope sandals (perhaps the greatest mortification of all for La Vallière, whose shoes had all been specially designed with heel lifts to minimize her limp, one leg being slightly shorter than the other).

Cards of admission were at a premium for the ceremony at which Sister Louise de la Miséricorde took her final vows and received her black veil from the hand of the Queen. Not a disparaging word came to Mme de Sévigné's pen as she described the spectacle to her daughter by letter on June 5, 1675: "That lovely and courageous person made her profession yesterday . . . in her customary noble and charming manner. . . . The entire congregation was struck by her beauty. . . . The sermon of the Bishop of Condom [Bossuet] lacked the inspiration one might have expected on such an occasion. . . ."

The comments of Mme de Scudéry, by letter to Comte de Bussy, were catty; "She never looked more beautiful or more content. She should be happy if only because she no longer has to lace up Mme de Montespan's stays. If the truth be told, she was a real martyr . . ."

If Louise de La Vallière had received gracious permission to

retire from the scene in 1674, the real reason was that the King and
Mme de Montespan could by then afford to dispense with her presence. By midsummer of that year, the Court of the Châtelet was
ready to grant Mme de Montespan the long-awaited legal separation from her much-feared husband.

"The high and mighty dame Françoise de Rochechouart," in
the wording of the decree handed down by the six judges in July,
"Lady of the Palace to the Queen . . . does and shall continue to
domicile separately from her husband . . . he, furthermore, henceforward . . . forbidden to frequent or haunt his lady . . ."

The process of law had been effected by a special formula (*é-
vocation*) best calculated to avoid publicity; witnesses had appeared at the Châtelet to attest to the Marquis's "profligacy in
financial matters" and to his "physical cruelty." Mme de Montespan had not appeared; all instruments bearing her signature had
been sealed and dated by her "in her apartment in the Palace of
Versailles." The judgment further specified that the couple's
community property should be separated and that the Marquise
was to be absolved from liability for any debts incurred during the
period of their marriage; the Marquis was ordered to restore to the
Marquise's family that portion of the dowry which had been paid
out at the signing of the marriage contract; he was furthermore to
pay the Marquise 4,000 livres annual alimony. In practice, however, these terms were considerably relaxed: the alimony awarded
to his wife was to be diverted to the advantage of the children;
restitution of the dowry sum was to be made to the children, too;
by the Marquis's will, upon his death. Having won her point and
her freedom, the Marquise could afford to show generosity: "It had
never been her intention" (according to an instrument dated July
21), "in this separation which she had sought, to bring about the
ruin of the house of the aforesaid seigneur, her husband; nor to
prejudice the interests of their children. On the contrary, she desired to contribute insofar as possible to the luster of the house of
Montespan, and to ensure that the education of the aforementioned children be of a standard consistent with their rank and
station. . . ."

Wherewith she may have considered her duty done to those children and their education. Marie-Christine would die the next year, 1675 ("aged approximately ten," according to the Toulouse Archives). The Montespans' son, the Marquis d'Antin, would write in his Memoirs that he never laid eyes on his mother until he was fourteen when he fell ill at the Collège de Juilly, near Paris, where she came to see him in 1679. "It was the first time I had had that pleasure. She evidenced me much cordiality but there were cogent reasons—reasons of court—why she could not visit me more frequently . . . and at this time I was deeply mortified. . . ." Here, the young Marquis speaks a kind word for his father, who has had few enough of them: "As for my father, he could not have shown me greater love and devotion . . . and, naturally, I responded . . ."

Their apprehensions about the Marquis de Montespan allayed by the court action in 1674, the King and the Marquise de Montespan could greet the birth, that year, of their fifth child—a girl, Mlle de Tours—more openly. From this time on, as the Duc de Saint-Simon points out, "Both the pregnancies and the births were public. . . . At first, the existence of the children had been kept secret. . . . Gradually, they were brought out of hiding, openly acknowledged. . . . Eventually, they and their governess were installed at the court . . ."*

The royal bastards—along with their mother, the royal Favorite—were now not only to be established in the official court hierarchy, they were to be integrated, by association and by marriage, into France's ruling family, blood brothers of the Bourbons (so

---

* Of the seven children born to the King and Mme de Montespan, three died before reaching maturity: the first child, a girl, had died at three, in 1672; Mlle de Tours would die in 1681, aged seven; the Comte de Vexin, born in 1672, would die in 1683. "All blighted by nature" (according to *Madame*) "with the sole exception of the Comte de Toulouse" (the last born); "the Duc du Maine, crippled; Mme d'Orléans, deformed, and Mme the Duchesse [de Bourbon], with a limp." The first-born is reported elsewhere to have been born with "a head so huge, the neck could not support it."

determined a policy of integration did Louis pursue that future generations of Bourbons would, almost without exception, trace Mme de Montespan's blood in their veins).

As for the Duc du Maine, the eldest born of the males among the royal bastards and favorite of all the King's sons, he was hailed as "Son of Jupiter" by La Fontaine, a protégé of Mme de Montespan's, who carried his friend Molière's *Amphitryon* analogy one step further. "You are the son of a hero," his mother once wrote to remind the boy, urging him "to show the ambition and courage appropriate to such a heritage. . . . It is well that you should know that you are fortunately spared any admixture of blood less noble —as is often the case with people of your kind. . . . You are the exception to the rule" (of royal bastards) "in that in both blood lines you can count nobility, courage, wit. While this gives you a singular advantage, to be sure, still it imposes an obligation to live up to both!" What she meant was that the Rochechouart-Mortemart blood was not less distinguished than the Bourbon.

Madame de Montespan considered herself more than the King's official mistress, as prize a role as that was deemed to be; she considered herself more than the Favorite, as significant a status nationally and internationally as the Favorite commanded. As her reign extended into a decade and beyond; as her children by the King grew and were legitimized, then integrated into the reigning dynasty, Mme de Montespan came to regard herself as the King's morganatic wife.

"The King's second wife," she was designated by the Ambassador from an African principality (to whom the idea of multiple wives was not surprising); he appeared at Versailles, bearing gifts for the French royal trinity; for Louis XIV, a tiger, a panther, and two lions for the new Versailles menagerie; for Marie Thérèse, a golden pheasant and a Moorish dwarf; for Mme de Montespan, pearls and sapphires.

"The real Queen of France," in the view of Primi Visconti. "At the table in her apartments, as at the Queen's, only ladies were received. She sat upon a chair with both back and arms . . . whereas even Princesses and Duchesses were entitled only to a *tabouret*. The King assigned four young cavaliers, smartly attired in His Majesty's own guards' uniform, to ride alongside her carriage everywhere she went. Except for the actual title, Montespan reigned; she was the real Queen of France."

The great years (if one concedes that any were great) of the reign of Louis the Great (if one concedes him the adjective) were the dozen-odd years between 1668 and 1680. These constituted the apogee of French glory and influence, power and prestige. If national greatness flows and ebbs with the tides of time, there was France at the flood. These were the years that would mark her with distinction for generations to come; this, the cultural phenomenon to be envied and emulated around the Western world. These were, as well, the years of Louis's great personal triumph, as master of Europe, if not of the world; as arbiter of war and peace, during his lifetime; as *arbiter elegantiarum*, for centuries to come. Well into the twentieth century, Western civilization would wear a French accent; the French, the tastemakers; the dictate would come from Paris in the graphic, the performing, and the decorative arts; in the art of living: in fashion, in cuisine, in manners, in speech, in social etiquette and diplomatic protocol.

That decade or more constituting the great years of Louis's reign over France coincided with the reign of Mme de Montespan over his heart (if one concedes he had one). If Colbert is often credited with being the real Augustus of France's Augustan Age, it is no more farfetched, no more fanciful to call this period "*L'Age Montespan*."

Louis XIV's Splendid Century would not have been quite so splendid without Athénaïs de Montespan.

If he presided consciously, an active Augustus, over his Augustan Age, his mistress actively and consciously encouraged, possibly guided him. Her orientation to the world of the intellect and the aesthetic could not but have had an influence on her lover. The King's mistress—and her family, all with highly cultivated literary and artistic tastes—gave direction to the cultural development of the era.

Mme de Montespan's taste was remarkable, remarked upon by all the contemporaries who knew the role she played as enlightened patroness of the arts. She early recognized the genius of the Four Friends: Racine, Molière, Boileau, and La Fontaine, all friends of hers as well as protégés. The Florentine musician, Lulli (Lully), had her to thank, along with the King—both ardent music lovers— for his appointment as director of the Royal Opera.

"It was Mme de Montespan—her views of glory as lofty as the King's—who selected Monsieur Racine and Monsieur Despréaux [Boileau] to write the history of the reign.* If this was a form of flattery, it was that of no ordinary woman, no run-of-the-mill mistress!" (High praise from another superior female, Mme de Caylus). "Despite Mme de Montespan's faults" (none of which were overlooked by Mme de Caylus), "she had uncommon qualities, grandeur of soul and loftiness of spirit. . . . She thought beyond the present . . . considered the opinion of posterity, as well," as when her choice fell on Bishop Bossuet, with all his "wisdom and erudition," as preceptor to the Dauphin.†

Madame de Montespan's tastes were as magnificent, as regal as His Majesty's. She shared his passion for architecture and landscape design. While he wrote and printed his own *Guide Book to the Gardens of Versailles,* she personally designed a fountain, "The Marsh," which featured a gilded willow tree weeping water from every frond; a hundred jets of water spurting from clumps of copper reeds and rushes (a total of 1,500 water spouts were counted by the time Louis XIV had completed those gardens in the last decade of the century—as many water spouts as servants at Versailles!). Mme de Montespan's pool was acclaimed the masterpiece of the

---

* History proved to be neither Racine's nor Boileau's forte. Mme de Sévigné might have been right when she claimed that her cousin Bussy would have done a better job as official historiographer of the Splendid Century.

† Mme de Montespan could not have guessed that, for all his "wisdom and erudition," Bossuet's fanatic and brutal discipline would cow and maim the Dauphin for life.

water gardens—just the touch of fantasy needed to relieve André Le Nôtre's rigid classicism, his acres of green geometry.* Since her every whim was gratified by her royal lover, there was cause for satisfaction in the fact that her taste was generally excellent.

She and the King would choose a promising young architect named Jules Hardouin-Mansart to design her Château de Clagny,† a miniature Versailles, close to the original in magnificence as well as geographically—the landscape architect for Clagny none other than Le Nôtre, his genius already manifest in Versailles's fabled gardens.

For Mme de Montespan's pastoral pleasuring, a porcelain pavilion—an exquisite and intimate trysting place—went up in the woodland edging Versailles park: the first of the Trianons, this one, with walls of blue and white faïence. (The second, the Grand Trianon—grandiose, rosy, marbled, colonnaded—was erected in its place in 1688, in what Saint-Simon refers to as the final phase of Louis XIV's "ruinous building mania."** Another name for the Trianon was the Palace of Flora, a flowerbower; flowers, the rage of the age; the parterres changed daily: one day, tulips; daffodils,

---

* Masterpiece though it was pronounced in Mme de Montespan's heyday, her water-tree fountain was later cut down to make way for the Basin of Apollo.

† "It beggars description!" Mme de Sévigné said of Clagny, then proceeded to describe it, noting over a thousand men still at work there in the summer of 1675. Its Courtyard of Honor was semicircular like that of Versailles; its Grande Galérie not quite so grand, but almost, with ceiling frescoes depicting the story of the *Aeneid*. Mme de Sévigné admired Le Nôtre's style: "He has left one small dark clump of woodland, to excellent effect. Then, there is a forest of orange trees, all in mammoth tubs . . . and to conceal the tubs, low trellises abloom with tuberoses, jasmine and carnations—the most exquisite, enchanting, original idea conceivable! A favorite promenade for all. . . ." Clagny, later the property of the Duc du Maine, was razed during the reign of Louis XVI to make way for a new twenty-eight-block addition to the town of Versailles.

** As for Louis's palace-building mania, in addition to Versailles, Marly —another weekend house—was erected during his reign; as well as Mme de Montespan's Clagny, and finally the Grand Trianon, restored in 1966 by President de Gaulle at a cost of $4 million for occupancy by himself and visiting heads of state.

the next; jasmine, another; et ceteras of stock and orange blossom and tuberose—the scent of the tuberoses so overpowering, one spring day, as Saint-Simon remembers, that the King and court fled, reeling, to escape it.

Mme de Montespan's Versailles apartment was to be larger than the Queen's: a layout sketch by Le Nôtre shows that eleven rooms were assigned to Her Majesty, in 1676, on the second floor of the new wing of the château, while twenty rooms were reserved for the King's mistress, on the same floor, adjoining the King's.

The Favorite's pearls were larger than the Queen's. Her train was carried by a Duchess; that of the Queen by a mere page.

"Bodyguards were stationed at Mme de Montespan's doors, and this was wise," *Madame* commented approvingly, "for the reason that the King was in her apartment, day and night. He even worked there with his Cabinet ministers."

"Madame de Montespan's court became the center of the court, the source of all pleasure, of all fortune—the hope and the terror of ministers and generals. . . ." (and because the Duc de Saint-Simon, while lavishly admiring Mme de Montespan, could never resist an opportunity to disparage the King, he added): "It was likewise a shame and a disgrace to all of France."

Saint-Simon is one of the few contemporaries to attribute any political influence to Mme de Montespan. An official mistress of the King's was generally considered a kind of political force in the court, but Louis XIV never permitted his Favorites any interference in the political arena. We have his own word for it in his Memoirs intended for his heir, speaking monarch to monarch: "Time given up to love affairs must never be allowed to prejudice affairs of state. . . . And if we yield our heart, we must never yield our mind or will. . . . We must maintain a rigorous distinction between a lover's tenderness and a sovereign's resolution . . . and we must make sure that the beauty who is the source of our delight never takes the liberty of interfering in political affairs. . . ."

Madame de Caylus might say that "Mme de Montespan had an ambition to govern and to make her authority felt," but most contemporaries agree that Mme de Montespan's influence was confined to the realm of grace and favor, and exercised primarily in behalf of her friends and family. She had the King's ear, and whenever possible put in a good word for her two sisters and her brother.

Generous pensions from the King and a choice apartment in all his palaces were enjoyed by the Marquise de Thianges, eldest of the three Rochechouart-Mortemart sisters. But then, Gabrielle had enjoyed the King's favor before Athénaïs ever came to court, and would never lose it. The youngest sister, Marie-Madeleine, had taken the veil at nineteen, in a "somewhat cavalier" fashion, in Saint-Simon's opinion. Veritable scholar of the family, she would turn the oratory into a study. Athénaïs caused the King's countenance to shine upon this sister: in 1670, Marie-Madeleine was named Abbess of Fontevrault, one of the richest and most important abbeys in France, a post hitherto reserved for ladies of royal blood. Favoritism was justified in this instance: Saint-Simon commends the Abbess's "talent for administration and for making herself beloved throughout her [Benedictine] order. . . . Her excellent homilies . . . her knowledge of theology and the Scriptures" (she had learned Greek, as a fifth or sixth tongue, in order to read the New Testament in the original) ". . . a truly remarkable woman. . . . At the height of Mme de Montespan's affair with the King . . . Mme de Fontevrault made frequent visits to the court. . . . If her nun's robes seemed out of place in such surroundings, she lost not a whit of her dignity. . . . The King took such a strong liking to her that he could scarcely bear to relinquish her company. . . ."

"The three most beautiful women of their age," Voltaire called the Mortemart sisters. And "enough wit between them" (according to Saint-Simon) "to furnish all of Europe! . . . Theirs, the gift of saying the most entertaining, most extraordinary, most original things—things no one expected, not even they! . . . A dazzling kind of talk peculiar to the Mortemarts. . . ." The Mortemart lingo, spontaneous, unpredictable, topical, universal, elegant, outrageous, fanciful, imaginative, literate, lyrical, ribald; now couched in stateliest, classical Académie Française French, purest of the century; now idiomatic, in the latest court jargon or raciest

Parisian *argot*. Voltaire, the conversational genius of his eighteenth century, paid tribute to Mme de Montespan as that of hers: she and her family "delighted everyone by a singular conversational line . . . a blend of jocularity, simplicity and finesse that was referred to as the Mortemart style." "I like clever, amusing people," the King once remarked to the Duchesse d'Orléans, and the Mortemarts all qualified.*

The Duc de Vivonne was "the most naturally pleasant fellow imaginable," by Saint-Simon's accolade; his easy, racy original sense of humor never failed to entertain the King, who used to tell, in Saint-Simon's hearing, "a hundred stories about Vivonne, one funnier than the other . . ." The Duc de Vivonne was one of the first great noblemen to treat artists and authors as social equals ("climbing three flights of stairs," as Boileau proudly noted, on a visit to that eminent literary critic). In the avant garde of both literary and religious views, born a century before his time, Vivonne was a man of the Age of Reason rather than of the Age of Louis the Great. Distinguished as both soldier and diplomat, swimming his white charger across the Rhine or serving as commander and viceroy in Sicily, his honors might have come to him on his own account rather than on his sister's; with the exception of the maréchal's baton, which came as a direct result of her intervention (at least in the Abbé de Choisy's version): "While searching through His Majesty's pockets, Mme de Montespan came upon the list [of newly appointed marshals]. Failing to see the name of her brother, she flew into a rage worthy of her mettle. The King, who could never resist her face to face, apologized by saying that it must have been an oversight on Louvois's part in drawing up the document. 'Send for him at once, then,' she said imperiously, and proceeded to a proper scolding. . . . The Minister

* Jacques Testu, that worldly and literary Abbé, made an interesting comment on the art of conversation as practiced by the three Mortemart sisters: "Mme de Fontevrault talks like a person who is talking; Mme de Thianges, like a person dreaming; Mme de Montespan, like a person reading." Mme de Caylus, who quotes him, takes issue: "He might be right about the other two, but he was wrong about Mme de Montespan . . . her eloquence was without affectation."

of War admitted to his error . . . and undertook to correct it instantly by appending Vivonne's name to the list . . . thereby appeasing the lady."

Both the Duc de Vivonne and his father, the Duc de Morte-mart, had made the gesture of resigning their court charges at the hour when Mme de Montespan's position as royal Favorite began to be publicly acknowledged. Not only had the King refused to accept their resignations; in 1669, he named his mistress's father as Governor of Paris.

It was Mme de Montespan, a devotee and a discerning critic of the theater, who suggested to her protégé, Molière, the theme for *The Magnificent Lovers,* * produced in 1670, a five-act comedy with choral interludes and ballets, in which the King danced the role of Apollo, the Sun God. It proved to be the last stage appearance of His Majesty's career, but confirmed balletomane that he was—and Mme de Montespan along with him—modern ballet may be said to stem from their enthusiasm: the art of choreography dating back to their court theatricals, where ballet movements and figures were, for the first time, recorded.

At thirty-two, Louis may have considered that his dancing days were over, but the Venetian Ambassador reported, "He is so vigorous and strong that before and after the ball, he goes to the riding ring or to the jousting arena." From the manège to the *carrousel* (tiltyard), from the *jeu de paume* (tennis court) to the hunt, from the Council Chamber (in session daily from ten to noon) to the chapel, to the table, to the boudoir, whither he repaired in the early afternoon, according to Saint-Simon—for a quarter of a century a daily observer of the royal timetable: "His Majesty slipped between the sheets with his mistresses after dinner."

If that was the mistresses' hour, the Queen's came at night, as a reward of patience. "Throughout the course of all his love affairs,"

---

* Molière's brilliant comedies of manners satirized the religious hypo-crite (*Tartuffe*, 1699), the female pedant or *précieuse* (*Les Précieuses Ridicules*, 1659, *Les Femmes Savantes*, 1672); the doctor (*Le Malade Imaginaire*, 1666); in 1670, it was the turn of the charlatan-astrologer. Visconti's resentment against Mme de Montespan may date from this lampoon of his profession.

Saint-Simon continues, "the King never gave up spending the night with the Queen . . . never did he fail to join her in her bed . . . though it was often late. . . ."*

"Marie Thérèse had made it her habit to wait up for him," as Mme de Caylus informs us, but the Queen did it without sulking, without reproach. "After all, the King renders her the full honors of her position," as astrologer Visconti adds. "He eats and sleeps with her . . . converses with her as gallantly as if there were no mistresses in his life . . . and fulfills his connubial duties. . . . He usually has commerce with her about twice a month. . . ." This last was inside information upon which Visconti cleverly based his calculations when required by Her Majesty to prognosticate the birth date and the sex of a child she hoped, on one occasion, to have conceived. Children of France continued to be born (six in all); continued to die (five out of six, all save the first-born, *Monseigneur*).

In his mid-thirties, Louis XIV began to wear a wig, and since he and his court set the fashion, all Europe followed suit. Too bad, really: the flowing curls, as shown in Bernini's bust of the young Sun King, are far more becoming than the massive, frizzly, leonine peruke. Not that His Majesty's luxuriant brown tresses had begun to thin, nor his vigor to diminish, but some of the earlier, the youthful "male and heroic beauty" of Voltaire's description was fading. His Majesty's legs were still the shapeliest pair in Europe, recognizable as his even at a masked ball. His body was still lithe and graceful, but the lines were beginning to thicken. Portraits of the decade by Van der Meulen and Testelin reveal a coarsening of the features: the eyes narrower, more glittery; the nose sharper, more salient; the lips more sensual but the mouth somehow compressed. "The pristine beauty," Saint-Simon comments, "had been succeeded by the imposing look . . . the aura of majesty. . . . It was a combination of his bearing, his walk, his manner, his expression

---

* The designation "the terrible Bourbons," in reference to their prodigious sexual proclivities, was never more apropos than to Louis XIV in his mid-thirties: the three to whom the line owes this reputation being the Sun King; his great-grandson, Louis XV; and his grandfather, Henri IV.

. . . all grand, regal, impressive . . . at the same time, entirely natural. . . . Long familiarity with his position had contributed to that
superbness. . . . His personal appearance, his face and form, likewise constituted an incomparable and singular advantage. . . . His
was, in sum, an awe-inspiring presence, a well-nigh terrifying majesty. . . . People were struck dumb at the first encounter. . . . On
state occasions, at Ambassadors' audiences and other such ceremonies, so imposing a figure had never before been seen. . . .
Indeed, one had to accustom oneself in advance to the sight of him.
Otherwise one might try to salute him publicly, and find oneself
speechless. . . ."

The Magnificent Lovers was not only a good title for Molière's
extravaganza, it was a good title for the royal paramours, the most
superb, prideful, and beautiful people of their time; partners in
splendor and imperiousness. Mme de Montespan's remark to the
King, quoted by Mme de Caylus, breathes a supreme arrogance:
"Mme de Montespan once reproached him for not being truly in
love with her: he had turned to her, she said, only because he
considered that he owed it to his public to have the most beautiful
woman in the Kingdom as his mistress."

When Mme de Montespan accused the King of loving her out
of vanity and personal glory rather than out of a genuine amorous
inclination, she proved that she understood the psychology of the
age. A love affair was "launched"—the popular seventeenth-century word for it—deliberately; the object of a gentleman's passion
carefully selected before he let that passion flourish. His reputation
as a gallant—the *beau idéal* of the age—rested upon the quality,
rather than the quantity, of his amorous liaisons. Athénaïs' love
carried the ultimate cachet: a great beauty, a great lady, a great
symbol of love.

The King himself equated love and glory, compared the
wooing of glory to the wooing of a mistress. "And this is how glory
must be wooed and won," he wrote in his Memoirs. "Glory is an
exacting mistress. . . . One proves oneself unworthy of her first
favors if one does not perpetually aspire to new ones. . . . In the

love of glory, one must display the same refinements—nay, even the same restraint—as in the tenderest passions."

"Madame de Montespan was imbued with the same sense of glory as was the King," Mme de Caylus conceded. Her hauteur was exceeded only by the King's: the Greek word for it was *hubris*, an ancient sin against the universe, an insolence, a wanton arrogance offensive to the gods on Olympus.

IX

The Easter Crisis

I F THE HEAVENS were slow to smite the royal sinners, the Church would assume the responsibility. What Bishop Bossuet, in the King's apartments, had been urging privately, the famous Jesuit Bourdaloue* thundered at His Majesty—making so bold as to use even the word "debauch"—in a Lenten sermon in the royal chapel in 1675.

It was on Maundy Thursday, April 11, of that year's Holy Week, that a humble priest of the Versailles village church dared deny Mme de Montespan absolution. "She stormed out in a tantrum" (according to another churchman, a protégé of Bossuet's) "and went straight to the King . . . to demand revenge for the insult suffered. . . . For a judgment, the King called on the Bishop [Bossuet] . . . who replied that 'In circumstances such as these, a clean break . . . an absolute severance of relations was an indispensable prerequisite for admission to the sacraments.' " ("A temporary separation . . . as in previous years" was not acceptable to the Church in 1675, as Visconti noted.)

The King's sins lay uneasily on him—all the comfort of previous Jesuitical casuistry now denied him. "He was, basically, a

* Chief in popularity of the sacred orators, Mme de Sévigné's favorite, Bourdaloue was the most stirring if the most longwinded. Fashionable ladies prepared themselves against emergencies by wearing, beneath their skirts, small porcelain receptacles popularly known as *Bourdalous.*

very religious man," Mme de Caylus observed, "giving evidence of his devoutness even during the periods of his most notorious misconduct with women—actually his one weakness. . . . Otherwise, he was decent and sober, so steadfast that he never missed Mass, in all his life, except on two occasions, and those when he was away with the army. He was especially remorseful on the high holy days when he could not perform his religious duties, or perform them only partially."

Until 1675, his personal confessor, Father La Chaise, had been more lenient. His Most Christian Majesty had performed his annual devotions at Easter but, in the past several years, had not dared to take Communion. He must do so, now, in 1675, as he prepared to go again to the Flanders front. He feared to meet death on the field of battle, unshriven.

Hosanna! On Easter Sunday, as the *Gazette de France* could officially announce, His Most Christian Majesty took Communion in the parish of Versailles.

What a commotion at court and capital when word got around that Mme de Montespan had been ordered to withdraw to Paris, with her four royal bastards and her friend, Mme de Maintenon (friend or foe? in pious league with the Jesuits? appointed by them to act as savior to His Majesty's immortal soul?).

"In the house outside the Vaugirard gates . . . Mme de Montespan received no one . . . [except] Bossuet, who went there daily . . . surreptitiously . . . wrapped to his nose in a great gray cloak. . . . Everyone was astonished at these developments" (the *Grande Mademoiselle* exclaimed) "though too discreet to admit the fact publicly . . ."

"Madame de Montespan made the rounds of the [Paris] churches, fasted, prayed, wept for her sins," says Mme de Caylus. "She shared the King's religious sentiments, and it was not solely to conform to His Majesty's views that she herself meticulously observed religious practices. She had been raised in a strict, religious household by an extremely pious mother, who had sowed the seeds of devotion in her daughter's heart from tenderest infancy —a devotion never to be lost. Of this she gave constant demonstration, as did the King, and I remember hearing it said that even during those years she lived as the King's mistress . . . she always fasted during Lent, so scrupulous as even to weigh her bread. The Duchesse d'Uzès, one day, astonished at such scruples, could not resist a comment. 'What, then, Madame!,' Mme de Montespan replied, 'Because I am guilty of one sin, must I commit them all?' "

Madame de Scudéry repeated the gossip as she heard it, by letter, to Comte de Bussy, writing on May 15 that the King had gone to Clagny, where Mme de Montespan was handily in exile, to bid her "a long and melancholy" farewell before he should depart to join the army on the morrow.

Apparently they were in secret correspondence during his absence, apparently with Colbert as the intermediary, although Bossuet continued to exhort the sovereign, throughout June of 1675, to strengthen His Majesty's resolve in his rupture with his mistress: "I do not expect you, Sire, to be able to extinguish, in one moment, a flame so violent; but seek, Sire, to diminish it, little by little. . . ." "A war more important, a victory more difficult," he called it, than any to be fought or won on any earthly field of battle. "May God give you victory, Your Majesty . . . both without and within . . . I see Mme de Montespan as often as possible, as Your Majesty commanded me. I find her fairly calm . . . occupied in good works . . ."

Not so, said the Bishop's secretary, the Abbé Le Dieu: "She spewed out reproaches; she told him [Bossuet] that it was his pride which had impelled him to cause her dismissal, to the end that he might hold undisputed sway over the King's mind. . . ." And when her rages failed to provoke the Bishop's ineffable calm, she resorted to the tactic of "flattery and promises—the highest honors of Church and State held out as glittering bait before him."

The three-year-old Comte de Vexin fell ill in June and his mother, for once, showed herself assiduous in her attentions, shutting herself up for six days and nights with him in a darkened room—unless it was all a touching scene of maternal devotion she had staged to be reported to the child's father, off in Flanders. She played to a substantial audience: all the court came to call; a sign that Mme de Montespan was not yet to be counted out. Even the Queen came to inquire and to visit Clagny, sign of an excessive complaisance.

Madame de Scudéry, Bussy's faithful correspondent, passed on the latest rumor: "It is said that Mme de Montespan will return to the court, although not lodged at the château, and that when she and the King meet, it will be always in the Queen's apartment. I have my doubts as to how long such conditions will prevail, for there would be great danger that love would gain the ascendancy again."

It was more than a rumor: the Archbishop of Paris, if not Bishop Bossuet, had agreed to consider Mme de Montespan's return to court, provided that the King gave his "word of honor that his conduct would be strictly honorable."

"Holy Week of the Jubilee Year once safely past, the question was whether Mme de Montespan could properly return to the court. Why not? asked her friends and relatives, even the most virtuous. Mme de Montespan, by right of birth and charge" (lady of the palace to the Queen) "belonged at court. She could lead a Christian life there as well as elsewhere. The Bishop de Meaux [Bossuet] agreed to this. . . ." (Herewith, two errors to be chalked up against Mme de Caylus's generally excellent memory: first, it was the year 1676, not 1675, which was celebrated as a jubilee by the Church; and secondly, Bossuet disapproved of any rapprochement whatsoever between the Magnificent Lovers.)

Back to her splendid Versailles apartment came Mme de Montespan in July, in advance of the King, whose return was scheduled for the twenty-first.

Out on the road to Luzarches—to meet His Majesty—went Bossuet, to make one final desperate plea; only to be told by the King (as Bossuet himself reports it): "Say nothing, Monsieur, say nothing. I have given my orders. They must be carried out."

"Should the meeting between Mme de Montespan and the King take place in public . . . without some advance preparation? Or should they meet first in private to avoid the embarrassment a surprise encounter might cause? . . . That was the problem," as

Mme de Caylus saw it: "It was decided that the King should come to Mme de Montespan's apartment but, to avoid any possibility of malicious gossip, it was agreed that the most dignified, most strait-laced ladies of the court should act as chaperones, and that the King should meet with Mme de Montespan only in their company. Thus, the King came to Mme de Montespan's, as had been decided but, almost insensibly, it seemed, he drew her aside, into a window recess, where they conversed at length together, wept together, and said to one another all the things a man and woman are apt to say on such an occasion.

"Then they both made a deep obeisance to that group of venerable matrons, and passed into another chamber.

"One issue of this famous reunion was the Duchesse d'Orléans" (the daughter born to Mme de Montespan and the King in 1677, who would be married to the Duc d'Orléans in 1692) "in whose face and in whose person I always think I discern the traces of this conflict between love and the Jubilee. . . ."

No surprise to those in the inner circle, this uncontrollable surge of passion, this tug of desire as irresistible as that of gravity; this yearning, this reaching, one to the other; this returning to a warm, familiar embrace, as ballet partners returning to a well-remembered, a virtuosic *pas de deux*.

No surprise to Mme de Scudéry: "They had parted purely because of religious scruples . . . still loving each other more than life . . ."

Once Mme de Montespan was restored to her pinnacle, all the courtiers began vying with one another to prove that their loyalty to her had never wavered, paying homage to her with lavish gifts, making pilgrimage to Clagny to salute her and to exclaim over the wonders of that recently completed château.*

---

* The Marquis de Dangeau's gift started Mme de Montespan's menagerie, according to Mme de Sévigné: "At a cost of more than 2,000 écus, he bought up the most passionate of all turtle doves, the plumpest of all piglets . . . the curliest lambs, the goosiest geese . . . and paraded the lot into Clagny. . . . Dangeau presented his gift so as not to be outdone by Monsieur Langlée" (another of the King's card-playing cronies). "Langlée's gift to Mme de Montespan had been a golden gown, gold on gold, and fitted over a

The Easter Crisis

The King himself had offered her a lavish gift of jewels, but this she had spurned as she had Mansart's first design for a small pavilion at Clagny—both more appropriate, she implied, "as gifts to be made to an opera singer." Like a Queen, Mme de Montespan preferred to help herself, upon occasion, from the crown jewels. "Mme de Montespan positively refuses to allow me to make her a gift of jewelry," Louis XIV wrote to his Minister of Many Portfolios Colbert: "This may seem extraordinary, but she simply will not listen to reason on the subject of presents. . . . Therefore, so that she may lack for no adornment, I want you to assemble a special collection . . . so that I can lend her whatever she may want. . . . Make up a jewel case including a necklace of fine pearls . . ." His Majesty's lengthy list began, ending with the injunction: "There will be considerable expense involved . . . but such is my will, my pleasure . . ." (this last, to shut off Colbert's nagging on the subject of the King's extravagance).

"The attachment" (the King's for Mme de Montespan) "is pronounced," a highly perceptive Mme de Sévigné could write in her letter of July 31, 1675. "There's ardor enough to fluster the parish priest and the busybodies, but perhaps not quite enough to

---

golden brocade sheath, which was cross-woven with threads of various shades of gold—all of which adds up to the most heavenly fabric imaginable. Fairies must have woven it on some secret, mysterious loom! Human hands could never have wrought it! The donor wanted to give the gift in a fashion as mysterious as its manufacture. So, Mme de Montespan's dressmaker came, one day, to deliver a dress she had ordered. It was a ridiculous misfit. What shrieks and scoldings went on, you can well imagine! The dressmaker spoke, all a-tremble: 'Madame, since time is pressing, please look at this other gown to see if it might not suit you as well as the one you ordered.' Whereupon the golden gown was brought forth. 'Oh, what a glory! What a fabric! Was it made in heaven?'—The gown is tried on. It fits to perfection. It is a picture! The King comes in. The dressmaker says: 'Madame, this gown was made to order, especially for you.'—It becomes clear that this is a gallantry on someone's part. But whose?—'It is Langlée's doing,' says the King.—'Of course, of course, it is Langlée,' says Mme de Montespan. 'Only he would be capable of so magnificent a gesture.'—'It's Langlée,' everyone starts saying. And all the world takes up the refrain: 'It's Langlée!' Even the echoes agree, and repeat: 'It's Langlée!'—Even I join the chorus, and chime in with the rest to tell you, my darling daughter, 'It's Langlée!' "

satisfy the lady, for—in the midst of her triumph—I detect an underlying note of melancholy."

What was wrong? A new, nagging sense of guilt, instilled by Bossuet and his terrible way with words? Guilt stemming from the sin of adultery, double adultery?

There came another reminder, another rebuff at the hands of a Fontainebleau curate, in September of 1675, who refused to hear Mme de Montespan's confession. It was only a harassment tactic, but it was embarrassing.

Love—or was it passion?—had triumphed, this time, over Archbishops, Bishops, and father confessors, but the Magnificent Lovers had been given to think that there might be an authority higher than the highest in the Church hierarchy, one upon which—for all their willfulness—they could not impose their will.

Things would never be quite the same again after the Easter crisis.

X

Dark Portents

MADAME DE MAINTENON, ever faithful to her charge, had traveled, that summer of 1675, to a spa in the Pyrenees, to try the curative effect of the waters there—as so many others had been vainly tested—for the young Duc du Maine's crippled leg.

Her spiritual adviser, Abbé Gobelin,* had doubtless sent her word that Mme de Montespan was basking again in royal favor. Strategically situated in the royal nursery, Mme de Maintenon had played her role in what appeared to be a Jesuit conspiracy, getting in a subtly barbed word, upon occasion, as adroitly as a *banderillero* setting his darts. ("Would not Your Majesty promptly cashier one of your beloved musketeers, were he to be discovered living in sin with another man's wife?")

When she returned to Versailles in late November, "the beautiful friendship" between her and Mme de Montespan had become "a bitterness, an antipathy," in Mme de Sévigné's opinion.

How could it be otherwise? "Mme de Montespan could not find in me views so diametrically opposed to her own without coming to hate me," Mme de Maintenon confessed to her father confessor in 1674.

---

* Most of the Abbé Gobelin's letters to Mme de Maintenon, along with most of her own letters and papers, were methodically destroyed in the final days of her long life: "I want to be an enigma to posterity," she said, and succeeded.

"As different one from the other as black from white. . . . The Lady Friend" (Mme de Maintenon, in the Sévigné code) "is so vainglorious that she defies the orders of the Other. . . . She seeks to please the Father of the children, not the Mother. . . . The Gentleman Friend [the King] is chided for his excessive cordiality to the Lady Friend . . ."

Madame de Montespan accused Mme de Maintenon of trying to alienate the childrens' affections (already a *fait accompli* in the case of the Duc du Maine). "The most terrible scenes go on between Mme de Montespan and me," Mme de Maintenon herself admitted to the Abbé Gobelin in a letter of 1675. "The King was witness to one yesterday. . . . 'If Your Majesty will accompany me into the adjoining chamber, mine will be the honor of explaining,'" she dared to say on this occasion. Things had changed. Six months earlier, as she had written her confessor, she "dared not address the King directly . . . Mme de Montespan would never forgive me for it. . . . The tales she tells the King about me are designed to damage me in his estimation. . . . I find it difficult to believe that it is God's will that I should go on suffering at Mme de Montespan's hands. . . ."

But if the pious claque continued to applaud her efforts to effect the King's salvation, she would persevere in what Saint-Simon called "her expert machinations . . ."

"Madame de Montespan's ill humors finished it off . . ." says Saint-Simon. ". . . She had never learned to control her moods . . . of which the King was most often the target. He was still in love with her, but he was suffering for it." (Mme de Maintenon may have felt that the Magnificent Lovers were well matched: the King, himself, was difficult in the extreme. "He lacked the faculty of making happy even those whom he most wanted to please," was the complaint of the first *Madame*, who spoke from bitter experience: "At least three times a week, his mistresses can expect a rough time of it.")

"Confronted with the necessity of conciliating his mistress" (Saint-Simon's account continues), "he became accustomed to discussing it with Mme de Maintenon, confiding his problems to her and consulting with her. Admitted thus into the innermost secrets of both lover and mistress . . . the clever *intrigante* knew how to cultivate that trust . . . to insinuate herself so thoroughly into the King's confidence that, little by little, she supplanted Mme de Montespan, who realized too late that the supernumerary had become indispensable to him. . . ."

Pregnant in late 1676, Mme de Montespan may have been relieved to see her perennially libidinous lover harmlessly occupied—or so it appeared—in the nursery with the children and their governess, whose pious and pedantic air had earlier displeased him ("Your highbrow friend!" he had once called her). Mme de Montespan may have thought, as did the court, that he was having his first experience of a Platonic feminine relation, what Mme de Sévigné referred to as "a brand-new country for him to explore" —the safest possible fields for him to roam during the months preceding the birth of their sixth child, expected the following spring.

Glory, the King's other passion, attracted his attention in 1676, away from the ladies in Versailles, to the town of Nijmegen where peace negotiations with the United Provinces were getting under way and where Louis's voracious appetite for glory and territory would be satisfied primarily at the expense of the mangy, decrepit Spanish lion. His triumph was complete when French replaced Latin as the official language of the Treaty of Nijmegen, signed in 1678. Out of all the annals of her history, that year marked the ultimate assertion of French supremacy; in the words of Lord Macaulay, France had at this time attained "over the surrounding countries at once the ascendancy which Rome had over Greece and the ascendancy which Greece had over Rome."

In that year, Louis ascended to his personal summit; the rest of the reign was anticlimactic. "Louis the Great": the Council of Paris made the title official with the minting of a gold coin on which that legend was engraved in 1678. (The last great King in the last Great Age of Kings? Was this a sobriquet loosely bandied about, with Peter the Great, Frederick the Great, Catherine the Great all wearing it within a hundred years of one another?) The

Century of Louis the Great did not last that long; a mere twenty-five years was actually the extent of it. "A brief moment of almost miraculous equilibrium" of genius, of power, prestige, and glory.

The château of Versailles was Louis XIV's monument to French glory and to his own. "Did ever the sun shine upon such a King before, in such a palace—or, rather, did such a King ever shine upon the sun?" as Thackeray sonorously propounded the question.

To see Versailles in all its glory one must have seen it in 1676, shortly after His Majesty moved in. And preferably with Mme de Sévigné, on a sunny Saturday in July:

"On Saturday, I went to Versailles, and here is how the day was spent: at three o'clock, the King, the Queen, *Monsieur* and *Madame* and the *Grande Mademoiselle*, all the Princes and Princesses, Mme de Montespan and all her retinue, all the courtiers . . . all, in sum, the so-called Court of France gathers in that handsome apartment of the King's, as you know. . . . The furnishings are divine, utter magnificence everywhere . . ." (the ceilings frescoed by Le Brun, the walls covered with Leonardos—including the "Mona Lisa"—Titians, Raphaels, Rubens; a hundred thousand candles blazing in giant silver candelabra and silver chandeliers). "There is music playing, as always . . . but the gambling constitutes the chief attraction. . . . There sits the King, with Mme de Montespan holding his cards; there are *Monsieur*, the Queen, Madame de Soubise, Dangeau and Company; Langlée and Company. Thousand louis gold pieces are scattered across the table; no other tokens . . . I saluted the King . . . and he returned the salutation as gallantly as if I were young and beautiful. . . . Mme de Montespan talked to me about her trip to Bourbon. . . . She said she had gone to the spa for relief of pain in one of her knees, and came back instead with a misery in both of them . . . I found her quite flat again in the rear end . . . but seriously speaking, her beauty is breathtaking. . . . While losing weight, she lost none of her radiance . . . her skin, her eyes, her lips all aglow. . . . Her costume was a mass of French lace; her hair dressed in a thousand ringlets; the two at her temples quite long, falling against her cheeks; her coiffure topped with black velvet ribbons and jeweled pins; her famous pearl necklace . . . caught up with superb diamond clips and buckles. In short, a triumphant beauty to show off, to parade before all the Ambasssadors. . . . This delightful hubbub in the King's apartment goes on from three to six . . . when the gaming ends . . . and then they are off in their carriage: the King, Mme de Montespan, *Monsieur*, Mme de Thianges. . . . The Earthly Paradise! . . . Later, everyone amuses himself according to his fancy. . . . Some go out on the Canal in gondolas, again to the sound of music. . . . At ten o'clock, they all come in for the performance of a comedy. . . . At the stroke of midnight, supper [the *medianoche*] is served. . . . And that's how Saturday is spent at Versailles . . ."

"Never has Quanto's sovereign sway been so firmly established!" Mme de Sévigné wrote, later that summer of 1676, using her favorite code name for La Montespan. "The rumor about La Théobon is totally unfounded . . ."

Rumors were flying: another linked the name of the Comtesse de Louvigny with the King's. What truth there might be to the rumors, no one could say with certainty except Bontemps, His Majesty's valet in charge of assignations. As for the beautiful Thianges girls, Mme de Montespan no more feared "those two snot-nosed little nieces of hers than if they had been carbonized!"* Far more likely, Mme de Sévigné thought, that it was their aunt, herself, who had introduced "the wolf into the lambfold," purposely tempting the jaded royal palate with those tender morsels of female flesh.

"Her beauty [Mme de Montespan's] is at its most glorious; her attire matches her beauty; her gaiety matches her attire."

Mme de Sévigné prided herself on the accuracy of her reportage but, in the autumn of 1676, in the tenth year of the royal liaison, Mme de Montespan's gaiety seemed somewhat strained. The royal wolf was on the prowl along the secret stairs, the back corridors of Versailles, as even the dullard Queen could see. Poor

* Brilliant matches would be made for the two Thianges daughters: the eldest would be married to the Duc de Nevers, nephew of Cardinal Mazarin; the youngest, to the powerful Italian Duke of Sforza.

Marie Thérèse! Another treacherous friend, another of her ladies of the palace, the beautiful Princesse de Soubise, had managed to attract the King's roving eye. And the Prince de Soubise, head of that proud and ancient Armorican Soubise-Rohan family, was not too proud to connive at his wife's amours with his sovereign.*

(Might the house of Montespan not likewise have prospered, had the Marquis been as complaisant a husband as the Prince de Soubise? Even in these latter years, Montespan was still a trouble-maker: a perpetual litigant, he was back in Paris, back in court; this time, a hopeless suit to obtain the succession to a dukedom on the distaff side. A letter from the King to Colbert proves that the intransigent husband still occupied the fears of the double adulter-ers: "Monsieur de Montespan is a madman. Keep a close watch on him . . . in order to deprive him of any pretext for lingering on in Paris, see to it that Parlement rushes through his case. . . . I know that he has threatened to see his wife. . . . Get him out of Paris as quickly as possible. . . .")

"It is said" (said Mme de Sévigné in late August of 1676) "that there is a scent of fresh meat in Quanto country . . . although no one is quite sure just where it comes from. A lady is named whose name I have already mentioned but since this clique is oh! so subtle, that lady may not be the one after all. The one sure thing is that the Cavalier" (the King) "is gay and sprightly whereas the Demoiselle" (Mme de Montespan) "is sad, mortified, and some-times tearful."

Madame de Sévigné simply could not keep up with develop-ments at Versailles. On September 2: "The Madame de Soubise episode has passed like a shooting star across a summer sky. . . .

---

* The story went that the Prince de Soubise snored on in unbroken rhythm when Bontemps knocked at their apartment door to summon the Princess to the royal rendezvous chamber. The Prince de Soubise could afford to serve as the butt of court humor: "Never was so prodigious a family fortune founded so speedily," Saint-Simon declared: "An abominable and magnificent heritage built up to be left to her house." The Hôtel de Soubise, the most magnificent private residence in Paris—today a museum and home of France's National Archives—stands as a monument to the Princess's beauty and the Prince's complaisance.

The reconciliation is complete. The other day, I am told, Quanto was seen at the gaming table, leaning her head, as cosily as could be, on the shoulder of her Friend. This was an affectation to be interpreted as: 'Never have I been in higher favor!' "

These were the years of the passing fancies, the amourettes, the dalliances. Mme de Sévigné called the King "a wolf," but was not the prey more forward than the predator? As His Majesty himself phrased it: "They lay siege to the heart of a Prince as to a citadel."

In the September 11 Sévigné communiqué: "Everyone believes that Quanto's star is paling. There are tears, moods of depression, airs of gaiety, fits of sulking, In fine, my dear, it's over. . . . The Beauty keeps to her apartments while the rest of the court continues in its round of revelry."

And by a September 30 bulletin, Mme de Sévigné flashed the latest news to Mme de Grignan: "Everyone is convinced that the Friend is out of love, and that Quanto is in a quandary—unable to decide which she most fears—the consequences of the return of the royal attentions or the dangers of withholding her favors . . . and seeing her royal lover turn elsewhere. Certainly she has not yet adjusted herself to the idea of a mere friendship . . . so much pride and so much beauty are not easily reconciled to take second place. Jealousy runs high, but when has jealousy ever changed the course of events?"

In 1677, it was jealousy of Madame de Ludres, a maid of honor of the Duchesse d'Orléans, who called her "an exceedingly beautiful creature." Visconti criticized La Ludres for "giving herself all kinds of airs. She wanted the court to think she was pregnant. . . . On the mere surmise that the King was in love with her, all the Princesses and Duchesses rose to their feet at her approach . . . just as was done in the case of Mme de Montespan. And it was by that mark of distinction, paid to Mme de Ludres, that the Queen learned of this new infidelity of the King's. . . . The Queen had, by then, resigned herself to his infidelities, but Mme de Montespan still flew into a rage . . . and did her best to disparage her rival. . . ."

Her best was very good indeed; to make sport of others was a specialty of Mme de Montespan's: she was a terror when it came to raillery and ridicule. "The courtiers avoided walking beneath her windows, especially when the King was there with her," Saint-Simon explains: " 'Running the gauntlet' was their expression for it, one that became proverbial at Versailles." "That rag-bag!" was one of her least scathing epithets for La Ludres. "Mme de Montespan could cheerfully have strangled her . . . led her a frightful life," as Mme de Montmorency notified the Comte de Bussy in 1677.

Heavy with child as La Montespan was in early 1677, there was little else she could do but fulminate against her rival. (If she tried something else, no one suspected it at the time.)

The King may have been glad to escape to his army, to the front, in February of that year, a campaign distinguished by the victorious assault on Valenciennes.

The birth of Mlle de Blois, on May 4, was surrounded, for some reason, "with great secrecy," by Mme de Caylus's account: the child "kept out of sight." She was born at the Château de Maintenon, Mme de Montespan and Mme de Thianges paying a long visit there. It could not have been too congenial a gathering: the châtelaine—the erstwhile paid companion and governess—had turned haughty and independent; would have no part of this sixth royal bastard; nor of the seventh, to be born the following year. "Monsieur de Louvois undertook their upbringing in the rue de Vaugirard house [in Paris]."

The King's return from the campaign was announced for the end of May: "We all await the King," wrote Mme de Sévigné on the nineteenth; "all the court beauties are on the alert to see which way he will turn."

He turned back to Mme de Montespan, away from Mme de Ludres.*

"Oh, my daughter, what a triumph at Versailles!" exclaimed Mme de Sévigné, describing a triumphant Montespan. "What pride redoubled! What a solid re-establishment of favor! . . . There's evidence of an added zest in the relation—all the sweeter,

---

* A princely honorarium of 200,000 francs was offered to Mme de Ludres with the suggestion that she betake herself, like Mlle de La Vallière and Mlle de la Motte d'Argencourt, to a convent.

now, after the lovers' quarrels and reconciliations. What a re-affirmation of possession! I spent an hour in her [Mme de Montespan's] chamber . . . the very air charged with joy and prosperity!"

By July 2: "Quanto and her Friend spend more time together, apparently more enamored of one another than ever before. . . . All the ardor, the urgency of the first years of the liaison are evident again today . . . all constraint is banished . . ."

By July 30: "Mme de Montespan was ablaze with diamonds the other day. The eyes are dazzled by the sight of such a glittering divinity. The attachment seems stronger than ever before; they are at the stage where they gaze into one another's eyes . . . never before has a love affair been seen to start up all over again like this one!"

"The return of the royal attentions" produced their inevitable "consequences": Mme de Montespan was bearing them for the seventh time when she set out with the King, the Queen, and the army, in February of 1678, toward Lorraine.

A military campaign in midwinter must have been a frightful hardship for a woman five months pregnant: "The roads are so bad and so torn up," Minister of War Louvois's agent, Saint Pouange, reported back from Provins, "that most of the court coaches have had difficulty getting this far. The coaches bearing the ladies of the palace frequently overturn or stick in the mud." And those ladies eternally on parade in full court regalia, laced and squeezed into those "monuments of whalebone and brocade."

The King left the ladies to dash off to Flanders, to lay siege to Ghent and Ypres, the former capitulating to the French in four days; the latter in seven.

On April 9, 1678, flushed with victory—"at the height of his grandeur"; "the terror of Europe over the last six years"—Louis XIV could issue an ultimatum to the league of his enemies, giving them one month's time to gather at Nijmegen and affix their signatures to the treaty he was offering. By autumn of 1678, his will was done: "His will, the law from one end of Europe to the other," as Voltaire defined it.

"Excesses of power," in Saint-Simon's definition, "from which one must pass . . . to others . . . even more fatal." Excesses of love: "The King's love affairs, the scandal of which filled Europe, confounded France, rocked the state, and doubtless brought down upon him the maledictions under the weight of which he saw himself brought so perilously close to the abyss, and his legitimate posterity threatened with extinction, the [Bourbon] line hanging on one slender thread" (the life of one frail great-grandson of tender age, the future Louis XV).

"Immediately after the fall of Ghent and Ypres, the King—still extremely enamored of Mme de Montespan—returned to Versailles several days before Easter, 1678. Père La Chaise, the King's confessor" (this eyewitness, the Marquis de Sourches, informs us in his Memoirs) "stayed on at Lille, claiming illness, although this may have been an excuse to avoid giving absolution to the King who, despite his resolves and promises, still would not break off relations with his mistress."

But with the birth, in June, of their last child, the Comte de Toulouse—again, a secret lying-in—the spell was broken. The King would love and favor the son, but he was becoming disenchanted with the mother (literally as well as figuratively, some would say, in the light of the sinister developments of the next few months).

The Italian Visconti, discounting the notion of the supernatural, attributes the end of the romance to strictly natural causes: "The King was tired of Mme de Montespan." (After a dozen or more years, a half dozen or more children!) "She had acquired an ascendancy over him which had developed into a kind of domination. And recently, since the birth of her last two children, she had gained so much weight that her legs—as I noticed, one day, as she was stepping out of her carriage—were as large as mine. . . . And this despite the fact that she spends two or three hours a day taking massages, rubdowns with perfume and pomade."

Opulent charms were fashionable, but Mme de Montespan's were now perhaps too substantial; she was gross with childbearing, with food and drink: "She was a heavy drinker, although never drunken," according to *Madame*. "She was a hearty eater," according to Saint-Simon, "loving her table to excess." (Of course, one cannot but sympathize with her dilemma: the King frowned on diets, as on dainty appetites—his own, gargantuan—expecting every lady in his carriage to do her duty by the huge hampers packed for his drives, as from Versailles to Fontainebleau, or for his hunting *pique-niques*.) Mme de Montespan was a gourmet as well as a gourmande; her chef one of the most renowned of the day.*

Madame de Montespan, thirty-eight in 1678, lush, velvet-petaled, was a full-blown rose. The King had reached an age (forty) when delicate, tight-furled rosebuds caught his eye, captured his fancy: such a one as seventeen-year-old Marie Angélique de Scoraille de Roussille, better known as the Demoiselle de Fontanges, whose noble but impecunious provincial kinsfolk made up a purse to finance a court debut and to promote their promising candidate in the competition for the King's favor. She had been "destined by her parents, since her early youth, to attain to this illustrious position," this glorious dishonor traditionally reserved for ladies of noble birth.

"Your beauty is a gift from the gods!" the fickle La Fontaine rhapsodized, dedicating the third edition of his *Fables*, in 1680, to the new Favorite, Mlle de Fontanges (the second edition he had dedicated, in 1679, to Mme de Montespan, his first and foremost patroness, primarily responsible for the success of his career at court).

"An extraordinary blonde beauty, the like of which has not been seen at Versailles in many a year," Ambassador Ezekiel Spanheim reported to the Elector of the Palatine, on the subject of

* Mme de Montespan's chef was Mouthier, one of a long line of distinguished chefs; his son would preside over the elegant table of Mme de Pompadour; his father had served the Grand Condé as *maître-chef* (successor to the Great Vatel, who had impaled himself upon his sword at the prospect of a fishless dinner party—his seafood order undelivered—a Friday dinner party, moreover, at which the expected guest was His Majesty, the King).

Mlle de Fontanges: "A form, a daring, an air to astonish and charm even that gallant and sophisticated court."

"Her head was empty," Mme de Caylus adds, "except for romantic notions inspired by her provincial education and by the panegyrics on her beauty. The King, in truth, was attracted solely by her face. He was actually embarrassed by her foolish chatter—except, of course, when they were tête-à-tête. One grows accustomed to beauty, but not to stupidity, especially when it is complicated by vanity; especially when one is living at the same time with a person of intellect and character, such as Mme de Montespan, on whom none of the ridiculousness of the situation was lost, and who knew how to satirize it so devastatingly, to point it up for all the world to see. Mme de Montespan would not have feared the duration of the favor of Mme de Fontanges—knowing full well that the King would eventually return to her—had there not been other complications. Being of a character more ambitious than tender, Mme de Montespan had often contemplated the King's infidelities with indifference . . . and had herself encouraged the King in his first interest in Mme de Fontanges." "Going so far as herself to present the newcomer to the King, during a hunt," according to Mme du Noyer, that sensationalist letterwriter from Toulouse, "going so far as herself to undrape the girl's bosom, saying to the King, 'See, Sire, what a beauty we have here!'" (A popular sport to picture the reigning mistress as pandering to the lusts of her royal lover, as Mme du Barry with hers, Louis XV.)

Differing with both these contemporary accounts, Mme de Sévigné depicts Mme de Montespan as "enraged" with jealousy. Jealousy not only of Mlle de Fontanges but of Mme de Maintenon! For if the Comte de Bussy refers to Mme de Montespan and Mlle de Fontanges as "The Two Sultanas," Mme de Maintenon makes Three—although, keeping to the shadows as always, her favor was hereto less easily discernible. Mme de Sévigné thought she could make out a romantic triangle, now and then, as when she relays this news from Fontainebleau, where her son was in attendance on the King: "He writes that the court is caught up in a whirl of festivities, which no one is enjoying; that Mme de Maintenon's favor waxes steadily while Mme de Montespan's perceptibly wanes. That of La Fontanges never higher!" And again, in some perplexity: "Mme de Fontanges's position is brilliant, solidly established. And yet, what to think—what to make—of that steadfast, that growing friendship . . . those endless conversations that go on between His Majesty and Mme de Maintenon?"

"What a comedy the court of France presents," the Italian Visconti laughed to think of it: "The King living with his Favorites, one on each side of him, as if in a legitimate family group. The Queen obliged to receive visits . . . from both, as from the illegitimate children. . . . In chapel, the two Favorites sit in full view of the King: Mme de Montespan, with her children, in the tribune at the left; the other one, on the right. . . . There they sit and pray . . . rosary or prayerbook in hand, eyes raised heavenward, as ecstatical as a pair of saints!"

"The comedy" that so amused Visconti may have, by then, begun to pall on Mme de Montespan: by then, His Majesty had created Mlle de Fontanges a Duchess (where Mme de Montespan was a mere Marquise; no rank below the ducal being considered "titled" by the standards of the Duc de Saint-Simon). Not only had La Fontanges been granted a duchy: "her handsome new pearl-gray carriage, marked with her cipher on the doors," as Mme de Sévigné described it, was "drawn by eight horses"—where Mme de Montespan's could boast only six. By then, Mlle de Fontanges "came walking across the ballroom floor, straight to the King—like someone intoxicated—looking neither to her right nor to her left, oblivious to all, even the Queen. . . ." By then, Mme de Montespan was constrained "to lend a hand to Mlle de Fontanges's toilette" —to adjust a ruffle, tie a ribbon, fasten a rose—as Louise de La Vallière had felt constrained to lend a hand to hers. "You can imagine what a cruel blow this is to her pride."

By then, "Mme de Montespan was close to bursting with spite," as the Marquis de La Fare tells it, "and like another Medea, threatened to tear their children limb from limb before the very eyes of the King."

"During these rages of his former mistress" (La Fare continues) "he turned for consolation to Mme Scarron who, day by day, rose higher in his esteem and his good graces. Just as Mme de Montespan alienated him by her tantrums, the other endeared herself to him by her complaisances."

"Three rivals for the King's favor kept the court in suspense," said Voltaire. "No one knew what to make of it," Visconti, least of all; "some thought that Mme de Maintenon must be the King's confidante; others, that she must be a go-between; still others, that she was a clever person who was helping His Majesty draw up the Memoirs of his reign." Others, still, and to this day, that she was a clever person who held His Majesty off with a virtuosic show of virtue and piety. Once again, the Sphinx speaks for herself in a letter written to her cousin, Mme de Frontenac: "I send him away, frequently in frustration, never in despair." (To control the fire without extinguishing it—clever, indeed! Her own word for it, to quote the lady again, again a rarity: "Nothing is so clever as to conduct one's self irreproachably.")

Was it the hand of fate or a human hand—white, shapely, bejeweled—that moved to eliminate one corner of the romantic triangle?

The line "The lovely rose that lives its little hour" might have been written expressly for Mlle de Fontanges. Mme de Sévigné sums up the Duchesse de Fontanges's little life in a few lines of her own: "Has the world ever seen such an example of a creature at once so fortunate and unfortunate? That beautiful Fontanges sadly languishing at Chelles" (the abbey of which her sister had been recently named Abbess, by the King); ". . . all her life's blood draining away . . . and the King's love with it! She would gladly exchange the 40,000 écus pension and the ducal *tabouret*, which are hers—for the King's heart and for her health, which she has lost!"

If her "life's blood" was draining away in hemorrhage, it was the result, contemporaries conjectured, of a miscarriage or of childbirth complications in previous months. "The beautiful Fontanges grieves over the death of a tiny person," Mme de Sévigné heard. "No one sees her, these days." If there had been a baby, its birth and death were both kept secret. If it had died, it was said to have been "poisoned," according to a rumor the Duchesse d'Orléans helped to spread. If La Fontanges had lost "the King's heart," it was because illness irked and inconvenienced him; he liked his ladies lively, lusty; not "languishing . . . pale, wan, despondent," as Mme de Sévigné describes Mlle de Fontanges. "Wounded in the line of duty!" she went on to say, to win a laugh from her daughter.

As for Mme de Sévigné's "Beautiful Beauty" herself: "It is said that she believes that she has been poisoned, and she is now requesting bodyguards."

The King would not refuse them to his invalid mistress. His own company of Royal Bodyguards was already on the alert. It was bruited about that a conspiracy was on foot to poison the King and the Dauphin. "A prediction of the King's death had been made by a mathematician named Pagani . . . a cause of apprehension to His Majesty," according to Visconti—probably the Count Pagani listed in the Archives of the Bastille, imprisoned there in 1659 "for having boasted that he could bring about the King's death by magic."

The strange and sudden deaths of the past decade were reviewed by nervous Frenchmen in 1680: the death of the first *Madame*, ten long years past but never forgotten; the deaths of such prominent personages as Hugues de Lionne, Secretary of State for Foreign Affairs, mystifyingly stricken in 1671; the Comte de Soissons, in 1673; the Duke of Savoy, in 1675. The Queen of Poland, French by birth, had narrowly escaped a poisoner's hand in 1677.

The capital as well as the court was edgy: the priests of Notre Dame would reveal no names, out of respect for the secret of the confessional, but they were agitated enough to report to the authorities that "the majority of the parishioners who made confession to them confessed to the sin of having poisoned someone."

The authorities had been baffled by the riots that broke out in Paris in 1676—women in several quarters of the city making sudden assault on midwives and abortionists. The police could not

make head or tail of the hysterical talk about kidnapping and blood
sacrifice . . . newborn infants snatched from their mothers' beds to
die under the knife in obscene rites on unholy altars.

The police arrived at the opinion that some connection did
exist between the riots in 1676 and the case of an unholy priest
named Tournet, arrested and tried, the next year, on charges of
sorcery and sacrilege. Some connection, as well, between Tournet
and a self-avowed witch named La Grange, sentenced to death
along with him, both defiant, both boastful of their diabolic powers, both burned alive at the stake in the Place de Grève in
1677.

A rash of police raids and arrests erupted in the capital in 1678
and 1679; the lower depths of Paris, roiled, yielded up a great haul
of criminals of every kind: abortionists, midwives, pharmacist-
alchemists, counterfeiters, astrologers, palmists, soothsayers, sorcerers, necromancers, and Satanists.

And not just common criminals, either. Else why so many
lettres de cachet? Letters under the King's seal, arrest orders on the
royal authority, signed and sealed in unprecedented number in
1679 and 1680, made out in the names of personages well known
in exalted circles, creating an uproar in the highest ranks of the
French social structure.

The government-controlled newspapers maintained a strict
silence, gave no hint of these sinister developments, but rumor
spread like wildfire. No gag could stifle word of mouth, and the
word on every tongue was that of poison. On every pen, as well:
the alarms are sounded repeatedly—though usually in cipher or in
Latin—in countless contemporary diaries, journals, memoirs, letters. What talk there was was sotto voce: political comment being
not only frowned upon by the regime, but subject to punishment.

Even so, the rumor of poison was rampant again. Actually, it
had never subsided since the shocking Brinvilliers murder trial in
1676. In 1679 and especially in 1680—with the mystery surrounding Mlle de Fontanges's mortal illness, and her openly expressed
suspicion of being a poison victim—rumor rose to a crescendo to

astonish and dismay France and all the nations of Europe. The Bastille was filling; a special tribunal being set up: the most sensational criminal trial of the seventeenth century was about to begin —a kermess of crime, a carnival of horror that would be known to history as "the Poisons Affair."

Never mind Racine's "divine Poetry," never mind the glories of Versailles, the elegance and refinement of the French language and French society, the symmetry and order of French gardens and French intellects: the Poisons Affair would reveal to the world and to history the sordid underside of France's Splendid Century.

PART TWO
The Affair of the Poisons

I

Poisons

"**B**Y A SINGULAR COINCIDENCE," Voltaire reflects, "the crime [of poisoning] contaminated France at her hour of glory, just as it had Ancient Rome during the greatest days of that republic."

Ancient Rome conceded to be a cradle of Western civilization, it was Renaissance Italy the Western world had to thank for its pharmacopoeia of poisons. To seventeenth-century France, poison was the Italian Crime, just as sodomy was the Italian Vice, and venereal disease, the Italian Malady. Poison was considered the importation of the two Medici Queens of France: first, Catherine de Medici, bride to the Valois King Henri II, disembarking with a sinister suite of poisoners and necromancers. Throughout her reign, she encouraged all the practitioners of the occult sciences and the black arts: the baffling poet-oracle Nostradamus enjoyed her patronage, as did the two astronomer-astrologers, Tycho Brahe and Cosmo Ruggieri. At the Château de Blois, on the Loire, to this day, the guide points out the four secret wall panels in the Queen Mother's apartments, cleverly contrived in the woodwork to hold and conceal her cache of poisons (although it might have been her hoard of jewels). Marie de Medici, coming from Florence to wed Henri IV, arrived in France with her equally sinister crew of Concinis. France shuddered at the Medici name, synonymous with poison as was the Borgias': Duke Cosimo III de Medici equipped and staffed full-scale laboratories for scientific research in toxicology and production of poisons.

Poison carried a special terror in that time for the reason that there was no chemical technology permitting detection of either inorganic or organic poisons in the tissues of the body; autopsies could not satisfactorily prove or disprove the presence of poison in cadavers. The only test was to administer remnants of the suspect food or drink (if such remnants were available) to a fowl or domestic animal; if the bird or beast succumbed, the substance was pronounced poisonous, and any suspect in the case might be charged; otherwise, no charges were preferred and the investigation was dropped. Toxicology had not progressed beyond the lessons of the sixteenth-century master, the French surgeon-chemist, Ambroise Paré.* Arsenic, the chief poison in use—"rat killer," as it was then called—was used in a form ("white arsenic" or "pure arsenic," usually arsenic trioxide) which was odorless and tasteless, and thus defied detection.† With any expertise at all—by the artful variation of ingredients and of effects, the lethal dosage administered gradually, over an extended period of time—the poisoner could avoid arousing suspicion in the naïve medical faculty, and the victim was usually declared to have succumbed to a wasting illness. With poison unidentifiable, undetectable, with no proof positive in the test tube to convict a poisoner, he—or she—enjoyed a relative immunity.

She rather than he. Poison was primarily a woman's weapon, most suitable to a woman's hand. And women, it must be remembered, occupied an uncomfortable and subaltern position, both

* With the advent of toxicological chemistry—and the development, notably, of the Marsh Test in 1838—the detection of metallic poisons became quite certain and the risk, therefore, of using these for homicide greatly increased. Even so, there are still a number of poisons which are not to be detected in ordinary or even sophisticated investigations of death. New chemical structures are being discovered constantly, many with a deleterious effect on living organisms. The majority are not produced, however, in significant quantity and therefore carry no serious threat of danger.

† Arsenic in less refined material, and under heat, emits a peculiar garlicky odor.

legally and economically, in seventeenth-century France. Not only the fortune of the female but her person were subject to often tyrannous paternal and conjugal authority: an errant, an uncongenial, an inconvenient wife or daughter could be shut away for life behind convent walls. It is not surprising that the majority of the poisonings in that day were committed by women.

France had been in the grip of a poison psychosis since 1670. People remembered a series of suspicious deaths beginning with that of the first *Madame*, Princess Henrietta of England; the horror of her sudden end still fresh in the minds of those who knew and loved her, most of them convinced that she had been poisoned. As Voltaire heard it, half a century later, from an old retainer of the Orléans household staff, "Diamond powder had been sprinkled instead of sugar on her strawberries." Not so.* Mme de La Fayette was only one of several in her entourage to see *Madame* clutch at her side in anguish the moment she had swallowed the chicory water: "She had no sooner put the cup back on the saucer than she cried out, 'Oh, what a pain here in my side! What an agony!'" Modern toxicologists know that there is no poison (none of the alkalis or acids, none of the metallic or vegetable poisons) which could have acted so instantly upon her stomach and intestines without burning her mouth and throat (oil of vitriol, for example, is highly caustic; mercury chloride, highly corrosive†). In the light of numerous recent analytical studies of the official post-mortem report, the consensus of modern medical opinion is that *Madame* did indeed die of "natural causes," as the corps of autopsy surgeons unanimously agreed, including two English medical representatives who were invited to attend: "*cholera morbus*," "aggravated colic," "excess bile," even "her grievous sorrows" were listed as the

---

* If the particles of diamond powder or of ground glass are sharp enough or large enough to damage the stomach or intestines, the victim would be conscious of them when he took them into his mouth.

† Mercury salt was introduced into the pharmacopoeia in the sixteenth century by the alchemist-metallurgist Paracelsus, although the poisonous properties of mercury had been known since ancient times. Oil of vitriol was the term in use in the seventeenth century—and for many years thereafter—for sulfuric acid.

"causes of death." In modern medical terms of reference, the diagnosis might be a perforated ulcer with peritonitis. The autopsy surgeons did not so diagnose, in *Madame*'s case, for the reason that a stomach ulcer was not then recognized by the medical faculty. Foreign Affairs Minister Lionne dispatched a special envoy to deliver reports of the investigation and of the medical findings to the brother of the deceased, Charles II of England. Charles accepted Louis XIV's explanations and condolences, but what else could he have done as long as he had to go on accepting Louis XIV's subsidies? Lord Montagu, the English Ambassador to the French court, was less easily persuaded that *Madame* had not been the victim of her husband, *Monsieur*, and his vicious favorite, the Chevalier de Lorraine, who was allowed to return to France from his Roman exile two short years later: "If *Madame* was indeed poisoned, as most of the world believes" (Montagu reported to London in indignation—in cipher—in 1672), "certainly the whole of France regards him as her poisoner and is justifiably astonished that the King of France should show so little consideration for our sovereign as to permit him [the Chevalier] to return to this court."

No sooner had Foreign Affairs Minister Lionne done dealing with the sudden death of *Madame* than his own was upon him. He had been beset by problems not only in foreign affairs but in domestic ones—problems, to be specific, with his wife. Her conduct was "scandalous . . . outright outrageous" to Mme de Sévigné, who was not easily scandalized or outraged: Mme de Sévigné's code of morals, like that of most seventeenth-century French aristocrats, highly elastic. In July of 1671, Lionne arranged to have his wife arrested: twelve policemen and an officer conducted her to the Convent of St. Marie. Scarcely a month later, Monsieur de Lionne was stricken with a malady which baffled his physicians: falling into a coma on the night of August 27, he was dead by the morning of September 1, at sixty years of age. Madame de Lionne recovered her liberty a month after her husband's demise, but enjoyed it only briefly: in December, she was shut away again in the convent, this time at the solicitation of her son, either because he suspected her of poisoning his father or because he did not want to see her continue in the dissipation of her fortune.

Next on the list of sudden deaths of prominent personages was the Comte de Soissons, in the year 1673, on a summer campaign across the Rhine. Again a mysterious, a sudden seizure, death upon him in three days' time . . . while only a few leagues distant, his wife, the Countess, disported herself gaily with her sister, the Duchesse de Bouillon, and their two lovers, the Duc de Villeroi and the Duc de Vendôme. Shortly after her husband's death, Olympe went brazenly to join the court and army at Maestricht. It was reported to Louvois that the Comte de Soissons had "died firmly convinced that he had been poisoned." Did he suspect the fine Italian hand of his wife, Olympe Mancini? She stood to profit on every count by his death: she gained her liberty from an obnoxious mate, she inherited an enormous fortune, immense appanages, plus 400,000 livres cash in hand for the late Duke's commission as colonel-general of the Swiss Guard, which was purchased by the King to bestow on the three-year-old Duc du Maine. Rumor was rife on the subject of the Soissons murder, but the Countess continued on at court insouciant, unmolested in her post as superintendent of the Queen's household. Who would presume to level charges against a niece of Cardinal Mazarin, an early love of His Majesty's, presently ensconced in the heights of the court hierarchy?

In 1675, death struck again, suddenly and inexplicably, this time upon a cousin of the Comte de Soissons, Charles Emmanuel II, sovereign Duke of Savoy. His case much like *Madame's*: a goblet in his hand, a tall chilled beverage to cool His Serene Highness on a summer's day—death within hours after.

Who dared accept a goblet or cup or plate from the hand of a friend or a relative or lackey? Danger seemed to lurk at every table. Crystalline water drawn from the deepest, purest fountainhead was apt to develop a bitter taste. At the first sign of a domestic difference, husbands looked askance at wives, parents at children, and the other way around. Charles de Sévigné, arriving in Paris at this hour, and addressing his "Pretty Little Sister" in Provence, could write: "Here I am back again with our darling *Maman*, but so far no one has accused me of trying to poison her which, I can assure you—the way things are going presently—is no small tribute to my reputation for filial devotion!"

The Marquis de Sévigné was jesting, but suspicion and fear paralyzed the nation. Sudden deaths and unexpected deaths—even when the causes were most patently natural—now stirred up questions, doubts, suspicions. The French courtier became as nervous as the Spanish: Never smell a flower. Never inhale perfume. Never open a letter except with a gloved hand. Fear of the unknown is the worst of fears. If the laymen shuddered in the dark of ignorance and superstition, the medical faculty was little more enlightened. The science of toxicology inexact, in its infancy, the poisoner operated with relative impunity and utmost effrontery; the crime of homicide by poison was on the increase. The myth and mystery surrounding the properties and effects of poisons intensified apprehension. Paris and Versailles approached a state of panic.*

Danger signals had flashed—unheeded—as early as 1668.

The French court had reason to think that *Madame* had not been the only poison victim there in 1670: they pointed to the sudden spell of illness which had brought Louise de La Vallière low, occurring the same year as *Madame*'s and similar in many ways to hers, save that it was not fatal. Attempts on the Favorite's life had been made previously: once it had been a midnight assailant climbing into her window at the Palais Royal; a narrow escape, after which the King had stationed guards about her residence. In 1670, the attack would be more devious: it would appear that a number of her dearest friends at court, plotting to eliminate her from the competition, had resorted to arcane, to recondite meth-

---

* Substances not intrinsically poisonous ("venom of viper," "blood of toad, bone of bat, dust of mole," and Spanish fly, for example, in vogue for a variety of nefarious purposes) were nauseous or irritating, the cause of vomiting or diarrhea. With the loss of body fluids, fatal effects could ensue, especially among the infirm, the very old, or very young. The mortality rate was high, and incidental death was frequently attributed to the intrinsic properties of poison when it was actually due to secondary causes.

ods, to the black arts: to conjurations, incantations, charms, spells, and magic potions—some very possibly poisonous—all designed to remove La Vallière from her place as royal Favorite, to make way at the top for another.

Practitioners of the black arts, as of all the others, were to be found among Paris's half million inhabitants. One needed only to know where to apply.

One applied, for example, to a sinister pair such as Le Sage, the sorcerer, and his apprentice, the Abbé Mariette, a renegade priest. Their arrest in 1668 came as the result of a city-wide alarm about poison and witchcraft; in midsummer, they were haled before the Châtelet Court on charges of sorcery—sorcery still a crime punishable by death in France in 1668, still on the statute books where it had been inscribed during the fifteenth and sixteenth centuries when all Europe had been obsessed by the witchcraft mania, engaged in a long, a giant, frenzied witch hunt.

Under interrogation, Le Sage and Mariette talked a gibberish about astrology, horoscopy, alchemy, chiromancy, cartomancy, phrenology, graphology, in all of which arts they were proficient. They jabbered to the judges about love potions they could concoct (out of "bone of toad, blood of bat, dust of mole, root of mandragore, Spanish fly," or some such!), all "passed under the chalice," "blessed" (or accursèd?) by an abjured priest (like the Abbé Mariette) upon a black-draped, unholy altar—dark rites performed in the dark of the moon and at the witching hour in the presence of and at the solicitation of some of the most high and puissant noblewomen in the realm. The purpose of those noble ladies, according to the testimony of Le Sage and Mariette, was "to dethrone Mme de La Vallière from her place in the King's heart and to capture his affections for themselves!" And who were the ladies of the court, addicted to such practices, who sought to supersede La Vallière? The judges may have regretted having asked the question—the answers scarcely to their liking: those two bold fellows in the dock at the Châtelet dropped some prestigious names; their clientele included, they declared, the Marquise de Bougy, the Comtesse du Roure, the Comtesse de Gramont, the Vicomtesse de

Polignac. Under pressure, still more exalted names were mentioned: that of the Comtesse de Soissons, that of the Duchesse de Vivonne.

Finally—and with supreme impudence—the two prisoners came out with the name of the Marquise de Montespan.

The judges gasped, proceeded to the verdict: Le Sage was condemned for life—that meant to death—to the galleys, those floating concentration camps of Bourbon France.

The Abbé Mariette, on the other hand, appeared to have been protected by one of his own most potent charms or amulets, for the presiding judge at the Châtelet turned out to be his own first cousin. And when the case was transferred to the Parlement of Paris, the presiding judge there turned out to be none other than Président de Mesmes, father of his client, the Duchesse de Vivonne. Needless to say, Mariette avoided any further mention of the judge's daughter's name—or that of her sister-in-law, the Marquise de Montespan—and drew a relatively light sentence, a short nine-year term of banishment.

The King, of course, would have been promptly informed—he expected to be kept informed on everything that went on in his kingdom—of a criminal affair involving ladies of his court, of his closest coterie.

Madame de Montespan may have learned of the trial and of the evidence from her lover, the King, or from her sister-in-law, the Duchesse de Vivonne. If so, she would have turned it promptly to account, to ridicule; exercising her devastating, coruscating wit upon it, treating it with her special brand of offbeat, malicious, piquant humor; tossing it on her tongue—that brilliant, wicked tongue of hers—and, in all probability, the King would have joined her in peals of laughter, as it was his wont to do.

Whether Mlle de La Vallière heard about the wizards in the Bastille working her downfall, whether she was aware that sorcery was being practiced against her by a number of her intimates, whether she thought she had been poisoned by one of them—or which one of them she suspected—there is no way of knowing. Her correspondence gives no hint, nor does her volume of *Reflections*.

As far as the general public was concerned, not a word leaked out from the courtroom of the Châtelet in 1668; no word of the Le Sage-Mariette trial was ever published; the scandalous affair was successfully suppressed by the authorities.

The blood-curdling Brinvilliers murder case and trial, on the other hand, was to be published to the far corners of the kingdom, to set an example—it was hoped—to all the King's subjects on the subject of crime and punishment.

II

The Brinvilliers Case

"PARIS CAN TALK OF NOTHING ELSE!"—nothing but the Brinvilliers murder case—Mme de Sévigné exclaimed by letter to her daughter in the spring of 1676: "Even the war news is forgotten!"

The scandal had burst like a thunderclap upon the aristocracy of the French court and capital—the Marquise de Brinvilliers, one of the most winsome little monsters in criminal history, being one of their very own.

Her capture was announced in March, in the town of Liège, whither she had fled from England with the French police hot on her trail. She had escaped from France three years earlier, deeply incriminated in a series of mysterious deaths including those of her father and two brothers. Tried in a Paris court in 1673, *in absentia*, she had drawn the death penalty.

The King followed developments with keen personal interest, sending instructions from Valenciennes—where he was heading his troops in sporadic springtime military forays against the Spanish in the Netherlands—instructions to the Premier President of the Parlement of Paris and the Prosecutor-General to see to it that "Justice be done" in this affair, regardless of the rank of the guilty party or parties.

The Marquise de Brinvilliers, as testimony in the case would develop, had resented her father's interference in an extramarital liaison which she had been flaunting as openly as her husband flaunted his. Not only that: the Brinvilliers, like most of the nobility, had lived beyond even their substantial means (their marriage, as was customary with the bourgeoisie was well as the aristocracy, had been made not in Heaven but in the countinghouse). So that the estate of her father, Monsieur d'Aubray, a prominent magistrate and chief civil law officer of Paris, came to represent a strong temptation to Mme de Brinvilliers. Furthermore, it so happened that her lover, one Godin de Sainte-Croix, not only dabbled in alchemy in his own laboratory, as was the vogue at that time, but frequented a renowned professional named Glaser, who was official "apothecary to the King and to *Monsieur*" and "alchemist-in-chief to the Paris Botanical Gardens." Sainte-Croix supplied his mistress with arsenical compounds; "inheritance powders" as she whimsically termed these "recipes of Glaser's," which she methodically tested on patients in the Paris charity hospitals. A touching picture she is said to have made on her errands of mercy—this pretty, dainty, patrician blue-eyed blonde, passing out fricassées of veal and chicken, pigeon tarts, arsenic-flavored *specialités* to tempt the flagging appetites of ailing indigents; then tabulating their symptoms.

"Who would have believed it of this woman of highly respectable family, of a delicate little creature such as this, with her apparently gentle disposition?" Not Nicolas Gabriel de La Reynie, the newly appointed police chief of Paris, who posed the rhetorical question.

No one would have believed her guilty, despite the rash of suspicious deaths in her family circle, had not Sainte-Croix died most inopportunely in 1672, leaving behind a red leather chest containing vials of assorted poisons and indiscreet letters from the little Marquise. She tried every conceivable stratagem to retrieve the red leather chest before the police should pry into it, but neither by bribery nor by political influence could she accomplish that mission. Closely related as she was to the Paris magistracy, her trial must have presaged an embarrassment to that powerful caste. Her flight to England may not only have been facilitated for her, but urged upon her.

Sainte-Croix's valet, La Chaussée, on trial before the Châtelet Court in 1673, inculpated Mme de Brinvilliers in the mass murders before his execution on the Place de Grève, where he was "broken on the wheel," as the sentence prescribed: attached and bound, spreadeagled, on a wheel, and there pounded to death, his bones broken by blows with stones or bastinadoes.

The tutor of the Marquise's children, a suggestible young seminarian named Briancourt—another of her lovers, another of her accomplices—had, by then, incriminated her, too. But even so, she might have faced down all her accusers, had she not been captured in Picardy, clutching in her hand a handwritten confession of her three murders as well as various and sundry abortive murder attempts on her sister and sister-in-law, on her daughter, on her husband and her husband's mistress, and on at least two of her own paramours, Briancourt and Sainte-Croix. The recital included also such "peccadilloes" (the word is Mme de Sévigné's) as sodomy and incest—the relations with her two brothers, beginning at the age of seven.

"Glory" was a word that came almost as often to her lips as to Louis XIV's; she had acted out of "ambition for her family and her children," she had told Briancourt, to ensure them a place high in the political and social hierarchy. She had killed her brothers to assure herself and her children the bulk of the family fortune and the magisterial posts which the brothers had inherited from their father, her first victim.

A hot debate would rage on the propriety of her confession's being used as evidence against her; the theologians arguing among themselves as to whether or not a written confession was entitled to the same sacred inviolability as an oral one, made to a priest in the confessional box.

The Grand' Chambre and the Tournelle courts of the Parlement of Paris were convoked in joint session, in April—a privilege of the nobility to be tried by this highest criminal judiciary body in the kingdom. In twenty-two grueling sessions over a period of two and a half months, the Marquise de Brinvilliers never lost her sangfroid—her voice and eyes, icy; her pride, fierce. Confronted with a sniveling Briancourt, she cut down her onetime accomplice with the disdainful comment that "his tears betrayed his lack of spirit."

Whereas "Her spirit horrified us!," Premier President of Parlement Lamoignon shuddered. She defied every witness, denied every charge.

There was "Only the evidence in her own hand to convict her . . . and this she claimed had been written when she was delirious with fever," Mme de Sévigné reported: "It took her eight months to finish off her father. . . . To all his caresses and his affection, her only response was to double the dose. . . . She tried frequently to poison her husband, too, to be free to marry Sainte-Croix; but the latter, wanting no part of such a wicked woman, gave the husband counterpoison. . . . So that, after five or six doses of poison, and five or six doses of counterpoison—poisoned and then disempoisoned, batted back and forth between life and death, the poor man somehow managed to survive!"

A suicide attempt by the Marquise was described in a letter of Mme de Sévigné's dated April 29: "She stabbed herself with a bâton. . . Guess where? Not in her eye. Not in her mouth. Not in her ear, not in her nose. Not *à la Turque*. So, try to guess. She would surely have died had they not come running to treat her wounds . . ."

"It is in the public interest," said parliamentary President Lamoignon to the Abbé Pirot, "that Mme de Brinvilliers's crimes end with her, and that she make a declaration that will help us to prevent the continued use of poison. . . ."

The Parlement of Paris was exceedingly anxious to discover the names of other possible accomplices of the Marquise's, as well as the purveyors of poison in the capital and the composition of the poisons and counterpoisons she had used.

"Half the people I know—people of quality—are involved in this same kind of thing," she had said repeatedly, "and I could drag them all down along with me, should I decide to talk . . ."

The cleric Edmond Pirot, whom Lamoignon called in to try to gain the confidence of the Marquise, was an eminent Jesuit theologian, a doctor of theology at the Sorbonne, renowned for his dialogues with the illustrious German philosopher-scientist Baron von Leibnitz.

The man's infinite compassion touched the obdurate heart of the prisoner in the Conciergerie Tower. Her constant companion during the last twenty-four hours of her life, the Abbé convinced her that no sins—not even such horrendous ones as hers—were beyond redemption, and that, by making a genuine contrition, she could hope for God's mercy on her soul.

So, she would freely confess; torture was unnecessary, she insisted: "I have nothing else to tell"; she had no other accomplices beyond those already named; the only poisons she knew were arsenic, vitriol, and venom of toad; milk, the only antidote.

Even so, she would not be spared the water torture which the court had ordered: vast amounts of water poured through a funnel into the prisoner's throat, the accumulation in the stomach and intestines causing excruciating pain. "They must be planning to drown me in those vats!" she quipped: "As tiny as I am, I could never swallow such quantities!" Her pride sustained her against physical pain, "but she was touchy on points of honor." It was the humiliation, the indignity to her noble person that sent her into those sudden, terrifying seizures to which a seriously disturbed, a psychotic personality such as hers was subject. One of these "sudden violent eruptions of her inner nature . . ." as Abbé Pirot described the phenomenon in his detailed record, "A storm boiling up from her lower depths . . . all her evil instincts reawakened . . ." her dulcet expression turned "vicious . . . her face contorted, scowling; her mouth awry; her eyes glaring murderously . . ."

One moment, she was all charm and graciousness, the great lady; the next, a maenad, a Fury, a Medea: "Medea was guilty of fewer crimes than she!" Mme de Sévigné commented.

The Marquise de Brinvilliers bore with Christian resignation and fortitude the sentence passed upon her on July 16, 1676: first, the Honorable Amend to be performed by her, upon her knees, crucifix and candle in hand, before the central door of Notre Dame Cathedral: enumeration of all her sins and expression of penitence. Second, decapitation by the axman's blade—a form of execution reserved for the nobility, regarded by her as her privilege. What she deemed an ignominy was the provision that her body be burned subsequent to execution. "Never mind," Abbé Pirot consoled her, "Your body will rise glorious from the ashes if your soul is in a state of grace."

What she bridled at was the sight of some half hundred sumptuously attired ladies and gentlemen of the court, crowding into the hall of the Conciergerie to stare at her as she entered the chapel for her last Mass. "What a morbid curiosity," the condemned woman remarked, staring coldly back and raising her voice so that it could be clearly heard. (A remark especially appropriate in the case of the Comtesse de Soissons, who headed the Versailles delegation, herself still under suspicion for complicity in the death of her husband, three years previously.)

What rankled in the Marquise's aristocratic soul was the means of transportation provided for her drive to the Place de Grève, the place of public execution in front of Paris's City Hall: a humble wooden cart, a tumbril, into which she was crowded along with the Abbé, with Guillaume, the executioner, and his valet; even logs and straw for the pyre.

What rankled was the tremendous audience to her shame: Mme de Sévigné, at the window of a house on the Notre Dame Bridge, exclaimed: "Never has Paris seen such crowds of people. Never has the city been so aroused, so intent on a spectacle."

Her hands bound, a rope around her neck, a blindfold over her eyes, she knelt and recited her last prayers with her father confessor, who says he was startled by a sudden sound, "a dull thud, like that of a butcher's cleaver upon the block. . . . The executioner had severed her head with one swoop of the ax. . . . 'Monsieur'" (Guillaume inquired proudly of the priest), "'have I not struck a fine blow? I always commend myself to God upon these occasions and, thus far, He has not failed me.'"

"Her confessor called her a saint," as Mme de Sévigné heard it. "The next day, the people went searching through the ashes for La Brinvilliers's bones . . ." (presumably as holy relics).

"She died as she had lived, most resolutely. . . . A loud murmur went up from the crowd at the final cruelty," Mme de Sévigné wrote on July 17, 1676, complaining in the very next line that all she had been able to see from her window on the bridge had been the top of the condemned woman's head, "nothing but her mob-cap! . . . But, now, at last, it's over and done with. . . . La Brinvil-liers has gone up in smoke; her poor little body tossed, after the execution, into a raging fire; and after that, her ashes scattered to the wind. So that now we shall all be inhaling her! And with such evil little spirits in the air, who knows what poisonous humor may overcome us? It may well be to the general astonishment . . ."

Madame de Sévigné wrote the words in irony, not prophecy —though that is what they proved to be: a very "poisonous humor" was shortly to "overcome" them all. And certainly "to the general astonishment."

III

Arrests

THE ALARM, IN 1677, came from the Jesuits on the rue Saint-Antoine: on September 21, they reported an anonymous letter dropped into the confessional box of their church, warning of a plot to poison both the King and the Dauphin.

Nicolas de La Reynie, Lieutenant-General of Police of Paris, went into action instantly to alert the King and the Royal Body-guards, to churn up the whole Paris underworld, to track down the ring of apothecary-alchemists and perfumer-poisoners operating in the area.

The King had appointed this new Lieutenant-General of Police with instructions that he was to create "Law and Order in His Majesty's good city of Paris," but the execution thereof was left up to La Reynie's ingenuity: up to him to regulate public safety, public health, public morals; up to him to formulate new city ordinances covering everything from gambling to garbage disposal, from prostitution to fire prevention; up to La Reynie to pass on the depth of the décolletage proper to lady worshippers, to put a stop to the practice of wearing masks in church and to that of hissing the actors in the theater.

The thirty years of La Reynie's expert administration saw Paris transformed from a dark, dirty, malodorous, pox- and pest-ridden medieval city into a relatively modern one.

La Reynie's first significant arrests came in November, 1677.

The gates of the Bastille closed upon Louis de Vanens and company; an unsavory company, composed of his mistress and his valet; his counselor, a parliamentary attorney by name of Sieur du Clausel, providentially possessed of government licenses for operation of "distilleries." Another associate of Vanens's, a physician named Rabel, made his escape to England where he became a favorite and pensioner of King Charles II (this empiric was celebrated for his elixirs; his Rabel Water in use until the end of the nineteenth century as an astringent in cases of hemorrhage). A third member of the mysterious confraternity, a Sieur de Bachimont, was picked up in Lyon and imprisoned there, on information found among the effects of the prisoners in the Bastille.

These, ostensibly, were alchemists and magicians, their laboratories filled with furnaces, crucibles, test tubes and retorts; with assorted ores and minerals, including those alchemic and magical indispensables, sulfur and mercury. But the police found also mercury chloride (sublimate) and arsenic, the two deadliest poisons then in use. In addition, counterfeit silver ingots were discovered. Obviously, these poisoner-counterfeiters had more than any mere academic, more than any mere esoteric interest in alchemy—that ancient art that was the precursor of the modern science of chemistry—which dated back to Egypt and/or China; which was dedicated to the age-old quest for the philosopher's stone or universal solvent, by which base metals could be transmuted into gold.

If these were not occult philosophers, neither were they the common run of criminals; their operations financed by a prominent and successful Paris banker, a secretary of the King, named Pierre Cadelan. At the moment of his arrest, this Cadelan was about to take over the operation of the Royal Mint in Paris. The counterfeit silver produced in Vanens's laboratories had already been purchased at market price for sterling by the mint agents.

The master mind of the cabal, a Captain de Chasteuil, scion of a distinguished Provençal family, was still at large. Were his life history not preserved in black and white upon police blotters across the Continent of Europe, such bizarreries would tax credulity: a Doctor of Law, a Captain of Guards under the Grand Condé, a Knight of the Order of Malta, decorated with the Maltese Cross, sailing under the banner of that ancient Crusaders' Order against the Paynim. It may have been during his two years of slavery in Algiers, and from the Arabs—for centuries, practitioners of the Hermetic arts—that Chasteuil learned his alchemic secrets; confiding them, in turn, to his friend Louis de Vanens, captain of a French galley, who was to snatch him from the hand of the public executioner in Marseilles.

That was after Chasteuil had returned to France, donned the robes of a Carmelite prior, smuggled a teen-age girl into his cell, strangled her late in her pregnancy, and buried her body beneath the paving stones of the monastery chapel. Condemned to hanging, he had been rescued by Vanens's troop from the very steps of the gibbet, and rushed up the coast to Nice. From there, it was only a hop, skip, and jump to Turin, to the court of the Duke of Savoy, where Chasteuil would serve as Captain-Major of the Royal Savoyard White Cross Guard and tutor to the Prince of Piedmont. A poet, a Platonist, and still a seeker after alchemy's "great secret," Chasteuil was joined in that quest by Vanens, Bachimont, and a Portuguese Count of Castelmajor, who had all gathered in Turin by 1675, the year the Duke of Savoy died a sudden and mysterious death immediately after quaffing a long and cooling draft, in all probability poisoned.

So rumor had it after this Duke's death, as after so many other inexplicable deaths in the Savoy royal family. Vanens and company promptly decamped from Italy; Vanens to Paris; Bachimont to Lyon; Castelmajor to England, where he became the official horoscopist-alchemist to the court of Saint James: adept—as was the case with most adepts—in more than one of the magical, or black arts.

With the arrest of Vanens and of Cadelan in Paris in 1677, Minister of War Louvois believed that La Reynie had come upon a spy ring. Of course, Louvois had a spy complex, director of his own espionage system and double-agent network throughout Europe; but it was clear, it was soon established, that Cadelan was linked with bankers in Venice and in Rotterdam.

As for Chasteuil, chief of the French organization, when he was eventually found, later in 1678, he was found dead; perhaps, as has been suggested, a victim of poison, perhaps on orders from some superior, superior even to him, in this perhaps international conspiracy with its chiefs, its hired assassins, its bankers in every capital of Europe.

The theory of the international conspiracy is one dear to the hearts of European historians and journalists in every century. It is postulated, in this instance, by Theodore Iung, an eminent and generally responsible nineteenth-century French historian, who seeks thereby to explain the long strange string of deaths in the French royal family, beginning with that of the first *Madame* in 1670, continuing through that of her daughter, the Queen of Spain, in 1689; and culminating, in 1711–12, with the deaths of three of Louis XIV's throne-heirs, three Dauphins, all within a year. As to the author of this plot against the Bourbons—in this period of violent religious dissension—Iung professes to discern the hand of the Huguenots, trying vainly to stave off their doom, which would be sealed with the signing of the revocation of the Edict of Nantes in 1685. Or if not the hand of the Huguenots, then that of the Jesuits? The hand of either aided and abetted by intransigent elements of a still untamed feudal nobility, and also by the governments of England, Austria, Spain, Holland; any and all of the nations of Europe under the threat of Louis XIV's arrant aggressions. Iung goes so far as to claim to identify a leader of this international conspiracy against France as the Man in the Iron Mask.*

The prisoner Louis de Vanens, whatever else he may have

---

* Dumas's solution to the mystery of the identity of the Man in the Iron Mask is the most popular; to the effect that the masked man was a twin brother of Louis XIV's, representing a perpetual threat to the security of the throne and, thus, for forty years imprisoned in a succession of the darkest cells, the remotest fortresses of the kingdom.

been, turned out to be a confirmed Satanist, an unreconstructed warlock, intrepidly pursuing his black arts' ritual in the very bowels of the Bastille, announcing to his shocked cellmates that "neither God nor King could stop him" from performing his blasphemous midnight Mass, in the name of Satan and Beelzebub, on the rump of his spotted spaniel.

Even more shocking was the fact that this rather handsome, well-born gentleman and former officer apparently had connections in loftiest court circles. There may have been some concern when news of his arrest and incarceration leaked out from the court of Parlement to the court of Versailles (never a word of such news to be found in the *Gazette de France*, primarily a court circular, carrying only an occasional report of a verdict or a judgment, its only political bulletins released by government bureaus, and confined to banalities and propaganda).

Could it be true that Vanens's valet, La Chaboissière, frequented the hôtel of the Comtesse de Soissons? Or that Vanens was on very friendly terms—as has been claimed—with Mme de Montespan? His valet told La Reynie (and La Reynie made a note of it) that his master "had given Mme de Montespan counsel for which he should be drawn and quartered!"*

While La Chaboissière did not actually retract this reference to the Favorite, he refused to sign the transcript of the interrogation until the reference was removed—the notation, nonetheless, indelibly inscribed in one of La Reynie's notebooks.

The King could have given such a fantastic statement little or no credence, had La Reynie taken it seriously enough to report it to him. Otherwise His Majesty would never have appointed Mme de Montespan to the highest court post available to a woman: head of the Queen's Council, superintendent of the Queen's household, one to which Mme de Montespan had long aspired, but which the incumbent, the Comtesse de Soissons, had been reluctant to surrender. In the spring of 1679, the King brought pressure to bear

---

* One of the cruellest forms of execution: each limb of the victim was attached to a separate horse, and the body rent apart; "quartered" by driving the four horses in four different directions.

upon her, and then compensated her royally for her compliance. The office of Queen's superintendent carried with it not only a tremendous pension but the rank and honors of a Duchess; the latter, privileges which Mme de Montespan had long coveted, of which her husband's intransigence had long frustrated her. Madame de Scudéry, one of Bussy's faithful correspondents, noted that: "Provided Mme de Montespan can get along without his love, she may still enjoy the King's consideration. What more can be expected of even the most perfect gentleman?"

No more seemed expected by Mme de Montespan, apparently resigned to her change in status, as evidenced in a holograph letter to a confidant, the Duc de Noailles, dated March 30, 1679: "All goes smoothly here. The King no longer comes to my apartment except after Mass and after supper. Still, these rare and tranquil encounters are better than frequent, stormy ones."

The King could scarcely have continued to deny Mme de Montespan the charge she had desired, in view of the fact that he was about to honor Mme de Maintenon with the charge of second mistress of the wardrobe to the new Dauphiness, the Bavarian Princess who would be wed to the heir-apparent in early 1680. If Christine of Bavaria was not much to look at, she was *gemütlich*, agreeable to the extreme, and put *Monseigneur* at ease so that he could perform his connubial duties, as to which some doubt had existed.

All this time, the Vanens Affair, as it came to be called, was under investigation by the judges of the Parlement of Paris, but a year went by and still no convincing evidence had been turned up against the gang.

La Reynie thought that a break in the case might have come in the closing months of 1678. A Captain of Police named Desgrez— notable as the arresting officer in the capture of the Marquise de Brinvilliers at Liège—received a visit, late one night, from a Paris attorney named Perrin, and the report of a curious company Perrin had just departed, at the home of a Madame Vigoureux, wife of a ladies' tailor. One of the dinner guests, Marie Bosse, a heavy, thick-set woman, a fortuneteller, held forth at length on the advantages of that profession: "What a marvelous trade it is!" she exulted, in her cups. "What a clientele I have—Duchesses, Marquises, Princes! Only three more poisonings, and I can retire—with my fortune made!"

Whereupon the other dinner guests laughed to split their sides, as at a stupendous joke. Only Maître Perrin caught the warning frown on the hostess's face, and went to ask his friend on the police force whether the fortuneteller's words had been spoken in jest or in dead earnest.

Captain Desgrez was sufficiently impressed with Perrin's adventure to send the wife of one of his lieutenants to investigate, to have her fortune told by La Bosse, inquiring how long she must endure the abuse of her husband.

Not long! La Bosse assured her, looking into her palm on the first visit; dispensing a vial of poison on the second, to ensure the fulfillment of the original prognostication.

On January 4, 1679, La Vigoureux was arrested. Likewise, La Bosse, along with her daughter and two sons, "all taken in one big bed together," all four snatched out, and "embastilled."

The fact that the four were all bedded down together—that the sorcerers' race was traditionally perpetuated by incest; the black arts a heritage, handed down from one generation to the other— was only the first of the abominations to be revealed in the course of the interrogations of this new lot of prisoners. For, if these were poisoners, abortionists, counterfeiters, as they were, they were something still more sinsiter: they were sorcerers—self-avowed, practicing, ninth- and tenth-generation diabolists, necromancers, witches, and warlocks.

La Reynie had walked into a chamber of horrors that was to shake even his iron nerve—steeled by a lifetime of police and court experience.

If he thought that the witchcraft mania and the witch hunts had ended earlier in the century, he had been mistaken. The years 1450–1600 had seen the worst of it: popular superstition whipped to a frenzy by the Inquisitional trials; by the executions in tens of thousands, batches of 500 to 800 witches at a time; from one end of Europe to the other, from the Scandinavian countries to France, Italy, Spain, and across to the British Isles. As late as 1609, some 600 sorceresses had been tried and burned in the Bordeaux region; smoke billowed up again in 1609–10 from the pyres in the Basque country near Bayonne. And the famous case of the Devils of Loudun—the demoniac possession of the nuns in the convent there —had been the sensation of the 1630's, with Cardinal Richelieu himself directing the prosecution, execution, and torture of the priest, Urbain Grandier, charged with sorcery, with calling up the fiends of Hell (a holograph compact signed by Beelzebub, Lucifer, and Satan themselves, and entered as irrefutable evidence for the prosecution).

Voltaire credited Louis XIV with having heralded in the Age of Reason with "the royal decree of 1672 ending legal prosecution on the simple charge of sorcery. . . . The spirit of knowledge and of reason . . . thus gradually prevailing over superstition." Louis XIV had stepped in at that time to call a halt to the auto-da-fé in Normandy; fifty or more stakes had been prepared when the King commuted the sentences of execution to sentences of exile—over the protests of the Parlement of Rouen, supremely witch-conscious ever since the trial of Joan of Arc in 1431. Those hardheaded, stubbornly conservative Normans warned the King of "the dangers of shelving the Devil so unceremoniously, reminding him that the Devil is nothing less than a dogma closely bound up with all the rest."*

La Reynie did research on witches, read up on the witchcraft trials of previous centuries, consulting the manuals compiled by the judges of the Inquisition in France, Spain, and Germany.†

* The Parlement of Paris took cognizance of and prosecuted profanations and malefices, but not as supernatural effects operated by the Devil, as Voltaire explains.
† La Reynie turned to the French jurisconsult Jean Bodin and his *Daemonomania of the Sorcerers*, published in 1588; and to the Dominican Jacob Sprenger, the Holy Office's High Inquisitioner, for the German witchcraft trials of the late 1400's. Sprenger's book for witchcraft prosecution, his manual for Inquisition (published in 1486 and widely reprinted under the title of *Malleus Maleficarum, The Witches' Hammer*) a hammer to be

As for the curious case occupying La Reynie's attention in Paris in 1679, what had at first appeared to be an international conspiracy seemed now to have developed into a carnival of crime, a Witches' Sabbath.

The vials, vats, jugs, jars, and packets, the crystals, potions, and potpourris found among the effects of La Bosse and La Vigoureux after their arrest in January—and rushed to a laboratory for testing by such elementary techniques as were then known—disclosed a witches' cauldron: arsenic, mercury, nitric acid, hemlock, hensbane (conine), wolfsbane (aconite), deadly nightshade (belladonna), witches' thimble (digitalis), root of mandragore (or mandrake, podophyllin), powder of cantharis, of toad and bat and viper, blobs of hanged-man's fat, nail clippings, bone splinters, specimens of human blood, excrement, urine, semen; all the ingredients for the then known aphrodisiacs and poisons, some genuinely efficacious, others merely nauseous—whatever was nasty or obscene, then considered toxic.

La Vigoureux was to die under torture before the year had reached the spring; but before succumbing, she would join with her confederate, La Bosse, in inculpating a score of fellow criminals, in implicating a dozen or more clients so prominent, so intimately allied with members of the ruling caste as to cause a general consternation among the police and magistracy.

La Reynie decided to consult with members of the State Council and the Cabinet when the names named by the prisoners proved to be exalted ones.

Such a one, for example, as the Marquis de Feuquières (son of France's Ambassador to Sweden), claimed as a client by La Vigoureux, whose help he had sought for "communication with the spirits." Then, a Madame de Poulaillon, daughter of a noble Bordeaux family, wife of the master of waterways and forests of the province of Champagne, named as a client by La Bosse. Even

---

wielded against heretics of all kinds in the bosom of the Catholic Church; a sense of urgency manifesting itself in the late fifteenth century for the extirpation of heresy, as if in anticipation of the great irrepressible heresy of the Protestant Reformation, just around the corner of the century.

more disconcerting, the next two ladies to be listed as La Bosse's and La Vigoureux's patrons were a Madame Leféron and a Madame Dreux, both married to magistrates in the Parlement of Paris, the latter's husband sitting in judgment on these very witches patronized by his wife.

On March 17, 1679, Louvois sent La Reynie official notice of an extraordinary tribunal to be set up by His Majesty to sit in judgment upon these extraordinary cases: twelve judges, including La Reynie; La Reynie to serve with another judge, Monsieur de Bezons, as co-chairman of the commission; Monsieur Robert named as Solicitor-General; Monsieur Sagot as court clerk.

To remove such a case from Parlement's jurisdiction was to violate its traditional prerogative, and aroused that ancient legislative and judicial body to vain but vigorous protest. Parliamentary justice had been less "immaculate" than was the boast of its Premier President in his petition to the King.

Such was the opinion expressed by Contarini, the Venetian Ambassador, in a confidential report to the Doges: "With the habit of poisoning becoming established in a nation, and with several members of the nobility and the bourgeoisie accused of complicity in so odious a crime, it seems that Parlement's judgments have not been pronounced with the severity required in so delicate a matter."

Louis XIV's and Louvois's real reason for preferring the small, specially constituted commission was to maintain a secrecy stricter than would have been possible in the large judiciary body of the Parlement of Paris. An effort apparently was made in the beginning to protect the names of certain privileged persons who had been incriminated. But, above all, secrecy was considered desirable for the public welfare, in view of the fact that poison promised to constitute the central theme of the proceedings—the composition, analysis, distribution, and application of poison. Clearly, the dissemination of such information could not but be considered dangerous, deleterious to the national interest.

Not only was this entire process of law to be secret; this court was a supreme court from whose decisions there was to be no appeal. This tribunal, composed of the elite of the magistracy, was to convene in a chamber of the ancient Paris Arsenal, and so would occasionally be referred to as the Arsenal Commission, occasionally as the Royal Chamber of the Arsenal, or even the Chamber of Poisons, but most frequently as *La Chambre Ardente*, a name harking back to medieval days when criminals of high estate were judged in the gloom of a chamber draped in black, and eerie with the flicker of torches, as the newspaper the *Mercure Galant* explained in one of its rare references to the events in Paris.

In the matter of the arrests, the decision rested primarily with La Reynie: if, in his opinion, evidence warranted, he ordered an individual brought in for questioning, and a copy of the interrogation submitted to the Solicitor-General, Robert. It was then up to Robert to decide whether the individual in question was to be released or held for confrontation with other prisoners. A transcript of the confrontation was submitted to the tribunal, which then decreed whether the suspect should be released or held for further questioning. If the latter, the interrogations would continue their full course, and transcripts thereof would be submitted to the tribunal. Upon this evidence, the judges would base their decision whether to acquit the suspect or to carry the inquiry further. The final phase of the inquiry was the Question, under torture; the Ordinary Question or the Extraordinary, depending on the degree of severity with which the torture was administered. The testimony thus extracted from the victim formed the basis of the evidence upon which his guilt or innocence was established by the court; upon which his sentence was founded.

The first session of the Chambre Ardente took place on April 10, 1679, less than a month after Louvois's order to La Reynie; even so the minister was impatient, importuning the Lieutenant-General of Police "to make all possible haste in this affair lest desperate people take their own lives or the lives of others to prevent Justice from penetrating to the truth, from getting to the bottom of this business."

Powerful as he was, Louvois was not to be so easily quit of

"this business." Three years would run out and the court would convene in hundreds of sessions; sentences of capital punishment, by the score, would be pronounced; and executions performed by the score, by fire, ax, or rope, on the place of public execution, before this Poisons Affair would be settled—if, indeed, it ever was.

IV

Revelations

THE MADAME DE POULAILLON CASE—such juicy details as inevitably filtered through the screen of secrecy in the courtroom, in 1679, and out to the general public—would have struck her many friends in Paris society as infinitely diverting, had they not reared up in indignation at the thought of a member of their own privileged caste put on trial like a common criminal, ignominiously interrogated on the *sellette* (the wooden stool for the Defendant) like a prisoner of the lower classes.

The young and attractive wife of a rich but aging husband (off often in the province of Champagne attending to his official duties), Mme de Poulaillon was ripe for extramarital romance, and fell into the arms of an expert operator in that line, a gentleman calling himself the Marquis de La Rivière (though his only claim to the title was as illegitimate son of the Abbé de La Rivière, Bishop of Langres). Lavish gifts and money were tribute this gentleman expected from his lights of love. Monsieur de Poulaillon tightened his purse strings and bolted his doors when the silver from the buffet, then the buffet itself, disappeared, apparently into the clutches of the pawnbrokers.

In desperation, Mme de Poulaillon consulted fortunetellers, entreated La Bosse and La Vigoureux to predict a happier future than she had any right to expect. She was too impulsive for even those harpies, who were the ones to give the police her name when torture loosened their tongues in the Bastille in January. She had complained to them of a perverse fate: even the professional swordsmen she had hired to assassinate her husband had botched the job, their blades failing to find a vital spot!

La Bosse feared to give this brash creature a complete course of poison for fear she would feed it to Monsieur de Poulaillon, all in one massive dose, and thus call the attention of the police to the murder method. La Bosse finally compromised by supplying arsenically treated chemises* which, if they could not kill, would embarrass the old gentleman by irritating the skin of thighs and groin, causing a reaction suggestive of syphilis. Other mild doses of arsenic and assorted toxic herbal brews were to be administered periodically in bouillon, wine, and enemas—the last, along with bleedings and purges, one of the chief panaceas of the era. It might require months to accomplish the purpose, but this was the artistic, the professional, and certainly the safest method of procedure—a slow death to simulate a natural decline.

Madame de Poulaillon was paying La Bosse handsomely for such prescriptions when an anonymous letter reached Monsieur de Poulaillon, warning him of his peril, on the strength of which he was able to secure a *lettre de cachet* to confine his wife in a convent while he instituted legal proceedings against her in the Châtelet Court.

* Arsenically treated chemises would produce a skin irritation which—with persistent scratching—could be regarded as potentially dangerous because of the risk of staphylococcal infection resulting in septicemia or blood poisoning. Paracelsus claimed that mercury could be introduced into the body by inunction—as by a mercury-treated chamois used to rub the arm or leg, with the result that fine mercury globules could be worked into the skin—but such a method would scarcely be practical for a poisoner since it would imply the cooperation of the victim. Arsenic or vitriol introduced into the body by enema or by douche could produce a deleterious effect on stomach and intestines, but the notion that poisoned gloves or fabrics could have a fatal effect was no more than a notion. The percutaneous application of poisonous agents is intricate. Curiously enough, there are, today, new organic phosphates—synthetic materials such as Parathion, a general insecticide—which can penetrate the clothing of workers handling these materials, causing symptoms of poisoning.

At this point, the Chambre Ardente, in one of its earliest sessions, issued a warrant for Mme de Poulaillon's arrest. (Mme de Poulaillon's loss was the Marquise de Coligny's gain: when the self-styled Marquis de La Rivière quit Paris for Burgundy to escape involvement in the trial, to whom should he next pay court but the Comte de Bussy's widowed daughter, who picked up where Mme de Poulaillon had left off.*)

The Solicitor-General, Robert, demanded the death penalty for Mme de Poulaillon, to be preceded by questioning under torture. But, brought into the Chambre Ardente on June 5, 1679, for interrogation, "her wit and presence of mind were so extraordinary as to win the admiration and sympathy of the judges," according to Sagot, the court clerk: after four hours of deliberation they let her off lightly, a sentence of banishment instead of capital punishment.

The judges' sympathy for well-connected and well-built ladies was to be tested more than once, that spring and summer of 1679. Louvois advised the King that there were some thirteen or fourteen witnesses to the crimes of Madame Leféron, who had succeeded where Madame de Poulaillon had failed, in disposing of her husband, a highly respected President of Parlement—dead in 1669, of poison admittedly supplied by prisoners presently in the Bastille. The widow, promptly wed to her lover, La Prade, was less than merry; La Prade, in the role of husband, wise to her ways, recognized the poison attempts the moment they began; took to his heels, and never stopped running until he reached Constantinople. At her trial before the court in April, Mme Leféron came off lightly, too, with a sentence of banishment; forbidden for ten years to set foot inside the walls of Paris; ordered additionally to make an "Amend," a donation of 1,500 livres to charity.

The most charming female prisoner to be summoned before the

* The Marquise de Coligny's pregnancy resulted in their marriage: their marriage, in the divorce court where she accused him of a false title; and he, her of a false pregnancy, all properly described and deplored by Bussy's sympathetic cousin, Mme de Sévignè.

court, and the youngest, was Madame de Dreux, not yet thirty, full
of grace and distinction, an ornament of Paris society; her husband
a distinguished member of Parlement, a special aide in the Department of Justice. Not only that, two of the judges on the
Chambre Ardente bench—Messieurs d'Ormesson and Fortia—
were the lady's blood kin.

La Bosse had substantiated her boast that she enjoyed the carriage trade. Her accomplice, La Joly, would later claim that
"Madame de Dreux was even worse than Madame de Brinvilliers
. . . the greatest poisoner of all. . . . Whenever her lover, the
Marquis de Richelieu, so much as looked at another woman, she
would promptly set out to get rid of the new rival. . . ." All
for love of Richelieu, she tried to poison both her husband and
a previous lover whom she now wished to shed. As for Mme de
Richelieu, a death spell had been laid upon her, though it proved
ineffective.

Possibly the Chamber of the Arsenal simply could not believe
such horrors of this charming creature; at any rate, she was finally
dismissed with the mildest of judicial Reprimands in April of 1680.

"The King could perform no greater boon for his city of Paris
or for his kingdom than to exterminate that whole miserable race
of fortunetellers!" La Bosse exclaimed to La Reynie (400 or more
of them in the capital alone, she estimated, including the magicians, all of them telling fortunes and making a fortune at it). "It
all begins innocently enough with a palm reading, but countless
women . . . women of all classes, ladies of quality along with the
others . . . owe their downfall to that apparently innocent first step.
Once the fortuneteller discovers her clients' weaknesses, she has
them in her power, and can lead them where she pleases . . ."

"Thank heavens, I have never bought rouge, pomades or potions; nor ever had my fortune told!" quipped Mme de Scudéry in
a letter to Comte de Bussy: "Paris can talk of nothing but the
people arrested for poisoning. Monsieur de Richelieu bewails the
misfortunes of Madame Dreux. . . . Everyone is frightened."

La Fontaine made his comment in poetry:

Revelations

Paris, one year, went daft over
A fabulous female fortuneteller.
Every happening was referred to her:
Whether you lost an earring or a lover,
Or had a husband who refused to die,
A jealous wife or a possessive mother,
Or any other suchlike bother,
Straight to the soothsayer you'd fly!

La Reynie, on the other hand, was grim, prosaic: "Human life is up for sale . . . and cheap. . . . There is a traffic in murder." And he soon concluded: "Poison is the sole solution to most family problems. Sacrilege, impieties, abominations are common practice not only in Paris, but throughout the countryside, across the provinces . . ."

But "What a scandal over nothing!" was Mme de Sévigné's reaction. (Class loyalty noticeably asserting itself; the privilege of the privileged class was threatened in the person of the prisoner before the bar, and the French aristocracy—including Mme de Sévigné—closed ranks behind her, expressing criticism of La Reynie and his Chamber of Poisons.)

On May 1, 1680, Mme de Sévigné reported the Chamber's verdict: "A mere admonition . . . the lightest possible legal penalty; along with a 500-livre Amend. That poor woman has spent one whole year in a cell lit only by a narrow slit high in the wall, cut off from all news of the outside world, as from all consolation! . . . Upon her release yesterday . . . she was welcomed back with open arms by her husband and all her family, who went to meet her in the Chamber of the Arsenal" (her lover present in the courtroom with her husband to greet her!). Madame de Sévigné's cousin, Philippe de Coulanges, "rushed to the Dreux home to pay his respects, along with so many other friends of the family"—his description of "the touching spectacle" moving Mme de Sévigné to tears.

If the King's justice and the King's tribunal could not be openly criticized, the round of fêtes honoring Mme de Dreux upon her acquittal were a subtle expression of anti-La Reynie, anti-Poisons Affair sentiment.

La Reynie and the Poisons Chamber were even more unpopular with the bourgeoisie for having inflicted the severest penalties on the statute books upon the widow of a prosperous bourgeois merchant, named Brunet, for crimes apparently no more heinous than those perpetrated by the ladies of the upper classes, who had all come off so lightly.

Macabre as it was, this *Affaire Philibert* set Paris tittering: Philibert, the fluteplayer, member of the King's own company of musicians, played solos in Monsieur Brunet's salon, duets in Madame Brunet's boudoir. Brunet, a patron of the arts and music lover, offered the artist his daughter's hand and a handsome dowry. Madame Brunet ran, like the rest of the Parisiennes, straight to a fortuneteller, who quoted her as saying that she was "ready to do ten years' penance if only the Good God would relieve her of her husband . . . for she could not bear to relinquish her lover to her daughter!" Her extravagantly erotic reminiscences embarrassed even the hardened criminal who later repeated them, although under protest, to La Reynie ("fit only," she said, "for the ears of priests in the confessional, not for judges on the bench"). Some of the spicier tidbits of testimony concerning Philibert's virtuosic sexual performances must eventually have penetrated to the outer world, for there is evidence that, after the case was over and Philibert released from custody, the ladies of the court and capital vied wildly for the flautist's favors.

Sentence was pronounced on Mme Brunet in May of 1679, and no mercy shown her: her wicked hand cut off at the wrist; her body hanged by the neck on a gibbet erected in the public square; her corpse consumed on a flaming pyre.

May was a month for burning in 1679; on the sixth, La Vigoureux and La Bosse were condemned to be burned alive at the stake on the Place de Grève; François Bosse, the latter's son, to be strangled and hanged; her daughter, Marie Bosse, to banishment from the kingdom; La Philibert and La Ferry, others of the criminal band, to hanging and burning. The Chambre Ardente, acting with vigor and dispatch in its first month in session, thus disposed of the first batch of fortunetellers and poisoners to make room in the Bastille and the Fortress of Vincennes for the second batch, incriminated on the allegations of the first. All the executions took place as scheduled, on May 8, with the exception of that of La Vigoureux, who died in the course of the Question, the final interrogation to which all the condemned were subjected, under torture.

Among the many names La Vigoureux had named during her agony was that of Primi Visconti, that fascinating man of mystery and of *mémoires*. "I had seen her only once in my life!" he exclaimed indignantly, "and that was at Madame de Vassé's. . . . She was very good at chiromancy, examined my palm and discoursed thereon as learnedly as a Doctor of Philosophy. She was accused of speaking words of comfort to women who complained to her of unhappy marriages, prescribing something to make their husbands more congenial or more openhanded. . . . She promised Louvois sensational revelations if her life was spared. . . . It was hoped that the water torture would make her talk, but it finished her off, instead. . . . La Reynie, who did not know me, proposed to the Chambre Ardente that I be called in for questioning, for he had heard that I was a man of scientific skills and had been, for that reason, much sought after, frequently consulted, and therefore in a position to make important disclosures about prominent people. But the judges laughed in his face, and the King must have stood guarantee for my innocence."

The King had been disarmed by Visconti's apparent frankness when the Italian first visited Versailles. Challenged by the King as to how he performed his "miracles" ("Primi, I give you a choice . . . either a 2,000-livre pension which I will pay you for your secrets —either that or the hangman's noose!"), Visconti freely disclosed to His Majesty the tricks of his trade: if he had recognized the handwriting of another man in the sample submitted as a specimen of the King's, it was because he had been forewarned that one of the royal secretaries could imitate the King's hand to perfection! If he had been able to tell the courtiers so many astonishing facts about themselves, it was because his friend and sponsor at the court had coached him, in advance; familiarizing him with the personality and background of the foremost court members!

Despite the royal favor he enjoyed, Visconti could not have been, in those uncertain days of 1679, as unconcerned as he would have his reader think: the Widow Léonard, a lady very close to him, languished in the Bastille at that very hour, one of the first ladies of quality to be arraigned by the Chambre Ardente, on a charge of poisoning her husband, and Visconti would not breathe freely again until her release in July. This Marguerite Léonard had come to him for a palm reading in 1678, at which time he had predicted that she would lose her husband before the year was out, and that she would remarry—none other than the palmist himself!

In view of the investigation then under way in the Chamber of the Arsenal—in the midst of the furore over divination and allied magical arts—how could La Reynie have overlooked Visconti, the foremost practitioner of them all . . . chiromancer, horoscopist, graphologist, the darling of the court, the rage of Paris and Versailles? His distinguished clientele included the Queen, the Duchesse d'Orléans, the *Grande Mademoiselle*, the Comtesse de Soissons.

He was "besieged," on his own admission, "overwhelmed, pursued by all Paris . . . by noble ladies . . . pulling me by the coat, by the hand . . . in the church . . . in the Tuileries . . . calling me oracle . . . prophet. . . . As many as two hundred and twenty-three carriages at a time waiting in the courtyard . . . clients crowding the staircases . . . eager for my services . . . the Comtesse de Soissons lavishing caresses on me, calling me her man of marvels. . . . Mme de Louvois coming to ask when her husband would break off his liaison with Mme du Fresnoy . . . Mlle de Poitiers offering herself up body and soul if I would only arrange to see a *tabouret* in her future!"

One name is missing—conspicuous by its absence—from the imposing list of Visconti's exalted clientele: that of Madame de

Montespan. Once only, when she was in the Queen's study whither Visconti had come on Her Majesty's summons, did the Favorite deign to test his powers on some samples of handwriting. Even so, their mutual antipathy was evident: at her "You seem unwilling to proceed in my presence," he bristled: "Precisely because you request it, Madame, will I oblige," and under his breath: "How well I knew the viper and her venom!"

There had been one other, one signal exception, one consulation she had sought of him, though not in person. The intermediary had been "her confidential maid," as Visconti describes Claude de Vin des Oeillets: "A demoiselle who gave me to understand that she herself had had carnal relations with the King more than once. She seemed quite proud of the fact that she had had several children by him. Not that she is such a beauty, but the King often found himself alone with her when his mistress was ill or busy...."

When Mlle des Oeillets came to Visconti on the mission for Mme de Montespan, it was to seek his interpretation of a dream: "A few nights earlier, Mme de Montespan had dreamed that she had lost all her hair. Mlle des Oeillets ... came to describe this dream to me, along with all the circumstances relative to the experience ..." Visconti's Memoirs are frustrating in that he fails to give the interpretation of the dream as he made it for the Favorite. As well as he read human nature, his interpretation was probably not too far off from the Freudian: If the dream is to be taken in the context of the Poisons Affair, bound up with the suspense and tension of the trial at that very hour coming to a crisis, then the loss of hair could be interpreted as signifying fear of exposure.*

---

* A Freudian analyst would require the very information Visconti did: "All the circumstances relative to the experience." According to one eminent practitioner of Freudian analysis, the loss of hair in dreams is a loss and grief for a woman: her hair one of her chief beauties; its loss symbolic of a sense of loss of attraction for, thus a sense of loss of power over men and, with this, anger and frustration. Or the attitudes might be ambivalent; in addition to the negative, a positive: the desire or intention to become a nun, symbolized by the shaven head; religious power as a restitution for sexual power; piety as a compensation for passion; heaven in Heaven instead of heaven on earth.

On the surface, all was serene at Versailles; the minuet of court life had been continuing, at least outwardly, at its usual stately measure; New Year's Day of 1679 was celebrated with the customary lavish exchange of gifts: the new Favorite, Mlle de Fontanges, presenting the old Favorite with a magnificent diary, the binding studded with precious stones.

Madame de Montespan received another volume, this one printed in gold, leather bound with an emerald trim, entitled *Diverse Works of a Seven-Year-Old Author*, a collection of letters addressed to his mother (*"Ma Belle Madame"*) by the Duc du Maine, who was undoubtedly precocious, although it was his governess, Mme de Maintenon, who served as editor and publisher: "Madame, Here is the youngest of authors come to ask your patronage. . . . If he reasons with some logic, if he expresses himself with some grace . . . these are qualities he has sought to learn from you . . . making a study of his mother rather than of his textbooks!"

Nor did Mme de Maintenon forget to pay the proper tribute to the young author's father. If the lad was "disdainful of ancient history," it was because "Past centuries pale in comparison to this one . . ."

"I am, Madame," Mme de Maintenon signed her dedicatory address to the boy's mother, "your most humble and obedient servant . . ."

"Humble and obedient" to Mme de Montespan she assuredly was not. "She triumphs over the other. Her empire extends over all," as Mme de Sévigné well knew, and added: "There are those who say that Mme de Maintenon will find herself in a situation likely to astonish all the world—with no thanks to Quanto, to be sure. For, as far as those two are concerned, the hottest hatred of our day and age seethes between them!"

"There is nothing new about the rages that break out against me," Mme de Maintenon wrote to her brother. "As my glory waxes, the reaction is violent. . . . I am the object of terrible tantrums and . . . a full-scale effort is being made to bring about my downfall. If it fails, I can afford to laugh about it; if it succeeds, I will bear up with courage."

It was still touch and go.

Frenzied gambling, as well as "the rages" and "the tantrums," were all symptomatic of Mme de Montespan's frayed nerves.

Even the sporting set at Versailles raised its eyebrows at the Favorite's spectacular winnings and losings, her towering high wagers. At the turn of the year 1678–9, the Comte de Rébenac wrote the Marquis de Feuquières: "Mme de Montespan's gaming has become so excessive that losses of one hundred thousand écus are common. On Christmas Day, she lost seven hundred thousand écus." And that same winter, by letter to Comte de Bussy: "In a nightlong session that began on Monday, Mme de Montespan lost four hundred thousand *pistoles* to the banker; then won them back again. At eight o'clock on Tuesday morning, Bouyn [a rich Paris financier], who was banking the game, asked permission to retire, but the lady insisted that she wanted a chance to recover previous losses to him, which she did before she finally went to her bed on Tuesday morning." And by still another bulletin came this, in an unidentified hand: "Mme de Montespan has lost, it is said, more than fifty thousand écus at *Hoca*.* The King expressed his disapproval vehemently, and became exceedingly angry with her."

"Tantrums," "rages," gambling fever. Suchlike exhibits of nerves and tension, on the part of the fading Favorite, caused comment by contemporaries in 1679.

Among them the Comte de Bussy, who—out of things though he was, in his fourteenth year of exile on his Burgundian estates—had a news item to relay to his friend, the Marquis de Trichâteau, Governor of Semur, on March 22: "Mme de Montespan left Saint-Germain for Paris in a great rush on Wednesday the 15th of this month. It is said that there is some squabbling going on in the ménage. . . ." Bussy attributed the sudden dash to Paris to the "squabbling" and to jealousy over La Fontanges. In his *Amorous History of the Gauls*, he says that "Mme de Montespan . . . was so furious that she began denigrating Mlle de Fontanges publicly . . ."

Bussy had his dates right, but whether Mme de Montespan's

* La Reynie tried to ban *Hoca* in Paris as it had been banned in Rome—most hazardous of all the games of chance.

sudden departure from Saint-Germain, her dash for Paris in "a great rush" is to be attributed, as Bussy attributes it, to "squabbling" and to "jealousy" is open to conjecture. The date Bussy quotes is significant in that three days earlier, on March 12, the key figure in the Poisons Affair had been arrested, imprisoned in the Fortress of Vincennes. Was it at news of this arrest that Mme de Montespan took sudden leave of Saint-Germain, took fright?

This arrest had been made on the basis of testimony supplied by La Vigoureux and La Bosse before they went to their deaths (and it is a reflection on that process of law that they should have been executed before other criminals with whom they had been involved had yet been interrogated). La Bosse, who had been arrested three years earlier on simple charges of counterfeiting, made the declaration that if she had started "amusing herself with chemistry experiments" (hemlock, nitric acid, mercury, and such!), it was the queen of Paris fortunetellers, the Parisian Pythia or Sibyl, the female impresario of crime who had "put the idea in her head."

That foremost pythoness, that sibyl, prophetess, seeress, soothsayer of the capital, that Delphian Oracle of Paris was Catherine Monvoisin, better known—worse known, known to infamy—as La Voisin, a name to conjure with, a name to shudder at, a relic of the Dark Ages.

Confronted with La Bosse, La Voisin would have torn her accuser's hair out by the roots and clawed her face, had La Reynie not intervened. La Voisin protested that hers was the most innocent of occupations: "A practitioner of chiromancy, a student of physiognomy. . . . Arts learned" (at her sorceress-mother's knee) "at the tender age of nine . . ." It was La Bosse, not she, she said, who went in for criminal practices!

La Bosse countered by accusing La Voisin of having supplied poison to both Mme de Leféron and Mme de Dreux to finish off their husbands. Not to mention a dozen abortive attempts to finish off her own—a bankrupt jewel merchant, a nonentity, nonwitch, spoilsport—in order to be free to take a more fitting consort to reign with her over her empire of crime: a king of magicians,

Prince de Legerdemain, a man of many aliases, currently Le Sage.

La Bosse's final suggestion to La Reynie was that he go digging about in La Voisin's garden.

Insofar as such statistics can be accurately compiled, no single individual—acting alone, unidentified with any penal, military, or state authority—has ever accounted for such a carnage as La Voisin. By her own admission, and numbered among her peccadilloes, the ashes of "some twenty-five hundred infants or embryos"—aborted, premature, stillborn, newborn—were fertilizing the greensward of her neat though isolated suburban villa at La Villeneuve-sur-Gravois, just outside Paris's Saint-Denis Gate.

La Voisin herself comprises a chapter in the annals of crime.

V

La Voisin

La Voisin was no common criminal.

She was a witch, in the true theological and anthropological sense of the word; La Voisin's, a figure to inspire fear and horror: a Witch of Endor, calling up the shade of the prophet Samuel from the tomb to satisfy King Saul's morbid curiosity about the future; or a Grecian Hecate, dark goddess of magic and sorcery, haunting the crossroads and the barrows—Shakespeare's Queen of the Witches, "Mistress of . . . charms and harms."

La Voisin was Queen of the Paris Witches, high priestess of the Paris covens and congregations; devout, deeply religious in her own interpretation of the word, a true believer and follower of the witch cult of western Europe.

When the witch cult came to be defined as a heresy, it was done so by and from the point of view of Christianity—the new religion, the exotic religion of the European Continent superimposing itself, from the third and fourth century on, upon a number of ancient pagan religions which had long flourished in that part of the world.

When the Holy Office's Inquisition set out to extirpate the heresy of the witch cult ("A sect deviating from the Catholic Faith," as Pope Adrian VI called it in a Decretal Epistle in 1521), it was merely one heresy among several with which the relatively new Christian religion had to deal; as it dealt with the Albigensian sect in southern France in the twelfth century; as with the Muslims and the Jews in Spain in the fifteenth.

The papal Bull, *Summis Desiderantis,* published by Innocent VIII in 1484, signaled the onslaught of the Church upon the witches, who "have intercourse with demons, Incubi and Succubi"; whose "sorceries and incantations, charms and conjurations . . . blight the marriage bed . . . suffocate, extinguish and cause to perish the births of women, the increase of animals, the corn of the ground, the grapes of the vineyards and the fruit of the trees."

Between the years 1484 and 1692—the date of the witchcraft trials in Salem—it is estimated that the number of persons executed for witchcraft in the Old World ran into the millions. If only one half of the witches executed were actually adherents of the Old Religion, still a figure so enormous gives some idea of the tenacity of the sect in Europe in the fifteenth to seventeenth centuries.

The first genuinely scientific studies of the witch cult—an anthropological approach to the subject—were made early in this century, notably by the late Dr. Margaret Murray, noted British Egyptologist. Her research into the witch trials of the fifteenth, sixteenth, and seventeenth centuries, into the original judicial records and contemporary chronicles, seems to have established the fact that basically the same beliefs, the same ritual, symbolism, and organization prevailed from Sweden to Spain to the Hebrides; apparent proof that this was the survival of the Old Religion, the well-established pagan religion indigeneous to western Europe, stemming probably—to judge by cave paintings in the Dordogne and Ariège departments of France—from the Paleolithic-Neolithic ages.

This was the cult of the horned god, a cult spread across all Europe, all the shores of the Mediterranean; representations of the worship of the horned god survive in ancient Egyptian, Babylonian, and Assyrian sculptures and artifacts; Pan is only the best known among the several horned gods of Greece and the Aegean Islands. The supreme god of ancient Gaul was referred to by the invading Romans as Cernunnos, The Horned One; it was upon the site of his principal shrine, upon the holiest of Gallic holy places, that Notre Dame, the cathedral of the new, exotic religion, would be erected; a stone altar from the earlier Temple of Cernunnos, with a carving depicting the horned and bearded deity of the Gaulish tribes, is preserved among Roman antiquities at Paris's Cluny Museum.

He was the anthropomorphic or theriomorphic deity of a widespread pre-Christian, perhaps even prehistoric religion—now designated as a religion of the "lower cultures"; the use of the word "Devil" or "Satan," in its Christian connotation, for the name of the deity of that ancient cult confuses the issue, as does the stigmatization of his worshippers as "witches."

The witch La Voisin had supreme faith in herself and in her craft: "Nothing is impossible to me," she told one of her clients. "Only another God can understand my powers," she said. "My God-given powers" was how La Voisin referred to them; cultivated from an early age, as she would tell La Reynie: inherited probably —indeed, traditionally—from a sorceress-mother. So great was the reputation of those powers of hers that it had reached the ears of even "the Emperor of Austria and the King of England," as she proudly told her daughter, and "those monarchs had written to invite her to come to their realm."

La Voisin's occult powers were exceeded only by her showmanship. She presided over her séances and magical ceremonies garbed in what she called her "Emperor's robe," a dalmatic vestment specially designed and woven for her (at the fantastic cost of 10,000 livres, as the tradesmens' bills, attest): a skirt of lace-trimmed sea-green velvet; a cloak of crimson velvet elaborately embroidered with "two hundred and five doubleheaded, wing-spread golden eagles"; the same motif stitched in pure gold thread on her slippers.

She was an imposing sight as she received her stream of visitors, the elite of court and capital, the *tout Paris* of that day. All Paris flocked to the rue Beauregard. It was all the rage to consult the oracle there, to hear La Voisin speak in sibylline tongue. She was the star attraction in the best salons of the capital: a not unattractive face; except for the eyes, so burning and piercing as to be disconcerting; a short, plump woman in her thirties, a clairvoyant, adept at crystal-gazing, telling fortunes with Tarot cards, reading palms and, best of all, reading faces. "The lines of the face far easier to read than the lines of the hand" was her shrewd observation to La Reynie: "Passion and anxiety are difficult to conceal." When the Comtesse de Beaufort de Canillac came to consult her, "She offered her palm to be read, but wanted to keep on her mask" (according to the transcript of a La Voisin interrogation). La Voisin's reply was that "She could do no reading of velvet physiognomies! Whereupon the lady unmasked. . . ." (Mask or no mask, if these great ladies thought La Voisin could not divine their real names, they underestimated her powers of divination.)

"She had a tremendous following," as La Voisin's maid Margot would later testify; "and that included people of all sorts and conditions."

"La Voisin had her terrible vices to be sure, but she was full of delicious little secrets for the ladies . . . for which the gentlemen could be grateful," wrote one of the grateful gentlemen, the "Marquis" de La Rivière (onetime lover of Mme de Poulaillon, who was paying for her romance with him in lifelong exile), in a letter to his new mistress, Mme de Coligny, Comte de Bussy's daughter: "La Voisin could make a lady's bosom more bountiful or her mouth more diminutive, and she knew just what to do for a nice girl who had gotten herself into trouble."

She was the talk of the town, provided the title for a hit play:

THE FORTUNETELLER

OR

THE FALSE ENCHANTMENTS

Was she not *the* fortuneteller of the capital? This was a comedy fantasy, performed by "The King's Troupe," and breaking all records with a four-month run (November, 1679–February, 1680) at the Théâtre de Guénégaud. The playwrights, Thomas Corneille and Donneau de Visé,* could thank their friend, La Reynie,

---

* Thomas Corneille was the younger brother of Pierre, the renowned dramatist. De Visé was the editor of *Le Mercure Galant*, the combination literary journal and society sheet.

for suggesting the title and the theme, and he could thank them for accomplishing his purpose—that of holding up to ridicule both the charlatans and their gulls, exposing the hoaxes and the flimflam. The director invented startling stage techniques, trick effects, optical illusions: a headless man, talking his head off! A man sawed in two and reassembling his own pieces! Wizards and genii flitting back and forth through stout stone walls as if they were cardboard —as, indeed, they were.

But La Voisin had made witchcraft pay. The figure of her yearly income, quoted in the coin of the realm and mentioned several times during the course of the court inquiry, was one to impress her contemporaries.

Better still, she had friends in high places, and in all the years of her career had never seen the inside of a prison, save that of the Bastille, whither she had gone, in 1663, of her own free will and accord to pay a visit to a friend in need, the dashing Captain Sainte-Croix, the Marquise de Brinvilliers's lover and purveyor of poisons.

Reports of the strange and nefarious business conducted at La Voisin's secluded villa did occasionally leak out to the outside world: mysterious comings and goings of mysterious characters, lanterns flickering among the trees and acrid smoke billowing up at midnight from a furnace somewhere on the grounds; voices raised too loud and too late at night in a vinous hilarity, the shrill of laughter and of violins piercing the shuttered windows and penetrating to the road. "The place had a bad name," Visconti said, restrainedly.

A pious group called The Missionaries (a congregation founded by Saint Vincent de Paul and dedicated to chastening the sinner and the heretic) had "persecuted" La Voisin, as she put it, "for the past fourteen years . . . but I rendered an account of my arts to the vicars general of Paris and to several doctors at the Sorbonne to whom I had been sent for questioning, and they found nothing to criticize." Had she not, furthermore, gone to the Sorbonne to discuss the science of astrology with some of the professors there? Did she not exchange social calls with the rector of the

University of Paris? Had she not been arrested—that famous day of March 12, 1679—just as she issued forth from early Mass at her parish church, Notre-Dame de Bonne Nouvelle?

The search of her house in the rue Beauregard revealed curious items: in a cabinet, under lock and key, an assortment of potions, powders, philters, prescriptions—many poisonous; shut away in upstairs cupboards, *Grimoires* or black books (primers for Satanists and necromancers, the ABC's of Abracadabra), sacerdotal vestments and paraphernalia, a cross, incense, black tapers; a mysterious oven in a garden pavilion, redolent of evil, noxious fumes; fragments of human infants' bones in the ashes. Of prime interest to La Reynie was a list of La Voisin's clients.

Brought in for questioning were Margot, her maid; her sons; Monsieur Monvoisin, her second husband; his daughter (her stepdaughter)—twenty-one years old, referred to throughout the investigation as *la Fille Voisin*, the Voisin Girl.

Evidence enough, testimony enough to produce mass arrests; the prisons of the Bastille and the Fortress of Vincennes overflowing now with fortunetellers, astrologers, alchemists, apothecaries, perfumers, midwives (and members of the associate professions: abortionists and poisoners); a hundred and more arrests, within a few weeks' time; all the congregations of the witch cult in Paris, La Voisin's coven and La Bosse's, plus associate cabals.

Heads of rival covens, viragoes La Bosse and La Voisin spewed invective at one another, charged one another with heinous crimes. La Voisin's murder attempts against her husband, according to La Bosse, had been frustrated time and time again, most of them perpetrated at the instigation of her lover, Le Sage, at that hour still at large. Monsieur Voisin had somehow, miraculously, survived the onslaught of charms and spells, conjurations, bludgeon blows, repeated poisonings at the family table dished up family style. Once, the maid Margot had saved him by jogging his elbow just as he raised a lethal bowl of bouillon to his lips; once a counterpoison had saved his life, although "he hiccupped for eighteen months thereafter . . . and suffered constant nosebleeds." He was "hard to kill," as he boasted to his daughter: "His soul glued, screwed tight to his body." It was all a great joke in La Voisin's circle: "*Bonjour. And how's your husband? Not dead yet?*"

La Bosse named La Lépère as La Voisin's abortion expert ("midwife-abortionist," the two words spoken as one, all in one breath). La Lépère, herself, would eventually admit to "some ten thousand abortions." But she had her scruples: "If girls were not really pregnant, she told them so and sent them off, whereas La Voisin accepted their money and gave them a prescription or a treatment."* When La Lépère questioned the practice, La Voisin jeered that "If her clients believed themselves to be sluts, she could see no reason to argue with them." When La Lépère complained that she barely eked out a living at her trade, her daughter gibed: "What's your gripe? . . . That all the women and girls in the world aren't hussies?"

La Reynie pressed the inquiry on the abortion traffic. There had been an abortion scandal among the Queen's own maids of honor, providing Mme de Montespan with the occasion to press for the disbandment of that band.† She was relieved to see the delectable young demoiselles replaced in 1673 by more staid, married ladies, Her Majesty's ladies of the palace. Mme de Montespan tried, but failed, to effect the same change in the household of *Madame*, the Duchesse d'Orléans, among whose maids the King had found not only La Ludres but La Fontanges, currently in competition with La Montespan for the King's favor.

"When the ladies to be aborted were ladies of quality," La

* The abortion methods were primitive: "a long pen," "a syringe and water," "an iron," all mentioned by the prisoners. The abortive ingredients were principally "Croton or Physic Nut," "laurel leaves, cinammon bark and cloves."

† The abortion traffic was so widespread at the time as to inspire poetic commentary. One verse of a sonnet by Hesnault, entitled "The Abortion," is quoted by Voltaire in his *Century of Louis XIV*:

You whom Love by crime in darkness made,
And Honor in its turn by crime destroyed,
Murdered while yet unborn, cast to the void,
Poor child! By Love and Honor both betrayed!

Lépère declared self-righteously in one of her interrogations (of which the official transcript survives in the Archives of the Bastille), "she [La Lépère] made every effort to protect their honor, to keep all the proceedings secret. . . . When she induced labor for a mother who had already felt life, she never failed to baptize the infant—herself carrying the body in a box to a gravedigger and giving him a thirty-sol coin to bury it in the corner of some cemetery . . . while the curate wasn't looking." La Voisin was not so scrupulous, burying the premature infants all about the grounds, but when La Lépère had warned her about "that garden full of bones," La Voisin had ordered her "to go to the Devil."

La Debraye and La Delaporte, "artists in poison" famous for their laughing-death powders (frog's tongue or *grenouillette*), formed part of La Voisin's coven and her crime ring. La Pelletier, another of the "Faithful," operated her own distillery (distillations of "toad and bat," cocks' combs and cocks' testicles, along with Spanish fly for aphrodisiacs and hanged-man's fat for candle tallow); her happiness powders and love powders came stylishly packaged in silk or taffeta pouches, like sachets. La Vautier specialized in perfume-poisons.

La Trianon, a great crony of La Voisin's, was hauled in with her inseparable, La Dodée . . . a pair of horoscopist-hermaphrodites, to quote their intimates. La Trianon was La Voisin's right-hand woman with a pestle; her pharmaceutical laboratory "a boutique and arsenal," according to La Reynie, when it came to putting up poison prescriptions. La Trianon's inventory of poisons contained fifty-seven varieties, affording her the opportunity—artist that she was—for improvisation; to vary the fatal doses and the symptoms from time to time to avoid creating suspicion. La Trianon was caught redhanded with a copy of *The Luciferian Credo*, along with a store of incense and black candles, which last, she impudently explained, served her "as shoeblack." Her collection of wax figurines, bristling with needles and pins like a pincushion—needles and pins inserted into the region of the heart, head, or bowels—was less easily explained away (explained today as a form of sympathetic magic; one still in use: the figurine representing a human enemy, who would suffer pain in corresponding regions of his body).

La Joly owed her large following to a repertoire of tricks which included conjuring up the Devil and sending heavy objects flying through the air.

La Deslauriers was credited with having been the Marquise de Brinvilliers's chief source of supply for poisons.

La Cheron, La Durand, La Bellier, La Pottereau, La Gontier, La Poignard, La Delahaye . . . and still they came. The "secret, black, and midnight hags!" "The weird sisters," a batch of witches, a coven,* a covey—a flight large enough to darken the Paris sky if they took to their broomsticks. But the *donjons* of Vincennes proved witch-proof, held them fast.

It was the arrest, on March 17, 1679, of Le Sage—La Voisin's onetime lover—that set off the fireworks at Vincennes. Le Sage set out to send La Voisin to the stake, and she reciprocated in kind.

Le Sage's name rang a bell in La Reynie's memory: the Lieutenant-General of Police would dig back into the files of the Châtelet Court and the Tournelle Court of the Parlement of Paris where Le Sage had gone on trial in 1668 with his accomplice, the Abbé Mariette (the latter still eluding La Reynie's dragnet in early 1679). Le Sage, found guilty of demonic practices and condemned for life to the galleys, had been released—a rare exception—while his galley lay at anchor in Genoa, in May of 1672. "At whose intervention," he insisted, "he never knew." And La Reynie never could discover. Nor could even mighty Louvois: the Minister of War wrote the Secretary of the Marine, Seignelay, to ask "at whose instigation" the pardon had been issued, but if there was a reply, it is missing from Louvois's papers. Ostensibly, La Voisin had exerted influence on one of her powerful patrons, for her paramour was restored to her arms in Paris in 1673.

* A coven being an assembly, a company or gathering of witches, usually thirteen in number. The genesis of the word "coven" unidentifiable in the mists of time; the first recorded use in 1522, in Pitcairn's *Criminal Trials of Scotland*.

Handsome Le Sage could not be said to be, "with his rusty wig, his heavy gray cloak wrapped about his ungainly body," as La Vigoureux told police in identification of this most wanted man on La Reynie's Wanted Persons list: whether under the name of Coeuret or Dubuisson or Le Sage. Obviously he was irresistible, under any one of several aliases, to the ladies, and to La Voisin in particular, who shared her most lucrative practice with him, recommending him as "the man of marvels" to her most illustrious clientele, to the inmost, topmost circle of the court: to the Vicomtesse de Polignac and the Comtesse du Roure, to the Duchesse de Bouillon—one of Cardinal Mazarin's nieces; to the Duchess's sister, the superintendent of the Queen's household, the King's erstwhile affinity—yes, to even the Comtesse de Soissons!

Both the Viscomtesse de Polignac and the Comtesse du Roure had come a number of years past, seeking charms and spells—and/or love potions—to win the affection of the King; charms and spells—and/or poisons—to do away with Louise de La Vallière, at that time in her heyday. "All these women are crazy," Le Sage told La Reynie. "All they can think about is doing away with their husbands. . . . What she [the Duchesse de Bouillon] was after was to become a widow."

Louvois, receiving these daily reports from La Reynie, promptly transmitted them to the King, especially where the allegations referred to persons in His Majesty's court circle. Much of the testimony given by La Voisin in her interrogations and confrontations with Le Sage was apparently omitted or excised from the transcripts of those interrogations and confrontations before they were submitted to the judges of the Chambre Ardente.

As for these confrontations between Le Sage and La Voisin, each was possessed of evidence enough to destroy the other, and each proceeded to produce it; each sought to push the burden of guilt for any given crime upon the shoulders of the other. Why the mortal enmity between them? Le Sage apparently smarted at having been superseded by other paramours and partners (the turnover in La Voisin's love life was rapid). A man named Latour had supplanted Le Sage in La Voisin's bed and coven. As for La

Voisin, she raged at the fact that Le Sage had betrayed her trust by appropriating those best clients of hers to whom she had introduced him: "Mme de Polignac's practice he had snatched right out of her hands!" (For which humanity owed him a debt of gratitude, Le Sage implied: thanks to him, La Voisin's clients had been weaned away from poison to the less pernicious practice of white magic, hocus-pocus, mumbo-jumbo, "and other suchlike trumpery." Not for him the sacrilege of black magic, Black Masses, necromancy! He confined himself to locating buried treasure, to forwarding romances and consummating marriages—to hoodwinking clients naïve enough to be taken in by such tomfoolery!)

La Voisin had herself been taken in, put upon by Le Sage, cruelly deceived as to his conversion to the cult: he was no true convert, no true believer in the craft or in his powers. He was a skeptic among the credulous, a charlatan among honest sorcerers. He scoffed at magic, called it trickery, called it "monkeyshines," monkeyish business (to use his word, "*singeries*").

He had astonished La Voisin by his sleight of hand: "Laurel branches and crystal cups locked in an armoire . . . retrieved in the garden! . . . Wonders such as she herself could not perform." His hand quicker than the eye of even his sharp-eyed accomplice, he had told her, and she had been so gullible as to believe and to repeat it: "that he was one of the original ten Sibyls of the Ancient World"; "that he belonged to the Apostolate"; "that he possessed all the knowledge and the science of the Cabala."* She hung her head in shame to think that she had allowed herself to be duped by him—as she herself had duped her clients! Le Sage had laid a death spell on La Voisin's husband by saying incantations over a ram's heart and then burying it under the porte-cochere. When Monsieur Voisin had cried out with pains in his stomach, his wife had relented and implored Le Sage to dig up the spell (all the while he laughed up his sleeve at her gullibility, he implied).

* The Cabala, a system of occult theosophy or mystical interpretation of the Scriptures among Jewish Rabbis and some medieval Christians; originally handed down orally, later written, and compiled between the second and sixth centuries.

Le Sage gave La Reynie detailed accounts of La Voisin's traffic in poisons, her sources of supply, her successes and her failures. She denied it all: "The only drugs to be found in her house were purgatives for her personal use and that of her family!" To Le Sage's accusation that she delivered her poisonous powders and potions to exalted customers at the Château de Saint-Germain, her rejoinder was that she supplied "nothing but beauty balms and skin lotions." She reacted violently, manifestly winced, La Reynie noted, at Le Sage's efforts to connect her with the court.

La Voisin's garden pavilion, Le Sage told La Reynie, was used as an abortions parlor. There was a small oven there, in the wall, "concealed by a tapestry, where the bones were burned if the infant body seemed too large to lay away in a garden grave." Margot, the maid, had warned him away from that "accursed oven," but when he had quizzed La Voisin about it, she had told him whimsically that it was for baking her *"petits pâtés."*

June and July of 1679 saw the Chambre Ardente go to work. Parisians, high and low, riffraff and upper crust, crowded the Place de Grève to watch the public executions: Belot, a bodyguard and an accomplice of La Bosse's, was broken upon the wheel; La Cheron, witch and fortuneteller, was burned at the stake; La Durand and La Pottereau, avowed poisoners, were hanged and burned.

In mid-September, Louvois sped a secret and urgent communiqué to the King: "La Voisin now begins to do a lot of talking. . . . Yesterday she said that Mme de Vivonne and Mme de La Mothe had come to her together to ask for something to do away with their husbands and that subsequently these ladies were in contact with Le Sage to carry out their projects . . ."

The name that leaped to the eye—to La Reynie's, to Louvois's, to the King's—was the name of Mme de Vivonne, the Duchesse de Vivonne, the wife of the Maréchal-Duke, the sister-in-law of Mme de Montespan! One of the high and mighty, one of His Majesty's most intimate coterie; a member, so to speak, of His Majesty's family circle.

On September 17 came even more startling revelations from

the lips of Le Sage: when La Voisin delivered her love powders—powder of cantharides or Spanish fly, *Cantharis vesicatoria*, the most ancient of aphrodisiacs—to the Château de Saint-Germain, it was into the hands of a girl named Cato, a maid in Mme de Montespan's household (placed there by none other than La Voisin!), and into the hands of Mlle des Oeillets, Mme de Montespan's confidential maid (His Majesty's sometime concubine). At the very moment of their arrests, La Voisin, La Vigoureux, and La Bosse had all been conspiring to place a second accomplice, La Vertemart, in Mme de Montespan's retinue.

Sorceresses, witches, poisoners, the most dangerous criminals in the land, in the entourage of the King's own mistress, with access to His Majesty's sacred person! The scandal was spreading alarmingly; reaching now into the King's own palace, contaminating the court of France of which he was so proud.

These were revelations which must not be allowed to reach the ear of the general public, not even the ear of the judges of the Chamber of the Arsenal—not allowed to go beyond the King's closest councilors.

On September 21, 1679, His Majesty addressed his Lieutenant-General of Police to advise of a decision: "Deeming it appropriate to continue the questioning of certain of the prisoners in my château of Vincennes on the subject of the facts mentioned in your attached report, I herewith write to instruct you to proceed as speedily as possible with such interrogations, but to make the transcripts of these responses on separate folios, and to keep these folios apart from the official records of the rest of the investigation . . . disposition of these separate folios to be made later, in accordance with my decisions . . ."

His decision would be to destroy them, to burn these separate, secret folios—sheet by sheet, and by his own hand—only La Reynie's notes surviving as a record of their content.

"As for any further charges against Mme de Vivonne or any other person of similar station which might be made in those interrogations that were being separately recorded," Louvois ordered La Reynie to send him immediate, daily notice.

Le Sage caused another sensation with the mention of a petition which La Voisin, on the very eve of her arrest, had been preparing to deliver by her own hand into that of the King of France. By royal French tradition, the monarchs accepted petitions —appeals for justice or relief from oppression—from any and all citizens in the land; upon certain appointed days, crowds gathered in the palace to lay such documents upon the table at which His Majesty sat to accept them, accessible to all in the ancient tradition of the king-magistrate.

Le Sage made curious, veiled, and confused suggestions as to the lethal properties of La Voisin's document—it was fatal to the touch; it had been prepared with poisonous substances; or it had been subjected to conjurations, charms, and spells.

If it was true that harm had been intended to the King's sacred person, then the Poisons Affair would become an affair of state.

"His Majesty listened with horror to the reading of your report," Louvois wrote to La Reynie on October 16; "nevertheless he wishes that these allegations be thoroughly investigated, that proof or disproof be sought throughout."

What horrified the King was Le Sage's charge that La Voisin had been in frequent contact with Cato and Mlle des Oeillets: "Negotiations taking place either at Mlle des Oeillets's house or at some rendezvous set by her on the road to Versailles on some affair having to do with Mme de Montespan."

Let La Voisin deny it if she could—deny knowing Mme de Montespan, deny knowing des Oeillets—then, La Filastre, La Voisin's right-hand accomplice in all this business, would corroborate Le Sage's story.

"If only you had La Filastre here," Le Sage exclaimed, "what dark secrets she could tell you!" Dark secrets about a conspiracy to poison Mlle de Fontanges! Even now, at this very hour, La Filastre was conniving to be assigned a place in the new Favorite's household!

Not only La Filastre but La Chapelain and La Vertemart, he insisted, would bear him out. He called on his former confederate, the Abbé Mariette, as witness to his word—along with a whole string of other defrocked priests about whose role he dropped hints of abominations too vile to speak aloud.

Louvois, notified daily by La Reynie, daily notified the King of every development in this ultra-secret investigation at the Fortress of Vincennes: "He [Le Sage] cites so many witnesses who substantiate his allegations that it is difficult to believe that he could be inventing these tales. . . . Yet, I find it even more difficult to believe that La des Oeillets could have been involved with La Voisin for anything except some harmless folly. . . . The crimes of those detained at Vincennes appear more extraordinary every day . . ."

By December 27, 1679, Louis XIV had reached a decision. On that date, at his command, Louvois summoned Boucherat, the President of the Chambre Ardente; Robert, the Solicitor-General; and the chairmen of the commission, Bezons and La Reynie, into a conference with His Majesty at Versailles.

La Reynie made note of the conference, and filed it among his personal papers: "His Majesty reminded us of our duty and, in forceful and explicit terms, recommended justice. He called our attention to the fact that he desired of us—for the public welfare—that we get to the root of this dreadful traffic in poisons in order that it might be entirely eradicated. He commanded us to do justice —absolute justice—regardless of rank or sex or position. And His Majesty made these recommendations to us in terms so clear and so vivid, and with a purpose so noble, that it is impossible to doubt his intentions in this case, impossible to misunderstand the spirit of justice in which he wants this investigation carried out."

VI

The Great and Near Great on Trial

"REGARDLESS OF RANK OR SEX OR POSITION."
The words of His Majesty ringing in their ears, the judges of the Chamber of the Arsenal proceeded to mete out justice.

A thunderclap shook and rattled court and capital.

On January 23, 1680, the Chambre Ardente issued warrants for the arrest of "high and puissant" noblemen and noblewomen —a Crown officer among them, a scion of an imperial house—the Duc de Luxembourg, the Marquis de Cessac, the Vicomtesse de Polignac, the Marquise d'Alluye. Last, but assuredly not least, the Comtesse de Soissons.

On that same day, writs of subpoena were issued in the names of the Comtesse du Roure, the Marquis de Feuquières, the Princesse de Tingry, Mme de La Ferté (wife of the maréchal) and Her Highness, the Duchesse de Bouillon—names as prestigious as any in the kingdom.

"We are all in a state of agitation," Mme de Sévigné exclaimed. Under the blanket of official secrecy, under the shroud of silence maintained by all the newspapers, tension mounted; rumor ran riot. "We send out for news," wrote Mme de Sévigné, who would suffer from writer's cramp before this affair was over, trying to keep her daughter posted on the sensational developments in Paris: "We go to other people's houses to hear what they have heard . . . we are consumed with curiosity." And in the next bulletin: "At the moment, the reaction is one of horror at the scandal. . . . The sentiment presently is one of sympathy for the accused . . . a feeling that they are innocent . . . though this may change overnight. . . . There is no other topic of conversation. No such scandal as this has ever been known in a Christian court!"

"The rumor is that His Majesty most charitably gave the Comtesse de Soissons time to get out of France," as Mme de Sévigné further reported on January 24. And the Abbé de Choisy corroborates the rumor: "The King, out of consideration for the memory of the Cardinal [Mazarin, uncle of the Comtesse de Soissons], sent the Duc de Bouillon to tell her that he offered her the choice of going the next day to the Bastille . . . or else leaving France immediately. The Duc de Villeroi [her lover] and the Marquise d'Alluye . . . urged her to go to the Bastille, in view of her constant protestations of innocence, but she did not dare take that risk. She declared to them: 'Monsieur de Louvois is my mortal enemy, because I refused my daughter's hand to his son. He has been powerful enough to have me accused; he has false witnesses at his command. Since things have gone so far that a warrant has been issued against a person of my rank, then I fear he will succeed in his criminal attempts, and will bring about my death on the scaffold or keep me in prison for life. I would rather keep my freedom, and exonerate myself later on.'"

"She protested her innocence in high key," Mme de Sévigné agreed, "but insisted that she could not face the indignity of prison nor the ignominy of being confronted with tramps and rascals. . . . For three days in a row, the official summons of the tribunal was trumpeted" (beneath the windows of the Comtesse de Soissons's apartment in the Tuileries Palace). "Due notice that her trial would proceed *in contumaciam.*"

But, by then, the Countess and the Marquise d'Alluye, her boon companion—her accomplice? likewise a client of La Voisin's; likewise on the tribunal's Wanted Persons list—were on the road to Flanders; "their carriage, drawn by eight horses," had been heard rattling over the cobblestones of the Place du Carrousel "at three o'clock in the morning of the twenty-third."

The King had gone in person to visit his cousin, the Princesse de Carignan (a Princess of the Blood Royal, a Bourbon-Condé, mother-in-law of the Comtesse de Soissons) to tell her that the Countess had taken flight at his warning. "I only hope," the King said, "that I shall not, one day, be called to account for this action by my God or by my people."

It was the family honor that was of concern to the Princesse de Carignan. No love was lost between the Princess and her daughter-in-law—the son of the former very possibly dead by the hand of the latter. At the mysterious death of the Comte de Soissons in 1673, the finger of suspicion had pointed at his wife, although no formal charges had been brought against her, onetime inamorata of the King's, first object of his youthful gallantries. Seven years later, in 1680, with an arrest order out against her, rumor had it that it was for the murder of her husband, but here rumor had it wrong.

La Voisin, in an official interrogation on January 16, had come out with accusations even more damaging to the Countess, as is evident in this official transcript to be found in the Archives of the Bastille:*

LA REYNIE: What did the Comtesse de Soissons say the day she came to your house? [This, in reference to a contact made several years earlier, in 1663 or 1664.]

LA VOISIN: I have told you before, and will uphold my previous declaration. I told her that I could see that she had once been loved by a great Prince. Whereupon she wanted to know whether that love could be revived. When I replied that a way might be found to revive it, the lady went into a rage, declaring that a way must be found! That if she could not get revenge on Mlle de La Vallière—get rid of Mlle de La Vallière!—then she would carry her vengeance to even greater lengths. She would do away with both one and the other.

* The transcripts of the original interrogations, in the Archives of the Bastille, are phrased in the third person singular, but have been transposed here—as by numerous French historians—into the first person, for the sake of clarity.

LA REYNIE: Did the Comtesse de Soissons say what method her vengeance would take?

LA VOISIN: No. All she said was that she would destroy them both. . . . At the end of the visit, the lady ordered one of her lackeys to give me five gold half-louis pieces.

LA REYNIE: Was it not true that the Countess's request to read her palm was merely a pretext, and that when you were alone together in the garden, the Countess asked you for something else?

LA VOISIN: When we were in my garden office, I looked at the lines in the lady's palm, and that's how I was able to tell her that I knew she had once been the love of a great Prince. . . . And all the rest occurred just as I have told it to you. . . .

Despite all the enjoinders to secrecy laid upon the investigating officers and the judges, there was talk. Within a fortnight, an almost verbatim account of the January 16 interrogation of La Voisin deep within the *donjons* of Vincennes had been repeated to Mme de Sévigné: "The Comtesse de Soissons asked [La Voisin] if she could rekindle love in a lover who had abandoned her—a lover who was a great Prince. And it is said that she said that if he did not come back to her, he would be made to rue it. The great Prince is understood to be the King, and anything like this having to do with the King becomes a serious matter. . . ."

A crime of *lèse-majesté*, a crime against the sovereign power, a threat against the sacred person of the sovereign; an affair of state, no less.

A sentence of perpetual banishment was pronounced upon the Comtesse de Soissons by the Chamber of the Arsenal, "announced by trumpeters in every quarter of the capital."

Madame de Sévigné clung to the theory of the Countess's innocence: "Such foolishness of which she is accused! Such silly stories as she has told on herself a thousand times . . . such as anyone tells after visits to these so-called witches."

But ugly rumors sprang up wherever the Countess passed. She had stopped at a Carignan domain, at Condé-en-Champagne, en route to the frontier, and Louvois reported two deaths there, in her wake: "A gentleman named Davery, dead of poison. . . . A chambermaid . . . named Gastine . . . who suffered the same fate."

So sinister was the reputation that preceded her that the gates of both Antwerp and Namur were closed against her when she sought refuge there after her flight from France.

"Louvois had sent cavalrymen after her, to make sure that she had crossed the border," Visconti relates in his Memoirs: "At Brussels . . . a soldier, set upon her traces by Louvois, loosed a sack of black cats in a Dominican church where she was attending Mass on a high holy day. . . . The people of the city, naturally superstitious . . . took the black cats for demons and the Comtesse de Soissons for a witch! And, aroused against her, forced her to travel on in search of another refuge . . ."

Wily, still attractive in her early forties, the Countess tripped up an Italian Duke in her toils, and he served as her protector until she made her way to Spain in 1688.

She was a harbinger of doom: her trail through Europe blazed by a series of strange, inexplicable deaths.

The Queen of Spain was next.

To bright, young, pretty, appealing little Marie Louise d'Orléans, "France was the very breath of life," to quote Saint-Simon. Her husband, King Charles II, was literally mad about her, but she was nonetheless a prisoner in the gloom of the Spanish court, in the straitjacket of its unrelenting etiquette, under its pall of fear. She dutifully reported to her uncle, Louis XIV, the sole item of international significance that she had been able to ascertain: that her husband was impotent. Yielding to pressure, the King of Spain finally allowed the Comtesse de Soissons to come to gossip with his homesick bride about Versailles and Paris. The Countess, an intimate of the Austrian Ambassador, entered into a conspiracy to eliminate the pro-French influence exerted by the French Queen, through her husband, on Spanish policy. One day in 1689, finding the Queen alone, the Countess tempted her with a glass of chilled milk—"a rare delight in a torrid Spanish summer," by Saint-Simon's telling: "The Queen died shortly after, in much the same circumstances as had *Madame*, her mother [after agonizing hours of cramps and vomiting]. . . . The Countess wasted not a moment's time in the palace. . . . Her flight had been arranged . . . her trunks, packed. . . . The King of Spain sent out after her in every direction . . . but she had laid her plans so well that she made good her escape from the country. . . . She lived, in obscurity, in Germany; now here, now there. . . . Finally, the Countess came to Brussels . . . where she died in poverty and opprobrium . . . French dignitaries forbidden to frequent her; shown little consideration even by her celebrated son, Prince Eugène."* (Though as Voltaire saw it, from another point of view in time, it was "Prince Eugène who avenged the death of his mother, in late 1708, by piling up the victories, by repeated triumphs over Louis XIV.")

As for the Countess's sister, Marie Anne Mancini, Duchesse de Bouillon, she bowed that proud and beautiful head of hers to answer the writ of subpoena issued in her name, arriving at the Chamber of the Arsenal on January 29, escorted by both her husband and her lover, the Duc de Vendôme (great-grandson of King Henri IV; the Vendômes another bastard but legitimized branch of the Bourbon family tree). She made it clear to the judges, as it is noted in the official court transcript of the hearing, "that she had condescended to appear before them only as a token of respect and obedience to the King . . . since it was within her ducal right to submit to no other judgment than that of the assembled high courts of the Parlement of Paris."

"She reigned like a kind of queen in Paris," by Saint-Simon's account: "The splendor in which she had lived . . . had spoiled her. . . . Her beauty and wit reinforced her pretensions . . . and the world gradually succumbed to her domination. . . . She treated Monsieur de Bouillon with disdain" (Grand Chamberlain of France though he might be; and his family one of the most power-

---

* Prince Eugène of Savoy, the great commander, who joined the Austrian forces when his services were rejected by Louis XIV. Prince Eugène proved the nemesis of France in the devastating campaigns of the War of the Spanish Succession at the turn of the century.

ful in the kingdom), "and all the rest of the world was lower to her than the grass she trampled beneath her feet."

"Her motto was 'To take a host of lovers, but one at a time, and in rapid succession,' " as Visconti heard it. (On which basis, he implies, she invited him to join the company.) "The Duc de Bouillon did not object to sharing his wife's favors with others . . . so long as she had enough to go around, for him as well as for them. . . ."

"The Duchesse de Bouillon went to La Voisin to ask for a little something poisonous to kill off an old husband before he bored her to death" (by Mme de Sévigné's report of January 31), "and for some magic charm or spell to bring about her marriage with a young man whom no one had suspected as her lover. . . . That young man was Monsieur de Vendôme, who escorted her [into the courtroom], taking her one hand, while Monsieur de Bouillon took the other. What a farce! When a Mancini is guilty of a mere folly such as this, is it not absurd to make such a fuss about it? These witches repeat all this nonsense in dead earnest, but what sense does it make to scandalize all Europe for such bagatelles as these? . . . As I hear it, from authoritative sources, Mme de Bouillon entered that Chamber [of the Arsenal] like a little Queen, taking her seat in a chair which had been especially placed for her . . . removing her glove to reveal her exquisite hand . . . and giving an honest answer to even a question about her age. . . . 'Why did you try to do away with your husband?'—'I? Try to do away with my husband? Ask him if he believes such a thing! He has escorted me here to this very door'—'Then why did you go so often to La Voisin's?'—'To see the Sibyls she had promised to evoke for me . . . a sight well worth seeing.' . . . When she rose to make her exit, she said in a loud tone of voice: 'Really, I would never have believed that such intelligent men could ask such stupid questions.' . . . All her friends and relatives were awaiting her when she came out, openly worshipful . . . so pretty she was, so natural, so undaunted, so superior, so serene."

The official transcript of the Duchess's interrogation, filed with the bulk of the trial documents in the Archives of the Bastille, shows her somewhat less flippant and less insolent than Mme de Sévigné describes:

DUCHESSE DE BOUILLON: La Voisin came one day to my house and told me that—knowing what a great curiosity I had about the supernatural—she could recommend a very exceptional man, a man of marvels. . . . And so, several days later [driving in her coach and six with a company including the Duc de Vendôme], it was decided to stop at La Voisin's to see the man known as Le Sage . . . to see what extraordinary things he could perform. . . . Le Sage told me that he could burn a paper in my presence and later make it appear in whatever place I should indicate. . . . Monsieur de Vendôme and I were to write down several questions or requests on a sheet of paper . . . which we did. . . . This sheet having been folded and sealed, Le Sage further tied it with a silken cord . . . then sprinkled it with sulphur . . . and set it aflame on a burner in La Voisin's room. . . . Afterwards, Le Sage told us that we would find the burned letter, intact, in a porcelain jar in my own house . . . although this did not come about. Instead, two or three days later, Le Sage came to me and brought the letter with him . . . which astonished me extremely . . . to see it folded and sealed just as it had been before it had been handed to him. . . . And having repeated this story to the Duc de Vendôme and the others of the company, they all found it difficult to believe, and said that it simply could not have happened thus, and that we must get Le Sage to burn another letter, and see if he could repeat the act. . . . So, I had to send for Le Sage again, and he came to me, and another letter was written and thrown into the flames . . . in which letter Le Sage said that we were to enclose two *pistole* coins for the Sibyls, as before. . . . And Le Sage, having said that he would have the burned letter restored to me intact again, withdrew. I sent for him several times to summon him to come; and even passed by his place, myself, but after making various excuses to me, he finally came three or four days later on to say that something had prevented the Sibyls from appearing, and that was why he had been unable to reply. From that day forward, I have not seen him again, and I found the whole thing so funny that I repeated it to a number of friends and even wrote an account of it to my husband, at that time away with his troops . . .

INTERROGATOR: Is it true that you wrote a letter which you turned over to Le Sage, sealed and burned like the others, in which there was included a conjuration to bring about your husband's death?

DUCHESSE DE BOUILLON: No, and the story is so patently absurd as to be incredible.

In another version of the Duchess's famous appearance before the Chamber of the Arsenal—this one by Visconti—she is quizzed by La Reynie as to whether the witches had ever conjured up the Devil for her. " 'Yes,' she replied to La Reynie, 'I saw him, and he looked just like you!' "

"Madame de Bouillon did so much bragging about her sharp rejoinders to the judges that she wound up with a *lettre de cachet* —an order signed by the King for her exile at Nérac, close to the Pyrenees (so Mme de Sévigné tells, by letter of February 16).*

There was talk that the Duchesse de Bouillon, given a choice by the King, had chosen exile—bitter as it was—in preference to the ignominy of confrontation with Le Sage and La Voisin.

The trial of La Voisin, already in progress in January, 1680, had been suspended on the twenty-fifth to allow time for her to be confronted with those who had been incriminated on her charges.

The inquiry was, meanwhile, to be diligently pursued—"No matter whose name comes up in the process!" as Louvois notified La Reynie.

Solicitor-General Robert was required by the same minister to

---

* All four of the Mancinis ended in exile: Marie, Princess Colonna, Louis XIV's first love, in a convent in Spain; Hortense, Duchesse de Mazarin, in England; the Comtesse de Soissons, at this time, in Flanders; the Duchesse de Bouillon now in Guyenne.

submit all his conclusions to the King, but was otherwise encouraged "to proceed with full freedom of action, in conformity with the rules of justice": "There does exist the risk, to be sure, which you mention—the risk that some of these inquiries might result in the denunciation of persons of very high station—but there would be even greater risk were it to be thought that His Majesty was shielding persons guilty of such grave crimes as these. For this reason, it is His Majesty's decision to leave the procedure to the discretion of the judges . . ."

Justice was to take its course—with one exception!

"There is only one matter upon which His Majesty requests you to proceed with caution," Louvois's letter continues: "This concerns the charges made against Mlle des Oeillets and against Mme de Montespan's maid named Cato . . . His Majesty being convinced that Le Sage could not possibly have been telling the truth in this instance. This particular charge will be further clarified by the judges in their interrogations during the trial of La Voisin and in the course of the trials of other prisoners involved. Thus, His Majesty believes that justice will not be prejudiced by your waiting to take further action on this particular charge of Le Sage's until such time as you may be convinced that there is any truth to it."

The Princesse de Tingry, one of the Queen's ladies of the palace, swept into the tribunal of the Arsenal on the same day as the Duchesse de Bouillon—the Princess, like the Duchess, accompanied to the gates by twenty carriage-loads of imposing friends and family.

"Up to this point," remarked Mme de Sévigné, "these ladies' crimes do not seem so black . . . not even a dark brown! If no further evidence is produced against them, it would seem that persons of such rank should have been spared from scandal." (The Princess's love life was something else again, and not a national issue: Mme de Sévigné had heard that "La Voisin's little oven for incinerating aborted babies was kept hot year in, year out, on La Tingry's patronage alone.")

Madame de La Ferté, wife of the marshal and notorious for

her debauches, answered her court summons that same week in January. Admittedly, she had gone along with the Comtesse de Soissons on visits to La Voisin, "But only to be sociable!" Her hearing before the court "provided her with a rare pleasure," Mme de Sévigné remarked maliciously: "For once in her life, she has heard herself proclaimed innocent!"

The Vicomtesse de Polignac took alarm at the action against her in the Chamber, and took flight to the provinces. When the Intendant of Auvergne, at Louvois's instance, descended upon her château at Puy-de-Dôme to take her into custody, he found the bird flown again, so her trial proceeded *in contumaciam*. The King was never again comfortable in her company, and later ordered her to depart the court. As a friend of Bussy's reported: "His Majesty had good reason to fear the proximity of a woman who had resorted to aphrodisiacs to arouse his passion for her."

"Deeply involved in the La Voisin scandal," as Saint-Simon phrased it, "she could never quite rid herself of the taint. . . . A tall and handsome woman . . . every inch the *grande dame*, she was exiled to Puy [-de-Dôme] in Languedoc, whence she never returned until after the death of the King. . . ."

Her sister-in-law, the Comtesse du Roure, stood up to her judges, and stood down her accusers on February 1, 1680. She flatly denied ever having gone to consult La Voisin, ever having summoned La Voisin to come to her, ever having offered or sent La Voisin money, ever having asked either La Voisin or Le Sage to "do away with La Vallière." The page in the Archives that bears the transcript of her interrogation—only twenty-five lines long—is all No's: "No" . . . "No" . . . "Never" . . . "No"; she had never dabbled in necromancy, never indulged in sacrilegious practices such as Le Sage described, "in the gallery of the King's own chapel." She had never joined him beside the altar in incantations over "a pair of pigeons' hearts."

"A blanket denial," as chairman of the commission Bezons reported to Louvois, "and somewhat of a surprise" to that judge, "in view of the fact that La Voisin's allegations had been given in such detail as to carry conviction . . ."

Despite all her protestations of innocence, the Comtesse du Roure—like Mme de Polignac—was "chased out of Versailles" (as Saint-Simon inelegantly but accurately stated it, years later): "After that adventure of hers [in the Poisons Affair], she was lucky to get off as lightly as she did, with a mere sentence of exile to her estates in Languedoc, whence she returned only once thereafter, by special permission, for a few months' sojourn. . . . She inspired fear wherever she went, in everyone . . ." (including her husband, according to Saint-Simon, who adds: "She lived in one château; he, in another").

The Marquis de Cessac, Master of the King's Wardrobe (whose function was to supervise the packing when the King traveled), decided not to wait for La Reynie's officers to pick him up, but to make a dash for it, across the English Channel. Cheating at cards—for which he had been briefly exiled in 1671—had not ensured his winning from those sharpers at the King's gaming table, and so he had resorted to sorcery, to good-luck charms, amulets, and talismans.

The Marquis de Feuquières had heard that he was next on La Reynie's list ("That mad fool!" he called the Lieutenant-General of Police), and wrote to his father, France's Ambassador to Sweden, to assure him of his innocence: "The accusations against me are ridiculous and baseless. . . . What all this amounts to is that a ring of professional poisoners have discovered a means of prolonging their miserable lives by denouncing a number of prominent people, who are being arrested and tried . . . and the time lost in that procedure is time gained for the criminals." The Marquis thus sat by calmly and coolly to await delivery of the warrant for his arrest which, happily for him, never came. The Chambre Ardente merely requested him to appear for questioning on a certain day. He complied, but refuted every accusation brought against him by La Voisin, Le Sage, and La Vigoureux, and was dismissed without further harassment.

His patron and cousin, Monsieur de Luxembourg, was less fortunate. The arrest of this powerful and popular nobleman was perhaps the greatest surprise of all: a Duke and peer of the realm,

Captain of the King's Bodyguards, "the last of France's great commanders," in Saint-Simon's esteem. Madame de Sévigné gasped as she reported it to her daughter: "The King told him [M. de Luxembourg] that if he was innocent he need only betake himself to prison; that he [the King] had appointed such fine judges to investigate this affair that he was leaving the entire conduct of the case to them. . . . You must by now have heard that poor Luxembourg acted as his own arresting officer, turned himself over to Bezemaux [the governor of the Bastille]. . . . He came in [to Paris] from Saint-Germain, encountering Mme de Montespan on the road. . . . They both descended from their carriages to go to speak together in privacy, and without constraint. . . . He, weeping bitterly . . ." (omniscient as Mme de Sévigné was, here her information is deficient; a record of that roadside conversation might have gone a long way in solving the major enigma of the Poisons Affair). "Monsieur de Luxembourg was shown, at first, into a very fine apartment [at the Bastille], but an hour later came an order to move him to one of those horrible, barred tower cells . . . where one can see only a scrap of sky, and cut off from all communication with the outside world. . . . Think of this man's brilliant career, his great fortune and high station, of the honors he has enjoyed as Commander of the King's Armies. And think of where he is now! Imagine how he must have felt hearing those great locks turned upon him!" A few days later, however, by January 31, Mme de Sévigné had lost patience with "poor Luxembourg": "He should have paraded his innocence across the border, and sent back word that he would return only to face his rightful judges in the Supreme Court of Parlement. . . . He has derogated the ducal rights by submitting to this special tribunal. . . . He will never again be able to take his place in the great world, after this catastrophe. . . ." (But he did, via the battlefield, and twirling a marshal's bâton) "Now he is entirely undone, has gone to pieces. . . . 'I have abandoned God; now God has abandoned me!' . . . If one lacks the stamina to stand up to the Bastille, one is better off making a run for it . . . as the King gave him every opportunity to do, up to the very moment of his surrender. . . . He has been subjected to a four-hour interrogation by La Reynie and Monsieur de Bezons. . . . The consensus is that he has not been charged with poisonings. . . . It must have been for some other *diableries*" (And the judges, agreeing with her, would acquit the Duke after some four months' incarceration. Intrigued as he was by astrology and horoscopy, he had undoubtedly run to the fortunetellers, but he was not alone in that. One of the marshal's biographers set out to vindicate his hero by proving that it was Bonnard, Luxembourg's intendant, who had signed his master's name to a pact with the Devil. Bonnard paid for this impertinence by a life sentence to the galleys, but the damage to Luxembourg's reputation had been done.)

A compact with the Devil, in the tradition of Dr. Faustus, traditionally inscribed on virgin parchment, proved one of the best-selling items in the sorcerers' stock in trade. Wondrous and fearsome privileges were implicit, according to the Devil's spokesmen: the ability to cast a spell on man and beast, to dry up or to taint a wellspring, to bring on a war, to call down a bolt of lightning, to raise up a tempest or a storm at sea, to summon demons to do one's bidding, to do away with a rival . . . to supplant a royal Favorite, such as a La Vallière or a Montespan.*

Le Sage accused the Princesse de Tingry, the Duchesse de Vitry, the Duchesse d'Angoulême, and the Duchesse de Vivonne of mortgaging their souls to the fiend in exchange for specific favors, to wit: a death spell to be laid on Mme de Montespan and a love charm on the King. Later, the quartet of noble ladies came to Le Sage to enlist his aid in retrieving the document bearing their signatures from the hands of La Filastre, who was obviously using it to blackmail them.

Here, again, was the name of the Duchesse de Vivonne. Here, again, in accordance with Louvois's instructions to La Reynie, her

---

* King James I accused the witches of having raised up the storm through which he had to sail home with his bride from Denmark. And if Scottish witches in the sixteenth century took credit for having roused the winds that helped to defeat the Spanish Armada, twentieth-century covens claim to have frustrated Hitler's plans for an invasion of their island.

name was to be erased, excised, expunged—effectively stricken, totally eradicated from the interrogation reports before these were submitted to the tribunal.

"These ladies and gentlemen believe in the Devil, if not in God," Mme de Sévigné quotes the pious old Maréchal de Villeroi as lamenting.

And he was right, for in the seventeenth century, the Devil was omnipresent: his image and his legend carved upon the stones of every Gothic cathedral in Europe. There, where the illiterate masses learned their theology pictorially, the Devil's effigy was prominent: on the tympana of cathedral doorways, in stained-glass windows and bas reliefs, among the gargoyles and the waterspouts, these latter aswarm with fantastic fauna presumably native to the nether regions. Nor is the witch—the high priestess of the diabolic church—neglected: a voussoir of the western doorway of Lyon Cathedral shows her naked, riding her goat, while figures in a castle tower cower in terror. Thanks to the medieval sculptor, the personnel of Hell took on classical anatomical and pathological deformities: squamous demons with horns and tails, with winged rumps, clawed hands, and taloned feet; with reptiles writhing in and out of every orifice. To the medieval mind, the existence of the Devil was as much an article of faith as the existence of the Most High—a dualism reminiscent of Zoroastrianism, Mazdaism, Manichaeanism; an antinomy existent between the eternally hostile principles of good and evil; the forces of darkness versus the forces of light; a conflict still unresolved in medieval days, as in these.

Not only Catholicism but Lutheranism was Devil-oriented: Luther's *Greater Catechism* cites the name of the Devil 67 times in comparison to a mere 63 citations for the Savior. In St. Thomas Aquinas' *Summa Theologica*, whole chapters are devoted to the variety of human and animal forms assumed by angels and by demons. The dialogue between demons and saints went on late into the Middle Ages. The medieval Church harped on the powers of evil—a dangerous policy. And even as late as the late seventeenth century, a churchman such as Bishop Bossuet, for all his mighty intellect, did not doubt the efficacy of sorcery. How, then, expect a Louis XIV or even the most cultivated elite of his court to doubt it?

The century of Louis XIV was the period of transition between the Dark Ages and the Age of Enlightenment, and it is not surprising to find curious quirks in the turn of the century mentality.

No more striking example is to be found than that of the Regent (the Duc d'Orléans, ruler of France between 1715 and 1723, the years of the minority of his nephew, Louis XV). He baffled Voltaire in that he was a notorious "freethinker," a proselytizing atheist and, at the same time, a practicing diabolist, astrologer, and alchemist (some said poisoner). Voltaire was shocked that a man of such enlightenment should fall prey to such superstition.

"Credulity is the indelible mark of ignorance," Voltaire would thunder out of the eighteenth century. "Superstitious practices debase religion"—superstition and religion synonymous to all the *Philosophes,* including Voltaire.

But the turn-of-the-century mentality still accepted magic as unquestioningly as it had accepted miracle (the distinction one of semantics: magic to be defined as "the operation of supernatural powers via a human agency"; miracle as "the operation of supernatural powers via a superhuman agency"). Montesquieu would shortly and derisively explain away both by proving natural causes. But Montesquieu would not be born until 1689.

In 1680, that celebrated and cultivated elite of Louis XIV's court and capital was being arraigned on charges of the practice of magic, black and white. And when Maréchal de Villeroi lamented that "These ladies and gentlemen believe in the Devil," he was right.

Meanwhile "all Paris," in Visconti's book, "ridiculed the procedures of the Arsenal Chamber, which was compromising the honor and the life of the most exalted personages in the kingdom . . . and this, over mere bagatelles!"

"All Paris" included the Marquis d'Alluye who, for his bold criticism of the royal tribunal, was "banished to Amboise . . . to his governance in Orléans," his eyes forever after denied the sight of the glory of his lord, the King. His wife, the Marquise, had by then parted company from her friend, the Comtesse de Soissons, and obtained permission to return to France; though not to Paris, not to Versailles, at least not for many a long year.

The judges of the Chamber of the Arsenal found themselves in a crossfire between the bourgeoisie and aristocracy, both up in arms against them. La Reynie felt the need of a bodyguard when he traveled beyond the walls of Paris to the Fortress of Vincennes.

"If they try to punish everyone who ever consulted a fortune-teller, then all the valets and ladies' maids in Paris will be trembling in their boots," the Prince de Condé's doctor, Bourdelet, scoffed in a letter to his patient.

The arrest of the great military hero, Luxembourg, had stirred up a hornet's nest; his acquittal, coming four months later, in May of 1680, would seem further to justify the resentment. The court, abruptly dropping its charges against the Marquis de Feuquières, seemed to be admitting to an error in having charged him in the first place.

On February 4, 1680, Louvois wrote to assure the presiding judge, Louis Boucherat, that the King had taken the entire bench under his special protection, and that "His Majesty expected of them that they should continue to render justice with the same determination with which they had set out, undeterred by any other consideration whatsoever."

Madame de Sévigné joined her voice to the chorus of protest: "There is no excuse for that Chamber's impudence in issuing warrants with so little justification against officers of the Crown. . . . This scandalous affair must be horrifying all Europe, and those who read of it in history books a hundred years from now will surely pity the victims of such baseless accusations."

A note of comic relief was struck now and then. As by Bussy in a message to La Rivière on January 27: "The King has returned a letter to the Duchesse de Foix—one written by her to La Voisin—in which appeared the phrase, 'The more I rub, the less they project.' When His Majesty demanded an explanation, the Duchess cleared up the mystery by confessing that she had gone to La Voisin to ask for a prescription to develop her bosom."

To everyone's amazement, the arrests and the citations continued, unabated: such a notable as the Comte de Clermont-Lodève, a Prince of the house of Bourbon, was arraigned, later dismissed. The pretty widow Marguerite Léonard disappeared into the fastness of the Bastille, leaving her fiancé, Visconti, disconsolate.

Even the renowned poet, official historiographer to the King, Jean Racine, knew a moment's danger, charged by La Voisin with having poisoned his mistress, the popular and beautiful stage star Thérèse du Parc, whom he had lured away—an act of gross ingratitude for which he was much reproached—from the theatrical company of Molière, the very man who had launched Racine upon his brilliant career.

Racine had produced a masterpiece, *Andromaque*, for La du Parc, in 1667, coaching and directing her in the demanding title role. And he had, unless himself a consummate actor, exhibited deep grief at her death, in 1668, presumably in childbirth, though possibly as the aftermath of an abortion. Now, twelve years later, La Voisin accused him of a crime of passion—just such a one as he excelled at plotting and motivating. She charged him with having poisoned his inamorata out of jealousy, of "having stood guard over her deathbed . . . never stirring from her pillow," denying access to her family and friends, even to La Voisin, a "long-time confidante."

On January 11, Louvois addressed a message to Bazin de Bezons, La Reynie's colleague, co-chairman of the commission: "The royal warrant for the arrest of the Sieur Racine will be sent to you whenever you request it."

Bezons never requested it; it was never issued. It may be that the King stepped in to protect his protégé, his favored playwright and historian. Or it might have been Bezons, Racine's friend and confrère in the Académie Française, who discouraged the court from taking further action against the tragic poet.

On the morning of February 6, 1680, upon Louvois's orders,

La Reynie presented himself at the Château de Saint-Germain, at the door of the royal apartments, immediately after the King's *Levée* (his Rising Up, the morning reception to which certain privileged courtiers were admitted).

As La Reynie scrupulously noted after the audience, "His Majesty brought up a number of very serious matters for discussion. He spoke of another crime against which war must be waged . . . although, on this point, His Majesty did not elucidate . . ."

Was it the crime of sodomy? La Reynie is silent; his notebook supplies no answer to the question.

The King was known to abominate the Italian vice, rampant as it was at his court, but his hands were tied by the fact that his brother, the Duc d'Orléans, was the most uninhibited pederast in the kingdom. A homosexual scandal, breaking that very year of 1680, and involving the Comte de Vermandois, Louis XIV's thirteen-year-old son by La Vallière, may have spurred the monarch to action. (The boy was banished from his father's sight; his death, in a garrison town, in 1683, would scarcely discompose His Majesty.*)

"All France trembled while this question hung fire," Visconti noted: "Countless ladies spent sleepless nights, and innumerable gentlemen tossed and turned in still crueler anxiety while waiting to hear whether there was to be an official inquiry into sodomy."

"Does it not seem to you there, so far away," Mme de Sévigné inquired of her daughter, off in Provence, "that, here, our very air is polluted with poison; that, here, we are living in a very den of iniquity, a very hotbed of sacrilege and abortion?"

What next? Who next? The questions were in every mind, though barely a word on the subject of the Poisons Affair was to be found in print, in either the *Gazette de France* or the *Mercure Galant*.

Column upon column was devoted, on the other hand, in mid-

* The young Count was little mourned. When Bishop Bossuet broke the news to his mother in her convent, she shed not a tear, remarking that "She could not properly weep his death since she had never properly wept his birth."

January, to the elaborate wedding ceremonies uniting the Prince de Conti and Mlle de Blois, Louis XIV's daughter by La Vallière; a "darling," a delight and joy to her father.

"The Princess was romantically beautiful," Mme de Sévigné exclaimed to her daughter: "She was magnificently attired and looked radiantly happy!" It was that rare exception in the royal family, a love match, as Mme de Sévigné rhapsodized, quoting two lines from the latest Lulli opera, *Bellérophon*:

> How sweet it is to find in the lover that one loves
> the husband whom one is obligated to love.

"The Prince de Conti's raiment was incalculably splendorous . . . his coat lined with black satin, tufted with diamonds! . . . I will write you more details as soon as I learn them. . . . Meanwhile I recommend your reading the gazettes. The reportage is excellent."

The coverage was excellent, too; in February when the King, the Dauphin, and all the court set out to meet the Dauphin's bride, as her cortège approached Vitry.

"All the court," to be sure, included Mme de Montespan.

Likewise Mme de Maintenon, reported by the *Gazette de France* as riding in the royal coach, "seated at the door curtain, beside the King."

Likewise Mlle de Fontanges, traveling in her "splendid new pearl-gray carriage," as Mme de Sévigné observed, without naming names: "This person will apparently be visited at night . . ."

"The King has three mistresses," Sainte-Beuve quotes Mme de Montespan as saying to Mme de Maintenon: "That young hussy performs the actual functions of a mistress; I hold the title; you, the heart." (If the remark is apocryphal, it is pungent.)

"Madame de Montespan was even more outraged," as Mme de Sévigné saw it, "at the honors paid Mme de Maintenon," the former governess of her children, than at the attentions paid to "that young hussy" who, by May, would have sickened and begun her decline, whimpering all the while that she was being poisoned.

Ambassador Spanheim would report to the Elector Palatine

that La Fontanges was suffering from "an obstinate ailment remaining from the period of her confinement, but which a widespread rumor, although perhaps baseless, attributes to a beverage supposedly given her on Mme de Montespan's orders."

To La Reynie it was more than a rumor. He was beginning to hear charges—not only from Le Sage but from La Filastre and her "weird sisters," La Chapelain and La Vertemart, recent additions to the cast of criminal characters confined at Vincennes—charges that pointed to an elaborate plot on foot to poison Mlle de Fontanges. As the evidence began to accumulate, as one criminal corroborated the fantastic charges of another, La Reynie found himself increasingly nervous. Not only the life of the King's mistress might be in danger, but that of the King himself.

Le Sage had named a name, and La Filastre and La Vertemart had echoed it: a name that was so closely associated with the royal family as to be almost sacrosanct. The name was that of Mme de Montespan.

The poisoning of Mlle de Fontanges was "a job being done for Mme de Montespan," or so La Filastre said she had heard somewhere in that murky underworld of hers, probably from La Chapelain. Indeed, "La Voisin and Mme de Montespan had been doing business together for the longest kind of time," from 1666 or 1667 on, or so La Vertemart declared, quoting Le Sage as her authority.

These denunciations of the King's official mistress—the mother of the Duc du Maine, the Comte de Vexin, the Comte de Toulouse, Mlle de Tours, Mlle de Nantes, Mlle de Blois;* if not technically Children of France, then certainly assured their places upon the lower steps of the monarch's throne and high in his affections— these denunciations of Mme de Montespan were all scrupulously extracted from the rest of the interrogation transcripts, kept separate and apart from the main body of the trial dossier, never allowed to go beyond La Reynie, never allowed to reach the eyes of

---

* The second Mlle de Blois—Mme de Montespan's daughter succeeding to the title relinquished by Mlle de La Vallière's daughter upon her recent marriage to the Prince de Conti.

the judges of the Chamber. The reports on this top-secret investigation, conducted personally and privately by La Reynie, were sent by him direct to Louvois, from Louvois direct to the King . . . to whom the latest developments must have been highly disconcerting.

On February 3, 1680, Louvois wrote to La Reynie: "With regard to that person to whom the use of poison is not unknown—that person whom you consider dangerous to allow to remain on at court—the King has judged it appropriate to receive you and to hear you on that matter. . . ."

This one scrap of paper, nothing more; not another to mark the trail. These few lines, no more; no others to be found in either Louvois's files or in La Reynie's to suggest the outcome of that conference with the King or his decision in regard to "that matter." The identity of "that person" referred to by La Reynie swallowed up in silence.

Who could it have been? He or she—"that person" whom La Reynie feared to see stay on at court?

Not the Comtesse de Soissons nor the Marquise d'Alluye, fugitives in the Netherlands. Not the Duchesse de Bouillon nor the Comtesse du Roure, both in exile, both leagues distant from court circles. Not the Vicomtesse de Polignac, far from court, in flight. Not the Duc de Luxembourg, at that time still in his tower cell at the Bastille.

Mademoiselle des Oeillets? But she had retired from Mme de Montespan's service, and removed from the court to Paris, in 1677 (according to a memorandum from Colbert to the King, dated 1680).

That left Cato, a maid of Mme de Montespan's, a creature of La Voisin's, owing her place in Mme de Montespan's household to the witch.

If not Cato, then the Duchesse de Vivonne, indicted by La Voisin, by Le Sage, by La Filastre, by a swelling chorus of accusing voices? Accused of repeated attempts to rid herself of Mme de Montespan in order to succeed her as King's Favorite, and by whatever means to that end the sorcerers might propose, whether by charms or by conjurations, whether by pacts with the Devil or by Black Masses, whether by death spells or by poison. The mounting pile of evidence against the Duchesse de Vivonne had thus far been kept secret from the tribunal, but Louvois and the King, alerted by La Reynie, would certainly have instructed that she be kept under a strict surveillance.

If not the Duchesse de Vivonne, then who?

Madame de Montespan, herself?

VII

Further Revelations

JUDGMENT IN LA VOISIN'S TRIAL, suspended on January 25, was resumed on February 15, 1680.

In the interim inquiry, she and Le Sage continued to exchange mortal blows: charges and countercharges of crime, one more heinous than the next.

With this difference: while it seemed probable that La Voisin would burn for her crimes, Le Sage was to be offered an opportunity to escape the supreme penalty for his. No less an emissary than Louvois was sent to Vincennes to interview the prisoner and to hold out the promise of the King's mercy in return for a full confession.

La Voisin, confronted with this relentless antagonist, admitted that her clientele included such noble ladies as Mesdames de Bouillon, de Polignac, and du Roure . . . even the Comtesse de Soissons. Even the Duchesse de Vivonne!

But she denied—with, literally, her last breath—Le Sage's allegation that she had had "years of commerce with Mme de Montespan."

"She had never seen Mme de Montespan!" La Voisin had insisted in an interrogation on January 16, 1680.

As for placing Cato in Mme de Montespan's household, La Voisin said "she scarcely knew the girl . . . had seen her only once or twice at the Palais Royal . . . where she had read her palm. . . . It was Cato's aunt who had coaxed her to make a supplication for the girl's good fortune, but all that she, Voisin, had ever done was to have three Novenas recited and three Masses celebrated . . . for which the aunt had given her a ring set with a paltry stone and worth only 45 sols for the gold mounting. She never saw Cato again after the girl went to Mme de Montespan's. . . ."

LA REYNIE: Why have you pretended, up to now, never to have known, never to have had dealings with Mlle des Oeillets?

LA VOISIN: I do not know Mlle des Oeillets . . . unless she came to my house . . . like all the others . . . [masked and using a false name is obviously La Voisin's implication].

LA REYNIE: Were you not aware of La Vertemart's scheme to get into Mme de Montespan's household, and did you not take a hand in it?

LA VOISIN: Vertemart did approach me once, somewhat casually, making mention of a plan she had in mind to get into Mme de Montespan's . . . offering a large string of pearls to anyone who could help her get such an opportunity. . . . But I replied that I could be of no assistance since I had no connections in that lady's retinue . . . no contact whatsoever with the lady herself. . . .

As to that petition which La Voisin had tried to present to the King in March of 1679, and to which Le Sage made such ominous and mysterious reference ("treated," he claimed, with poison or conjurement), why, it was a petition like any other, such as any other humble subject might present to her sovereign to seek his intervention in behalf of a friend ("her latest gallant," according to La Reynie), a man named Blessis, unjustly held in durance by a nobleman, the Marquis de Termes. Le Sage claimed that he had warned La Voisin that she was "heading for trouble in such a business." La Trianon said that she, too, had warned La Voisin about "getting mixed up in a crime against the state, a crime of *lèse-majesté*"; disaster showed up clearly in the stars of the horoscope drawn up by La Trianon for La Voisin for that very occasion.

It was the questioning on the subject of the petition, La Reynie noted, which gave La Voisin her sharpest anxiety: "Her great fear was lest something be discovered pertaining to that particular Saint-Germain expedition," her cellmates at Vincennes reported to the Lieutenant-General of Police.

She was less sensitive to Le Sage's charges of sacrilege, serious as were the implications of such a crime in a seventeenth-century Catholic kingdom: charges of Black Masses; dark, evil, and obscene rites performed under her roof and at her direction.

Le Sage began to reel off a list of apostate or defrocked priests who had officiated at La Voisin's desecrated altar. It was to give one more turn of the screw to the impact of the unholy ritual if the officiant was a member or former member of the Holy Orders.

By Le Sage's indictment, La Voisin had a stable of such hierophants to choose from: Father Davot, her confessor at her own parish church, Notre-Dame de Bonne Nouvelle; Abbé Gerard of the Church of Saint-Sauveur; Abbé Cotton, who would confess, *in extremis*, to having performed the ceremony at which Mme de Vivonne pledged herself to the fiend; the Abbé Mariette, Le Sage's own former colleague. Not to forget the head of that hierarchy, the hideous and infamous Abbé Guibourg, sacristan of Paris's Church of Saint-Marcel, the "High Priest," the "Grand Master" or "chief," the "God Incarnate or Devil of the Paris congregations."*

As quickly as Le Sage reeled off their names, La Reynie tracked down these renegade priests.

By February 14, Mme de Sévigné had heard rumors of an astonishing new turn of affairs in the Poisons Case:

"The Chamber of the Arsenal is back in session. One of the judges, who remains anonymous, said to M. de La Reynie: 'But, Monsieur, as it now appears, we are being called upon to deal with cases of witchcraft and daemonomania, whereas the Parlement of Paris no longer prosecutes on such charges. Our tribunal was set up

---

* It is by Dr. Margaret Murray's analysis in *The Witch Cult in Western Europe* that the Abbé Guibourg's rank has been designated as that of grand master, chief, God Incarnate, or Devil of the Paris congregations.

to deal with poisons. How does it happen that we are now asked to consider something else?' La Reynie looked surprised, but answered with the words: 'Monsieur, we are under secret orders'— 'Then let a new law be promulgated,' replied the other, 'and we will adjudicate in accordance with it. . . . Meanwhile, lacking the special information at your command, I must stand by my original opinion, which is based on law and reason. . . .' "

The new ruling was forthcoming, that same month of February: letters patent, signed by the King, extending the competence of the Chamber of the Arsenal to include "Cases of sacrilege, impiety and profanation. . . ."

Called before the bench, seated on the *sellette*, La Voisin was subjected to intensive interrogation by the judges on February 19, 20, and 21.

The final interrogation was under torture, a method known as the Question of the Boot, whereby the victim's legs were encased between wooden planks into which metal wedges were driven by hammer blows; a steadily increasing pressure applied to grind, crush, crunch on flesh and bone. The *Question Ordinaire* consisted of the insertion of four of these wedges into the boards; for the *Question Extraordinaire*, four more.

The Vincennes torture chamber was crowded on February 22.

The team of torturers, traditionally garbed in black, trained from youth to their profession, which was generally hereditary, moved swiftly and silently to their task, followed by their apprentices and assistants carrying their grim armamentarium. The corps included a medical man, who counted the victim's pulse occasionally, and warned the judges if there was any danger of the prisoner's expiring under the questioning.

The court clerks or scribes hovered over the prisoner in order to catch every moan or shriek or whisper, while making their official transcript of the question-and-answer period.

The questioning was usually done by one or both of the commission's two chairmen: most frequently, by La Reynie; occasionally, by Bezons.

In this instance, the interrogation was concentrated on the matter of La Voisin's delivery of powders and potions to Mlle des Oeillets and to Cato at the châteaux of Versailles or of Saint-Germain; on the plot to place La Vertemart in Mme de Montespan's household; and above all, on the subject of the petition which La Voisin had tried to present to His Majesty.

She continued to deny Le Sage's charges on all three counts. Nothing more was to be extracted from her, not even in the agony of the "Fifth," "Sixth," "Seventh," or "Eighth Corner," in the torturers' term of reference for the procedure.

Like the Marquise de Brinvilliers, La Voisin would take her secrets with her into the hereafter.

Sardonically, scornfully, as if to toss a sop to her interrogators, she delivered herself of a few platitudes, such as "For the sake of clearing her conscience, she would state that a large number of persons of all sorts and conditions had come to ask her help in killing off a large number of other persons . . . and that it is debauchery which is at the root of all this evil. . . ." And in the understatement of the day: "One hears strange things in this profession!"

But she would name no more names; none in the inner, upper circles of the court.

La Reynie posed his questions and watched the court clerks inscribe the answers on the official record, but he later noted in his private notebook that the Question of the Boot had been *pro forma*; that "La Voisin had not been subjected to the real torment; thus it had been ineffective."

Upon whose orders the executioners had spared her, La Reynie does not state. But only Louvois or Colbert could have exerted such power, acting on instructions from the King or in response to pressure from some individual very close to one or the other minister of state. By whom the directive was issued remains a mystery, as does the motivation . . . whether out of fear of what La Voisin might reveal, *in extremis*, or whether in fulfillment of a bargain for her silence on certain classified subjects.

There must have been sharp anxiety in certain quarters at Paris and Versailles while word was awaited from the courtroom and from the torture chamber where La Voisin had been brought for the final rounds of questioning.

"There was mention of Mlle des Oeillets and of Mme de Montespan while La Voisin was being interrogated," according to La Reynie's notes; "and, in truth, something of what was said did leak out to the general public." But, "be it said to the credit of the judges," as La Reynie said it, security was fairly tight.

Mme de Sévigné corroborates in a letter on February 23: "There is still no report on what she [La Voisin] said, but everyone seems to feel that sensational developments can be expected in this affair."

La Voisin's maid, Margot, under interrogation by La Reynie (and confronted with Le Sage, whom she vituperated as "You traitor!") would later make it clear that she had never for a moment doubted that her mistress would go to her death, lips sealed; "Saying nothing, not even at the end, to incriminate me or anybody else!" Indeed, silence in the presence of the infidel or unbeliever was an article of faith in the witch cult: "The Devil makes them [the witches] swear very solemnly never to accuse one another, never to report anything which has passed between them," as Henri Boguet reported in his *Discours des Sorciers* (*Discourses of Witches*), published in Lyon in 1608.*

Not only did La Voisin not confess, she went unrepentant as well as silent to her end.

Inquisitor Pierre de Lancre had something to say about that,

---

* Cases of infant cannibalism cited in the Scottish witch trials in 1661 and 1695 are explained as a form of sympathetic magic: by eating of the flesh of an infant whose tongue had never articulated a word, the witch's own tongue would be prevented from articulation; a form of insurance against any betrayal of their faith or of their co-religionists. Pierre de Lancre, the prosecutor in the Basque witch trials in the first decade of the seventeenth century, referred to this as "The virtue of taciturnity": "In order not to confess the secrets of the school, they [the witches] make, at the Sabbath, a paste of black millet made with the dried liver of an unbaptized child . . . so that whosoever eats of it will never confess. . . ."

too, in his handbook for witchcraft prosecution published in 1613:* "There are witches so besotted in his devilish service that neither torture nor anguish affrights them, and who say that they go to a true martyrdom and death for love of him, as gaily as to a festival of pleasure and public rejoicing."

La Reynie was reminded of another, earlier "martyr," La Grange, the very first to appear in the Poisons Affair, whom he described in his notebook as "A real artist, a professional, highly skilled in the manufacture of poisons. . . . Interrogated, judged, condemned, subjected to the Question, she had died for this and other crimes [in February, 1677] without breathing so much as one word of confession. . . . This miserable creature . . . maintained to the end her resolve not to talk," but she dropped hints of a conspiracy on foot to poison the Dauphin. "Triumphant, so to speak, in her silence . . . she gloated in intimations that her own innocent death and martyr's crown would shield the conspirators' machinations, and contribute to the success of their mission. . . . As to the widespread traffic in poison, all she would say was that there was a divine purpose in it which the judges would never penetrate."

La Voisin's purpose—whether divine or hellish—was never to be penetrated by the judges, either. Her last hours were lived in a "triumph" similar to La Grange's, as they are described by Mme de Sévigné by letter of February 23:

"She had learned her fate . . . on Monday. . . . That night, she twitted her guards: 'What? Are we to have no midnight supper?' She ate with them at twelve o'clock, drinking heavily of wine and singing twenty drinking songs. On Tuesday, she was subjected to the Question, both Ordinary and Extraordinary. . . . That night, broken in body as she was, she ate her supper and started up all over again on her scandalous debauches. The people around her tried to shame her, telling her that she would do better to think of God and to sing an *Ave Maria* . . . or a *Salve* . . . which she proceeded to do . . . but as a mockery. That night she ate and slept.

* Pierre de Lancre was the author of *Tableau de l'inconstance des mauvais anges*, published in Paris in 1613, and of *L'incrédulité et mécréance du sortilège*, Paris, 1622.

Wednesday, she spent in Confrontations, in debauch and song. She refused to see a confessor. . . . She was brought by carriage from Vincennes to Paris. They again urged her to make a confession, but there is no news on that. . . . At five o'clock, she was bound into a tumbril, a torch placed in her hand. . . . Her face was flushed. . . . She was seen to repulse the priest and to shove the crucifix aside with a gesture of violence. . . ."

"She was roaring drunk the day of her death," Visconti commented, "just as she had been almost every day of her life."

Mme de Sévigné counted herself fortunate to have been invited to the Hôtel de Sully on the rue Saint Antoine, directly on the line of march of the execution cortège:

"We saw her pass . . . Mme de Sully, the Countess [de Fiesque] and I, along with many other guests. . . . At Notre Dame, she [La Voisin] point-blank refused to perform the *Amende Honorable* and, at the [Place de] Grève, she fought fiercely against being removed from the cart. They had to use force to drag her out and up to the stake . . . to seat her against it and to fasten her with iron bands. They covered her with straw, the while she cursed them. Five or six times, she pushed aside the straw, but finally the flames leaped up, enveloped her, and she was lost to sight. . . . So, there you have the death of Mme Voisin, notorious for her crimes and impiety. It is generally believed that some surprising developments will be forthcoming . . ."

Antoine Coypel, one of the King's official artists, caught a glimpse of La Voisin on her way to the place of execution, and sketched her in that voluminous white hooded robe which Mme de Sévigné described as "the costume apparently traditional for victims of the stake."*

---

* Coypel was one of many painters to be tempted by the iconography of witches; his, only one in a vast gallery of witches drawn by famous artists, beginning with Leonardo da Vinci's nude and narcissistic young "Witch with a Magic Mirror," and including Albrecht Dürer's "Four Witches," a shapely quartet caught in the act of stripping off their clothes to fly away up the chimney, and off to a Sabbath gathering (one obviously a great lady); and David Teniers's "Departure for the Sabbath"; his, the traditional old hag drawing her magic circle on the hearth with the "arthame" or ritual dagger.

Coypel framed his head of La Voisin in a garland of snakes and skulls, intertwined with sprigs of hellebore and witchweed, fresh from the pits of Hell.

"So, now her ashes are on the breeze," Mme de Sévigné wrote as the tagline to her story on the La Voisin execution (much the same as she had used at the Brinvilliers's execution, but a good one and perhaps worth repetition).

The next day she could add, as postscript, an anecdote told her by her son (whose charm and whose unwavering devotion to his mother could never strike so much as a spark of response in that heart utterly monopolized by a daughter). Young Charles de Sévigné had complained to a magistrate of the brutality of the executions in the Place de Grève: " 'Ah, Monsieur,' the judge replied, 'You should know that certain small concessions are made for the weaker sex'—'What, then, Monsieur, do they strangle a female victim before the fire is lit?'—'Not that, but they pile up branches about her while the executioner's assistants rip off her head with iron hooks.' So, you see, my daughter, it's not as terrible as it appears. And are you feeling queasy after hearing my little story? When I first heard it, I admit, it set my teeth on edge. . . ."

(Can this be, in the words of one of her votaries, "the tender Sévigné"? If so, André Guillaume, public executioner of Paris, might be said to have displayed sensibilities more exquisite than the Marquise's, on this occasion, declining to perform his official duties on February 23, on La Voisin, a bosom friend and former light of love.)

If the trials and executions in the early spring of 1680 relieved

---

Goya's two canvases at the Prado Museum are occupied by nightmare figures such as haunted his last years of madness: his "Witch Preparing a Philter" is a loathsome crone stirring some evil brew in her cauldron, while a confederate with a skull for a head parodies the episcopal gesture of benediction; and his "Sabbath" shows another hideous witch sacrificing a child on the altar of the Goat-God. Hieronymus Bosch, Lucas Cranach, and several Breughels have likewise contributed to the iconography of the witch cult and Satanism, with macabre scenes of Sabbath orgies and demon-ridden Last Judgments.

the congestion at the Bastille and at Vincennes, a new crop of prisoners would shortly fill up the cells again.

Marie Marguerite Montvoisin, the Voisin Girl, joined her voice with Le Sage's in wholesale denunciations of La Voisin's coven and accomplices. She took up where La Voisin had left off. She gushed into confession, spilling secrets her stepmother had known how to keep.

She only wished, she told La Reynie, that she had started talking sooner: "But now that her mother had been judged, there was no longer reason to hold back. . . . She was unfortunate, indeed, to have been left by her mother with this terrible mess on her hands! It was obvious from the questions they were asking her, that her mother had withheld information. . . . Otherwise, they would not be quizzing her, the daughter, for answers her mother could better have supplied. . . ."

She whines and snivels her way through half a hundred interrogations, confrontations, declarations; the tattered, yellowed, crumbling sheets in the Archives comprise one long wail for pity.

How could she and her father have stood up to La Voisin? Since his unfortunate venture into the jewelry business, he had been dependent, along with his children, upon the bounty of his second wife. He had had forebodings about "the strange goings on in that house," and had once "threatened to smash a locked cabinet" in which La Voisin kept her stock of poison powders. "Nothing good could come of it," he told her, but his warnings merely earned him the epithet of spoilsport. Another time, "He had come upon a curious little wax figurine, its hands clasped as in prayer . . . wrapped in cotton batting, inside a metal box . . . left lying by Le Sage. Her father had smashed the mannequin," but all he had gotten for his pains were blows upon the head and poison in the soup tureen.

And what could she have done, young and helpless as she was? "She was appalled at the things she saw going on . . . the poisonings, one after the other . . . and would have escaped from that criminal household, had only she had some other means of liveli-hood. . . ." During her early years, she had "always been ordered out of the room" by La Voisin, Le Sage, and the others when their maleficent liturgies began, and only later on admitted to their mys-teries.

The garden pavilion had likewise been forbidden her, when abortions were being performed or when La Voisin and La Vautier lit the oven. "The minute she stuck her head in the door, her mother ran her out." But she had peeped at them at their work, "preparing toads. . . . Both of them holding their noses while they worked . . . such a stench it made. . . ."

The Voisin Girl was "a queer one," by La Reynie's analysis, after long hours of interrogation. "A wild one," too, an impas-sioned, violent nature, "and yet not without wit."

She revealed the whereabouts of the Abbé Mariette, who had been spirited, by La Voisin, out of Saint Lazare Prison in 1668, to various hideaways in the provinces, finally to a monastery near Toulouse, where La Reynie's men took him into custody in March.

The Voisin Girl also pointed an accusing finger at a dapper villain by name of Romani, "a highly personable young man with a fine physique; a jack-of-all-trades, widely traveled, the cleverest and slipperiest fellow imaginable," in La Reynie's appraisal.

So clever and so slippery as to have seduced the Voisin Girl, a year or so earlier. He had offered, be it said to his credit, to make an honest woman of her; an offer, at first, to be gratefully accepted. Only later did La Voisin decide that if some of her grandiose projects, then under way, were to be successfully consummated, Romani would no longer constitute a suitable *parti* for her step-daughter.

Romani, on the other hand, had been "the very man for the job," just the smart and subtle operator needed to undertake the ticklish mission of finishing off the Duchesse de Fontanges. (By June, the Duchess would be moved from her apartment in the châ-teau to the Abbey of Chelles, first way station to the tomb—illness and death alike to be banished insofar as possible from Saint-Germain and Versailles.)

The plan was for Romani ("man of a thousand disguises," in the Voisin Girl's admiring term) to pose as a silk merchant from Lyon, with his friend Bertrand posing as assistant; the merchandise already on order: "Silks from Lyon and gloves from Grenoble, irresistible," as La Voisin told her daughter, "to ladies of quality." Romani knew not only how and where to have these items treated with poison so as to make them fatal to the wearer; he also had the most excellent opportunity imaginable to gain entrée to La Fontanges's presence. Through the good offices of his brother, a priest, Father La Pierre, father confessor to none other than Mlle des Oeillets!

Another reference to Mlle des Oeillets. So many, and by so many different witnesses, as to become dismaying to La Reynie.

Another interrogation to be sequestered and suppressed, to be kept from the judges, to be kept off the record, as was the case with so many of the Voisin Girl's interrogations; only La Reynie's notes relating to them to be found, today, in La Reynie's private papers, to reveal their substance.

These notes, in his private papers, in his own hand, constitute the only record of another interview with the Voisin Girl, unidentified by date, but probably late spring or early summer: "Mlle des Oeillets had been in the habit of coming to her mother's house for two years or more. She was never addressed by her own name. Nor were any of the other ladies, none of them wanting to be recognized. So when she [Mlle des Oeillets] happened to come when La Voisin was out, La Voisin was told upon her return that 'the young lady with the dark hair' had called . . . 'the young lady with the double-trained dress,' as they referred to her. . . . Mlle des Oeillets served La Voisin and Mme de Montespan as go-between."

To the reader of La Reynie's notes, it is clear that the Lieutenant-General of Police was, by then, convinced that Mme de Fontanges's illness was the result of poison, and that she might still be in danger from machinations even then under way. Guards were posted at the Abbey of Chelles.

La Filastre—"One of the most extraordinary characters" in all that extraordinary cast, in the words of La Reynie: "Dangerous with a dagger, dangerous with poison, one of the most dangerous criminals of the lot"—had been arrested at the very moment when her scheme to gain admission to Mlle de Fontanges's household seemed closest to success.

Poisoners, murderers, witches, and warlocks had infiltrated the palaces of Versailles and Saint-Germain. Self-avowed poisoners such as La Dumesnil and La Bretesche had had access to Mme de Fontanges's household, and La Filastre had applied for admission. At Mme de Montespan's Château de Clagny, Cato had found a place through La Voisin's good offices, and La Vertemart had been about to join her colleague in the Favorite's entourage.

La Reynie had cause for alarm when he discovered La Vertemart's brother, Lemaire, serving as a wine steward in the King's own cellars. And for alarm still more acute when Lemaire accused a co-worker in the royal catering staff of involvement in a plot to poison His Majesty—a man named Duchêne, recommended to the post by Mme de Montespan!

La Reynie decided to intensify the inquiry into the matter of the petition which La Voisin had tried to deliver—by her own admission—into the hand of the King, although she herself would not admit, not to her dying day, to the fact that the petition had been poisoned or otherwise "treated."

Whereas the Voisin Girl was now saying that it had: that Romani had "treated" it with poison . . . or had it been La Filastre or La Chapelain or La Trianon? She, herself, had not been taken into her mother's confidence, but she had overheard La Trianon warn La Voisin that "she was getting into something she would never get out of alive . . . a direct attempt on the life of the sovereign." To which La Voisin had replied that this was her golden opportunity; she must seize it, and then escape to England, thanks to powerful protectors who would arrange her crossing.

"How grateful we can be for lovers' quarrels!" La Voisin had exclaimed to La Trianon that day (the very day before her arrest):

"What a boon it is to our profession when lovers resort to desperate measures!"

Who the lovers were; or what their quarrel: which lover had been brought to desperation, La Voisin had not said; nor, as yet, had her daughter, in quoting her. The identity of the mysterious "lady who had sent her carriage to transport La Voisin and her petition to Saint-Germain" had not yet been revealed.

The King instructed La Reynie "to leave no stone unturned in his efforts to get to the truth concerning the petition . . . about which so many prisoners are now talking . . ."

La Voisin's arrest had come, in La Reynie's opinion, in the very nick of time, on Sunday, March 12, 1679. For La Filastre, La Trianon, La Chapelain, and Romani all agreed that La Voisin had planned a return trip to Saint-Germain, a second attempt at delivering her petition; and that this had been scheduled for Monday, March 13.

La Reynie's anxiety communicated itself to the King. Even in his "ineffable majesty" (as Saint-Simon described it), Louis XIV betrayed signs of nerves, even in public, and for all the world to see, including some courtier who reported it to Bussy who could, in turn, report it to another of his numerous correspondents: "The day the King was leaving Saint-Germain" (for the usual spring campaigning), "just as His Majesty was about to step into the coach with the Queen, he had a sharp exchange of words with Mme de Montespan on the subject of the strong scents she always uses and which sicken His Majesty. He addressed her first, most civilly, but when she snapped at him, His Majesty grew hot with anger. I doubt that she will remain much longer at the court."

Bussy could not have known what His Majesty knew from reading the daily reports from Vincennes: that "La Vautier had been proven to be a poison artist . . . notorious for her poison-perfume"; that "La Vautier had been one of La Voisin's chief suppliers"; and that La Voisin (according to her stepdaughter's charges) "had delivered love potions and love philters to Mme de Montespan at Saint-Germain, at Versailles and at Clagny, time and time again. . . ."

"A bitter quarrel broke out, the other day, between His Majesty and Mme de Montespan (Mme de Sévigné had heard a report much like Bussy's, and within the same fortnight): "Monsieur Colbert did his utmost to effect a reconciliation, and finally won the King's consent to make his customary visit to her apartment for midnight supper, but His Majesty agreed only on the condition that the entire court be present, too."

Mme de Montespan may have "suffered a serious fall from favor"; may have "sunk to an incredibly low estate," just as Bussy told it: "The King no longer notices her, and you can be sure the courtiers take their cue from him."

But she was nonetheless included in the royal caravan that set out to join the King in Flanders, in the summer—another dress parade, another gala tour of conquered territory. She was, after all, superintendent of the Queen's household, and she had little Mlle de Nantes in tow, aged seven, eldest of her three daughters by the King; she and her children an integral part of France's royal family.

La Reynie's reports followed the King and the Minister of War, all along the route of the military expedition.

On July 21, Louvois acknowledged receipt of the most recent declarations made by the Voisin Girl, and advised La Reynie that he had read them aloud to His Majesty.

A few days later, Louvois notified the Chamber of the Arsenal that further judgment in the Poisons Affair was to be suspended until such time as the sovereign should return to the capital.

Since the day of La Voisin's execution, throughout the spring and early summer, the Voisin Girl had claimed to have been telling all she knew (more, perhaps, than she knew, in the view of some investigators).

But there had been one name on which the Voisin Girl had choked.

"She tried to do away with herself, to strangle herself in her cell," La Reynie noted, "before she could bring herself to make these final declarations."

By letter, from Lille, on August 2, 1680, Louis XIV issued an order, direct to La Reynie: "Monsieur de La Reynie, Having seen the declaration made on the twelfth of last month by Marie Marguerite Montvoisin, a prisoner in my Château of Vincennes . . . along with your interrogation of the prisoner on the 26th of last month, I write this letter to tell you that it is my will that you make every effort within your power to get to the truth of the statements made in her declaration and in her answers to your questions. It is my intention that you take every precaution to make sure that all reports dealing with this particular inquiry be filed in special dosiers, kept separate from the rest of the records of the investigation. . . ."

The name that the Voisin Girl had finally brought herself to speak, on July 26, was that of Mme de Montespan.

It was Mme de Montespan, she said, who had commissioned La Chapelain to set up the elaborate poison plot against Mlle de Fontanges; La Chapelain, in turn, commissioning Romani and La Filastre to execute it. Mme de Montespan was an habituée of the Abbé Guibourg's infamous Black Mass. Mme de Montespan was the mysterious "lady," whose "carriage had transported La Voisin and her petition to Saint-Germain," in a direct attempt on the King's life.

Before the month of August was out, the Voisin Girl's fantastic tales—"Too fantastic and in too elaborate detail to have been invented!" in La Reynie's opinion—were being corroborated by other prisoners.

VIII

Black Magic

"EVERY TIME SOMETHING NEW CAME UP to upset Mme de Montespan, every time she feared a diminution in the King's good graces, she came running to my mother for a remedy, and then my mother would call in one of the priests to celebrate a Mass, and then she would send Mme de Montespan the powders which were to be used on the King."

The transcript of this interrogation is not to be found among the Archives of the Bastille, but La Reynie's résumé and comments survive in his personal papers.

Le Sage and the Abbé Mariette had had much the same to say as had the Voisin Girl. Only they had said it much earlier, twelve years earlier, at the time of their trial in 1668. Now, in 1680, their charges were reiterated and, to this fact La Reynie attached—to use his own words—"great significance."

In 1680, the prisoners at Vincennes might hope to save their skins by naming a name as exalted as that of Mme de Montespan, the King's "second wife," "the real Queen of France"—their hope being that they would not be brought to trial because their testimony against such a personage would have to be kept secret, could not be allowed to be uttered in even a closed courtoom.

But such had not been the case in 1668. Then, Mme de Montespan was not generally known to be enjoying the King's favor; she had not yet been openly acknowledged; Louise de La Vallière, to all appearances, reigned as official mistress. Indeed, at that time, Mme de Montespan, alone, could have revealed to Le Sage and Mariette some of the facts they recited, pertaining to her relations with the King, the court, and La Vallière.

La Reynie reasoned thus; then underscored the paragraph in his memorandum to himself: If the testimony of these men, as given in both 1668 and 1680, should be true—and it had "the ring of truth" to La Reynie—then, he thought that it might constitute strong proof of the truth of the other charges presently being made against Mme de Montespan, in the testimony of the other witnesses in the case.

Le Sage and Mariette had told in 1668, and repeated in 1680, tales of exotic but innocuous rituals invented to titillate their blasé, noble clientele—the Duchesse de Vivonne prominent on the list; Mme de Montespan heading it. Le Sage and Mariette never pretended to lay a death spell on La Vallière, but they could offer Mme de Montespan a potent love charm whereby to bewitch the King and, to that end, arranged a thrilling, chilling ceremony in the Bois de Boulogne at the witching hour of midnight: the blood sacrifice of a pair of snow-white doves (bird of passion as well as bird of peace, sacred to Venus); the pair of bleeding hearts conjured, and then encoffined in a fancy vermeil box for burial. ("The heart of a dove, the womb of a swallow, the kidney of a hare," the very things "to make one's self beloved," according to one medieval *Grimoire*, the *Zekerboni* of Pierre Mora.)

Between 1666 and 1668, the critical years in which Mme de Montespan maneuvered to supersede La Vallière as royal Favorite, Le Sage and Mariette staged special Masses for her at various secluded or abandoned chapels; once set up an altar in the Marquise de Thianges's apartment in the King's own Château of Saint-Germain, where they "chanted the Gospel" over the bowed head of the Marquise's sister, and "passed love powders under the chalice" (a consecration in reverse, a curse rather than a blessing, an invocation of supernatural powers upon the object).

But they were only amateurs, mere neophytes, the pair of scoundrels made clear to La Reynie. Not for them the ultimate evil of black magic, the ultimate sacrilege of the Black Mass. For that awesome, gruesome, and obscene rite, they said, Mme de Montespan had had to turn to the High Priest of the diabolic church in Paris, the iniquitous Abbé Guibourg.

Even La Reynie, case-hardened policeman that he was, seemed at a loss for words in describing Guibourg: in all his years of experience, he had "never come across such a man as this one. . . . A man who confesses to abominations so vile as to be inconceivable to the normal mind . . . guilty of every known crime against God and man and sovereign. . . ."

No professional make-up artist of stage or screen could have surpassed Nature's job on Guibourg's face. It was that of a natural villain, eyes crossed, and with purple veins that seemed about to burst, seaming his hideous, bloated cheeks.

"A man in his seventies," when La Reynie saw him: "A libertine . . . claiming to be the illegitimate son of the late Duc de Montmorency . . . having served as vicar at Issy and at Vanves, presently attached to the Paris Church of Saint Marcel. . . . Engaged for twenty years in the traffic of poison and sacrilege. . . . A man who had slit the throats and sacrificed countless numbers of infants on his unholy altar. . . . A man who seems, at times, a raving maniac; at others, speaking calmly of what he will do and say when he is subjected to the Question, or when he burns at the stake . . . threatening to choke everyone he can lay his hands on so as to hasten the day of judgment and of punishment.

"A man comparable to no other," La Reynie concluded, unless perhaps to Gilles de Retz (whose case history and trial documents La Reynie began to study) condemned for a hundred or more self-confessed ritual murders, and executed for sorcery in 1440 in Brittany . . . a marshal of France, commander-in-chief and special protector to Joan of Arc (against whom not entirely unsubstantiated charges of witchcraft have also been leveled).*

Guibourg had made sacrifice of several of his own children by

* Gilles de Retz or Raïs is considered by some to be the original Bluebeard.

his concubine, La Chanfrain (enough and to spare, evidently, in the course of their twenty-year liaison).

La Joly, with her flourishing trade as midwife-abortionist, was one of the cult's chief sources of supply for sacrificial victims . . . newborn, stillborn, or premature. Failing which, there was resort to kidnapping or to purchase on the open market, where the going price, as quoted by Guibourg, was "1 écu." (The Voisin Girl, at the onset of labor pains, fled trembling from her home to a secret place of refuge, as she told La Reynie, lest her baby be snatched from her breast by her stepmother.)

"A bloodbath!" was what La Reynie called it, and repeated the expression several times over, in horror: "This constant talk of children sacrificed, throats slit, eviscerated!" reminded him of the sudden, mysterious riots in Paris in 1676; "the wild rumors of child sacrifice and kidnapping" suddenly comprehensible in the light of these recent revelations. "There may have been a foundation in fact," La Reynie noted, in 1680, "for the mass hysteria that gripped the lower classes of the capital four or five years ago."

The Abbé Guibourg had officiated at the ritual murder of La Filastre's own newborn babe, her own flesh and blood "delivered over to the holocaust" by her own hand, as she herself readily conceded.

In an interrogation, dated August 2, 1680, La Filastre made the astounding announcement that the Abbé Guibourg "had been working for Mme de Montespan."

La Reynie took notes on La Filastre's interrogation and, then, in going over those notes, jotted down his impressions and his line of reasoning:

"La Filastre's testimony has to be carefully sifted, weighed and considered, but then it should serve to throw some light on Mme de Montespan's connection with this case. There is reason to think, following the case from the beginning, that it will be found that charges against her constitute pure braggadocio on the part of these criminals, mere boasts to enhance their reputations. Either that . . . or there has been, in very fact, some intricate intrigue afoot, some obscure and complex machination in operation . . . something sinister in the wind . . . someone after something unsavory. . . . La Filastre must be made to divulge what she knows, what she has done and how she has done it, under what circumstances . . . and by whose orders. . . ."

By the orders of Mme de Montespan? Or by those of someone acting for her? Or by those of someone using her name, perhaps purposely to incriminate her?

The questions filled up and overflowed La Reynie's notebook and his brain.

On August 6, from Valenciennes, Louvois forwarded La Reynie the latest instructions from the King: "In view of the fact that La Filastre is so ill that you fear she may not survive until His Majesty's return, he has decided [to make an exception] and to allow her trial to proceed. . . . But only upon the condition that she has not mentioned the person of exalted station named by the Voisin Girl in her declaration, last month . . ."

At the mention of the name of "the person of exalted station," an interrogation would be halted, the court clerk dismissed, the questioning taken over by La Reynie (as in the case of La Bellier, when she said that it was "in the interest of Mme de Montespan" that La Filastre had sought placement in Mme de Fontanges's household; as in the case of the alchemist Galet, when he said that he had "made up powders out of bread and cantharides to be given to the King . . . at the orders of a lady . . . whom they called Mme de Montespan . . .").

More and more of the prisoners at Vincennes were being isolated, withdrawn from the official court investigation, and consigned to the top secret inquiry conducted by La Reynie and Louvois.

Of the August 13 interrogation of the Voisin Girl, not even La Reynie's own personal copy is extant; only a résumé and analysis made by him from his notes: "She said that her knowledge of the criminal design against the person of the King is based on what she heard her mother say, and that such a design had first been contemplated at the hour when Mme de Montespan realized that all the expedients to which she had had recourse for so many years were now unavailing. Her mother told her that the lady was prepared to go the limit to have her way, to impose her will, and sought to compel La Voisin to resort to means for which the latter had great repugnance. . . ."

"In her interrogation of August 13," La Reynie's notebook reads, "the Voisin Girl denied ever having had direct personal contact with Mme de Montespan, ever having seen her face to face, ever having spoken to her. . . . But in the interrogation of August 20, it turns out that she has seen Mme de Montespan, has spoken to her, talked with her once at the door of her carriage when they met by appointment . . . on the road between Ville d'Avray and Clagny . . . to effect the delivery of a packet of powders. . . . Thus, clearly, here, the Voisin Girl has been caught in a lie . . . yet, all the rest of what she has to say is said with such an air of ingenuousness that one may easily be taken in by it. I put little reliance on her testimony because there seems to me . . . though I am not quite sure why . . . more reason to believe her statements false than to believe them true. . . ."

In the interrogation of August 20, the Voisin Girl described a Black Mass: "An altar had been set up in my mother's bedroom . . . the cross in place, the candles lit. . . . A lady was stretched out, stark naked, on a mattress, her legs dangling off one end of it, her head hanging down on the other, propped up on a pillow which had been placed on an upended chair. . . . A linen cloth was folded on her stomach . . . the chalice reposed on her groin. . . . I saw a Mass like this performed by Guibourg for Mme de Montespan at La Voisin's, about three years ago. Mme de Montespan arrived at ten in the evening, and did not leave until midnight. . . . La Voisin promised to have the other two Masses [three such were required to obtain the desired effect] performed on her own body. . . ."

And in another interrogation, the Voisin Girl elaborated, adding grisly touches: "At one of Mme de Montespan's Masses, I saw my mother bring in an infant . . . obviously premature . . . and place it in a basin over which Guibourg slit its throat, draining the blood into the chalice . . . where he consecrated the blood and the wafer . . . speaking the names of Mme de Montespan and the King at the moment of the offertory. . . . The body of the infant was incinerated in the garden oven, and the entrails taken the next day by my mother to La Dumesnil for distillation, along with the blood and the consecrated Host . . . all of which was then poured into a glass vial which Mme de Montespan came by, later, to pick up and take away. . . ."

The Black Mass, as it has been practiced throughout the centuries, is a deliberate travesty, profanation, and perversion of Catholicism's supreme sacrament, mystery of mysteries—the Mass, the Holy Communion, the Eucharist. In the Black Mass, everything is performed backward (as the sign of the cross made with the left hand); everything is black: black bread, black potions, black candles, a black goat enshrined at the Sabbath.*

At the Sabbath, in the wildwood, among the menhirs on the meadows of Brittany, at the Blockula in Sweden, atop the crags of the Brocken in the Harz Mountains (the site of Goethe's famous *Walpurgisnacht*), wherever the congregation of the Old Religion gathered, the High Priestess was ensconced in intimate communion with the incarnate deity—a relic, possibly, of the ritual sexual abandon of the priestesses at the Dionysia and other ancient Grecian religious festivals. At the conclusion of the Sabbath's ritual and feasting, the congregation scattered into the shadows beyond the torchlit circle for orgiastic mating dances.

The cult of diabolism stressed sexuality, magic power being theoretically polarized by the release of sexual energy. Christianity, on the other hand, exalted the spiritual life at the expense of the physical, in a stigmatization of the pleasures of the flesh. Thus, the

---

* The derivation of the word "Sabbath" in this connection is unknown, having nothing to do with the number seven, nothing to do with the Jewish ceremonial; most probably a derivation of the medieval French verb, *s'esbattre*, to frolic or to gambol. The word "*Esbat*" was also used to indicate a congregation of witches.

Jules Michelet saw the witch cult, along with the ritual of the Black Mass, as a development of the Dark Ages, a reflection of the desperation of the serf oppressed by the lords of the Church as well as the lords of the castle.

Black Mass came to require a sexual as well as a blood sacrifice, perhaps as a second deliberate desecration of the holy altar.

This feature of the Black Mass was described in lurid detail to La Reynie, at Vincennes, by Le Sage, by La Filastre, by the Voisin Girl and, finally, by Guibourg—the similarities of the several accounts striking to La Reynie: "Guibourg and the Voisin Girl have corroborated one another on circumstances so extraordinary and so shocking that it is difficult to believe that such horrors could have been invented or imagined by two separate and distinct individuals, each on his own. Such things as these must actually have taken place to have been described like this, in such detail—the details of one report coinciding with those of the other."

The transcript of Guibourg's interrogation is missing, as are so many others; the only record of its substance in La Reynie's notebook: "Leroy, the governor of the pages of the King's small stable, had been the first person to talk to him [Guibourg] about working for Mme de Montespan, promising him 50 *pistoles* and a bonus of 2,000 livres. . . . He had heard that others had been doing this kind of work for Mme de Montespan before he was called in. . . . The first Mass he said for her was at Ménil, near Montlhéry, and performed on the body of a woman who came in with another taller woman. At the moment of consecration, he had recited the following conjuration [in the name of the woman on whom the Mass was being said]: 'Hail, Ashtaroth and Asmodeus,* Princes of Friendship, I conjure you to accept the sacrifice of this child in return for the favors asked of you: that I should have and keep the love of the King and that of *Monseigneur*, the Dauphin . . . that the Queen should become barren . . . that the King should leave her bed and board to come to mine . . . that he should grant whatever I ask of him, for me and mine . . . that I should be included in the councils of the King, a party to all state business . . . and that the

---

* Princes of Hell, demons, or rather incubi; Asmodeus is identified in the Apocrypha. Most of the nomenclature of the infernal legion is supplied by the Bible: the Old Testament performed the introductions for Satan himself, for Lucifer, Leviathan, and Belial; while the New Testament presents "the Prince of Devils . . . Beelzebub."

King's love for me should wax and flourish . . . so that he shall
abandon and no longer look upon the face of La Vallière . . . so
that the Queen shall be repudiated . . . so that the King may marry
me. . . .' And he [Guibourg] said that, in conclusion, he named the
name of the King and that of Mme de Montespan [hers being the
signature on the pact]. . . . After he had pierced the infant's throat
with a knife, and drained the blood into the chalice, the body of the
child was removed. . . . Later they brought him back the heart and
entrails for a second consecration . . . this last to be used, they told
him, to make powders which Mme de Montespan wanted to use on
the King. The lady in whose name the Mass was celebrated always
kept on her *coiffes* [head veils] covering her face and part of her
breast. The second Mass had been performed in a hovel on the
ramparts of Saint-Denis, on the body of the same woman, with all
the same ceremonies as before. The third Mass had taken place at
La Voisin's . . . some eight or nine years ago, again on the body of
the same person who . . . or so they always told him . . . was Mme
de Montespan. . . ."

"Impossible for a man of Guibourg's mentality to have invented the story of the pact in such detail," La Reynie noted, much
as he might have liked to think otherwise. "His mind is simply
incapable of manufacturing such a story, following through on it,
sticking with it. Nor is he in a position to know that much about
the world in which Mme de Montespan lives. Furthermore, his
memory is such that he simply could not have retained, over all
these years, so many of the words of the supposed pact . . . unless
he had seen and read and recited some sort of a similar conjuration, many times over."

The precarious state of La Filastre's health convinced the King
of the necessity of proceeding immediately with her trial.

Attention suddenly focused, in September of 1680, on the
Duchesse de Vivonne. She came within an ace of arrest. On the
twenty-fifth, Louvois instructed Solicitor-General Robert: "His
Majesty has learned with extreme displeasure that much evidence
points to the Duchess's involvement with La Filastre and other
prisoners at Vincennes. . . . However, until all the evidence is in

and final proof forthcoming, His Majesty believes that the wisest course is to postpone an arrest order against a person of Mme de Vivonne's standing. . . ."

In other words, action was to be postponed until they had seen La Filastre's answers to the Question. Not that the judges in the Chamber of the Arsenal were to see them, but the Solicitor-General would, and the decision would be left up to him as to what action should be taken against such persons as might be named and incriminated by La Filastre.

The Chamber wound up La Filastre's trial, along with that of the Abbé Cotton, on September 30, although no reference was made in the text of the judgment—"Thanks," as La Reynie said, "to the discretion of the judges"—to any possible connection between La Filastre and the King's mistress.

Both La Filastre and Cotton were sentenced to the Question, and to the stake: "At the Second Corner of the Extraordinary Question [as La Reynie noted], La Filastre, exhorted to tell the truth about her trip to Normandy and to Auvergne . . . cried out, 'Oh, my God, have mercy on me! It was Mme Chapelain who commissioned me, and it was Mme de Montespan who commissioned Mme Chapelain . . . and the purpose was to procure poisons to kill off Mme de Fontanges, and love powders to restore Mme de Montespan to the King's good graces . . . powders for death, powders for love . . . all for Madame de Montespan!' "

But she had no sooner been released from the instrument of torture, and removed to Paris, to the chapel of the Bastille—her last stop en route to the Place de Grève—than she sent for La Reynie and made partial retraction of her accusations against Mme de Montespan.

La Reynie was skeptical: "Most judges," he comments, "attach little significance to such retractions, for the reason that once the condemned prisoners fall into the hands of the confessor and the executioner, the poor wretches can be manipulated, intimidated or abused, and made to say almost anything." (The Curé of Saint Laurent had been hand-picked by the King to extract a confession from La Filastre.)

On October 1, 1680, the day following La Filastre's torture and execution, Louis XIV—to prevent her charges against Mme de Montespan from reaching the tribunal—called a halt to the proceedings; instructed Louis Boucherat, the chief justice of the court, "to discontinue the session."

A King is loath to reverse a position; above all, a King such as this one. None but the most cogent motive could account for this embarrassing retreat from his original, public posture.

If one seeks to substantiate the theory that Mme de Montespan was involved in the Poisons Affair, the most potent argument is to be found in the action of the King in arbitrarily discontinuing the course of justice set in motion by his own letters patent.

If the King's official mistress and mother of his children—the symbol of French grace, beauty, pride, elegance, and culture; the symbol of the French heyday—if Mme de Montespan were to be involved in a scandal as sordid and as squalid as this one, then the King's own majesty and prestige would be attainted; the dignity and splendor of his court diminished. Public disgrace could not be visited on the head of Mme de Montespan without complicating his already delicate family relations, without embarrassing him on the domestic as well as on the national and international scene.

Above all, his male ego was involved. Anathema and censure for his arrant military aggressions, for his rapine of Europe, Louis XIV was prepared to accept; as even for his flagrant personal moral delinquency. But he could not withstand ridicule. Better an ogre than a figure of fun. His imposing image might dissolve at one titter of laughter were the news to get out that this cock of the international walk was crowing on a craw full of aphrodisiacs; hand-fed for years by his mistresses on a mash of blister beetles, cocks' combs, and cocks' testicles.

Once Mme de Montespan had been identified at the center of this web of criminal intrigue, as the chief instigator of this nexus of crime, then the Poisons Affair belonged in a council of state rather than a hall of justice.

No further public reference to the King's official mistress, in such a context, could be tolerated in his kingdom, not even in a closed courtroom.

And yet, since "these execrable, chronic crimes . . . this accursed traffic in poisons," in La Reynie's term of reference, had to be prosecuted and extirpated, he agreed to carry on the investigation, singlehanded and in secret.

Then, before the week was out, he began to hedge, writing Louvois that he was "torn" between his "duty as a judge and as a loyal subject of the Crown . . . overwhelmed with doubt as to the legality and propriety of the procedure."

It was, to say the least, irregular—in even an absolute monarchy where the monarch was justice incarnate, "the source of law"—to withhold testimony from the very judges appointed by the monarch to hear and adjudicate the case.

"I must have time to think this out, to find my way . . . through the shadows that envelop me," La Reynie wrote to Louvois: "Thus far, I can think of no other course than, somehow, to continue the search for the truth. . . . But I trust to God . . . to indicate the appropriate method . . . to uncover this sink of iniquity . . . to inspire the King to make the best decision in this crisis. . . ."

Meanwhile, La Reynie would continue his solo "search for the truth," at Vincennes, on into the winter; with repeated interrogations of the Voisin Girl and Guibourg, Le Sage and Mariette, Romani and Bertrand, La Chapelain and Galet.

In January of 1681, the transcripts of this secret investigation, along with that of La Filastre's responses during the Question, were consigned—on Louvois's orders—to a black leather coffer, under lock and key; the key, enclosed and fastened under seal, into separate cover; the lot—coffer and key—transmitted by Captain Desgrez, La Reynie's confidential aide, into the hands of Louvois himself, at Versailles.

This secret dossier, read aloud by Louvois to the King, behind locked doors in his study, made anything but pleasant reading: "It caused His Majesty distress to listen to it," Louvois reported to La Reynie—as well it might, with its repeated indictments against Mme de Montespan.

Four months after the Chamber of the Arsenal had been ordered into recess, the King—not ordinarily a hesitant man—still hesitated as to whether or not to reconvene it. In early 1681, he summoned Colbert to join Louvois and La Reynie in consultation.

Some special formula would have to be devised to deal with the special circumstances by which they were confronted; some special royal decree to regularize the irregular proceedings, to legalize the withholding of evidence from the court legally appointed to hear it.

Until then, the case was at an impasse.

IX

The King's Justice

RARELY CAN A POLICE OFFICER, an officer of the Crown, have
found himself in so cruel a predicament as did La Reynie
when the King demanded that he pronounce himself as to whether
he considered Mme de Montespan guilty or innocent of the crimes
of which she stood accused.

If Mme de Montespan was guilty of criminal intent—thus constituting a threat to the safety of the King and to that, perhaps, of
others at the court—then La Reynie must be considered guilty of
criminal negligence if he failed to give warning. If, on the other
hand, Mme de Montespan should be proven innocent—or if she
should be able to convince the King of her innocence—then La
Reynie stood to pay with his life for his temerity in speaking out
against her.

All La Reynie's expertise as a magistrate and police officer had
been brought to bear upon this inquiry. He had cudgeled his brain
and searched his conscience. His notebooks bear witness to his
unceasing, untiring, and relentless effort, to his lack of bias and his
integrity, to his keen critical sense, to his acuity as an investigator.
As he studied the prisoners' faces, so he studied the transcripts of
their interrogations, confrontations, and declarations; comparing
one statement with another; balancing contradictions against cor-
roborations; juggling pros and cons. His analyses are models of
logic, penetration, and application. His cramped and careful script

fills page after page of his notebooks, wherein his train of thought is tracked, his ratiocinations charted. Frequently, he resorts to a diagram form once popular in history and rhetoric class: at the far left of the page, extending from top to bottom, a giant bracket outlines the premise; its arms embrace three shorter, auxiliary brackets, providing the data in substantiation; these three are, in turn, supported by additional facts and figures, within brackets successively abbreviated, and so on and so forth, all the way across the page.

Reluctant to commit himself, La Reynie addressed to Louvois a memorandum indicating the various inconclusive Conclusions at which he had arrived: "Appointed judge by the King, it is my duty to maintain an open mind. . . . If I seem to lean more to one side than to another, such is not my intention. . . . In examining both the proven and the presumptive evidence, I have done my best to convince myself that this evidence is true, but I cannot do so. Conversely, I have done my best to convince myself that it is false, and this has proven equally impossible . . ."

If La Reynie clung tenaciously to his ambiguities in his letters and memoranda to Louvois and to the King, he confided his conclusive Conclusions to his notebooks. In these, the researcher finds strong indication that La Reynie was convinced of Mme de Montespan's guilt, if not on all, then on several counts. First, that she had ordered Black Masses, including even blood sacrifice (doves' hearts, first; later, infants') to be performed in her name by the Abbé Guibourg, herself participating in some; all to the purpose of ensuring to herself the favor of the King, by means of both a compact with the Devil and of love powders "passed beneath the chalice." Second, that "from 1667 on, she had been in the hands of La Voisin"; that "she had likewise then been in contact with Le Sage and Mariette . . . both of whom undoubtedly know Mme de Montespan . . ." and "in whose testimony," La Reynie found "great credibility" (this despite the fact that La Reynie was well aware of the disreputable character of these witnesses). To these people, La Reynie believed, Mme de Montespan had early turned for charms and spells, for love potions and love philters to be used on the King; originally, to win his love away from La Vallière; later, to hold it against a succession of rivals. "From 1667 on, there had evidently been such a design in operation." More recently, in La Reynie's analysis, the Favorite had sought stronger, more potent doses from La Filastre and Galet, through La Chapelain. "These facts," La Reynie considered to have been "well substantiated by the testimony not only of La Filastre, under torture, but by that of Guibourg and Galet . . . the account of one confirming the account of the other . . . in practically every detail. . . . Many of these charges appear to be substantially proven."

Of the fact that Mme de Montespan had been spooning aphrodisiacs into the King's food and drink for years on end, there can be little doubt, nor did La Reynie seem to doubt it. Not that she ever dreamed these might be poisonous.

If La Reynie had medical advice to the effect that cantharidin, the principal ingredient in all such preparations, could prove fatal when taken internally, the advice rendered him was not entirely accurate according to modern medical theory.* As to the King's frequent vertigoes and migraines, noted by his staff of physicians in a voluminous case history known as "The Journal of the King's Health," these attacks might have been caused, if not by cantharidin, then by the other foul ingredients of the love powders prepared to order for Mme de Montespan. So Michelet implies when he calls her "the King's malady"; his implication being also that, with her constant nasty doses, she overstimulated Louis XIV's sexual desires, as is witnessed by other reports of the royal physicians, who complained that His Majesty overtired himself at night

---

* Cantharidin, the active ingredient in any preparation of cantharis (Spanish fly or blister beetle) is a vesicant; when taken internally, an irritant to mucous membrane of stomach and intestines. Deaths reported in connection with its use appear in most instances to be due to loss of body fluid from vomiting. The preparation in the seventeenth century was unsophisticated: a powder from ground-up insects or a decoction from ground-up bodies of insects, thus a relatively weak compound, was obtained, containing only small amounts of the active principle. Despite the claims made since antiquity for *Lytta vesicatoria*, its actual aphrodisiac effect is still subject to question.

(although not too tired to continue those nocturnal overexertions well into his seventies, as witnessed by the complaints of Mme de Maintenon to her father confessor in 1705).

If La Reynie suspected that Mlle de Fontanges had fallen victim to poisoners, as he gave evidence of doing, then Mme de Montespan must have struck him as the most likely suspect; hers most likely to be the hand behind the several obscure plots described by and involving La Filastre, Romani, and Bertrand.

But when it came to the petition which was to have been delivered by La Voisin to the King to effect his death by conjuration or by poison, this must have seemed to La Reynie the least credible of all the allegations (no poison, then or now, fatal "to the touch," as even the Voisin Girl had surmised and commented). And although Shakespeare, within that very century, had already advanced the argument that "Hell hath no fury like a woman scorned," it does not seem to be applicable in this particular instance. Mme de Montespan was unlikely to have gone to that extremity; her position of supremacy, and that of her children, was assured only for the King's lifetime. She had more to lose by his death than to gain.

What struck La Reynie as a distinct possibility, however, was that "someone else may have intended an attempt on the King's life, causing poison to be added as an ingredient" to what Mme de Montespan considered simple aphrodisiacs, "using Mme de Montespan as an unwitting accessory before the fact."

Throughout the pages of the Archives and of La Reynie's notebooks, mysterious and shadowy figures appear and disappear, never to be identified: very possibly, in La Reynie's opinion, agents of the still active, still vengeful Fouquet faction. (Fouquet, the once mighty superintendent of finances under Mazarin; disgraced and sentenced to life imprisonment by the young King on his accession, on charges of massive peculation.)

By a second theory, Louvois's undoubtedly, these were the agents of an international conspiracy: here, a "Stranger"; there, a "Foreigner," or an "Englishman," an "English Milord"* frequently

---

* As to the identity of the "English Milord," François Ravaisson (assistant director of the Library of the Arsenal in the late nineteenth century)

mentioned by the prisoners, in connection with Mlle des Oeillets, at the most obscene Black Mass of all; an English Milord who promised to arrange flight for Guibourg, La Voisin, and the Voisin Girl, out of France and into England.†

La Reynie finally brought himself to sound a stronger note of warning to the King. Forwarding one batch of the secret interrogations, he apologized for the fact that it was his unpleasant duty to pass on "reports which must be so offensive" to His Majesty's eye.

Not only that; La Reynie's "suspicions had been aroused," he wrote, "by an unnatural silence" prevailing in certain quarters: "La Filastre's accusations against Mme de Montespan, made under the torment of the Question, were made in the presence of ten people: the executioner and his two valets; the torturer and his valet, the doctor and the surgeon . . ." (the other three consisting of La Reynie himself; Bezons, his opposite number, and Sagot, the court clerk). "Of these ten, there were several who would have felt no moral obligation to keep secret what they had heard. To the contrary, it must be presumed that some of them did talk. . . . With all these people in on the secret . . . I find it difficult to believe that secrecy could have been preserved . . . and yet, until now, nothing has been said . . . not a word has reached the general public. . . .**

---

takes an educated guess at either the Duke of Buckingham or the Duke of Monmouth, both corrupt, both visitors to France during the 1670's.

† Extract from the Interrogation of the Abbé Guibourg, October 10, 1680: "He [Guibourg] said that, garbed in alb and stole, he had officiated at a conjuration at La Voisin's in the presence of La des Oeillets, who wanted to lay a death spell on the King, and who was accompanied by a man, who supplied the text for the conjuration. For the composition of this death spell, the sperm of both sexes was required, but since des Oeillets was menstruating, she had to give blood instead; while the man who accompanied her went behind the bedrail with him [Guibourg] to empty his semen into the chalice. . . . In addition, a powder of bat blood mixed with flour was added to give body to the concoction. . . . And after he [Guibourg] had recited the conjuration over the chalice, he poured the contents into a small vial which La des Oeillets and the man took away with them. . . ."

** La Reynie was right: no word is to be found, not even in the pages of those omniscient telltales, Bussy, Sévigné, Saint-Simon.

And it is this silence which surprises me. . . . Indeed, it strikes me as ominous. If the persons who have been implicated have any idea of the charges leveled against them—and if they are innocent—then, is it not reasonable to assume that they would have risen to refute such dreadful accusations? On the other hand, if they are guilty, and know with what they are being charged, then must they not be living in a state of panic and desperation? . . . And if so . . . to what lengths might they not go . . . having already gone so far in crime and abomination? And even now, while this investigation is under way, while they are threatened by imminent exposure, is not this the crucial moment, the hour of danger? Must not precautions be taken against some sudden outbreak of violence? . . ."

At the next writing, the cautious man cast caution to the winds, exclaiming: "Sire, beware a hand that has already been raised against you! Take care that fear does not now impel it to strike again!"

That La Reynie's reference was to Mme de Montespan, that La Reynie found her guilty on several counts, is evident.

Secretary of State at Large Colbert protested her innocence, rose to her defense.

Called into conference by the King and given access to the secret dossier, this powerful and trusted counselor, in turn, called in an authority on criminal law to make a study of the evidence against Mme de Montespan, and to draw up a brief in her defense.

With this brief as basis for his *Mémoire*, Colbert took up his own pen to indite a lengthy document for presentation to His Majesty.

Madame de Montespan's legion of detractors point out that strong family ties bound the minister to the ex-Favorite—his daughter having only recently been married to her nephew, the Duc de Mortemart, son of the Vivonnes. But Colbert makes a good case for the defense.

"If all the people who had gone to have their fortunes told or to purchase good-luck charms were to be brought to trial, the century would not be long enough to see the end of the affair!" (If Mme de Montespan, that is to say, had actually patronized fortunetellers and magicians, she may have been naïve, superstitious, credulous, gullible, indiscreet, but still innocent of criminal motive.)

As for the motive of the prisoners in dragging her name into the case, that, according to Colbert, was easy to decipher: it was to draw a red herring across their trail; the implication of a person of such prominence was calculated to obstruct the due process of law and to put off the prisoners' evil day of judgment—as, in very fact, it had. Even such evidence as these criminals had produced would not hold up under examination, was insubstantial, subject to re-buttal.

Take La Filastre, to begin with: if she had inculpated Mme de Montespan, she had later retracted one of the charges made earlier under torture. Furthermore, she had never claimed to have met or to have seen Mme de Montespan face to face; her claims were all based on hearsay: it was La Chapelain who had told her that the poisonings were being done on Mme de Montespan's order. While La Chapelain, herself, had never named Mme de Montespan. Nor had the Abbé Cotton, nor La Vigoureux, nor La Trianon, nor La Vautier, nor Blessis; while it was to be noted that Romani and Bertrand had denied any contact with her. As for the Abbé Guibourg, though he named Mme de Montespan, he admitted that he had never seen her face through her veils, that he only knew her name as it had been named to him by others. And as for the Voisin Girl, a low-lived, common whore, a confirmed criminal, grasping desperately at any dodge to save her skin . . . what reasonable judge would listen to her denunciations of a Marquise de Montespan? Denunciations, moreover, made only subsequent to the death of her mother.

For La Voisin, it must be remembered, denied to the end any connection with Mme de Montespan, and this Colbert considered to be the most telling point in favor of the Favorite (as must all history; as did La Reynie, when he made rueful admission: "It is true that La Voisin said absolutely nothing" on the subject of the King's mistress).

If the riddle of the Poisons Affair remains unsolved, La Voisin is the Sphinx who propounded it. It is difficult to understand what motivated her silence on the subject of the Marquise de Montespan—if, indeed, she had been in contact with the Marquise over long years' time, as so much evidence indicates she had. Might there have been spoken some unfulfilled promise of mercy in return for La Voisin's silence? Might she, like La Grange, have died a "martyr" to the cause, to "the purpose"—to shield the conspirators still active in some conspiracy she was willing to forward at the cost of her life? Evil for evil's sake? For the sake of the cult, the coven: some obscure "purpose" referred to by La Grange as "divine."

"Execrable calumnies," Colbert termed the denunciations made against Mme de Montespan, "the babble of lunatics!

"His Majesty, who knows Mme de Montespan to the depths of her soul," as the minister concluded his *Mémoire*, "will never persuade himself that she could be capable of such abominations as these."

Of what His Majesty "persuaded" himself: how he found Mme de Montespan—whether innocent or guilty—remains a mystery, now, as then. No hint is to be found in any of his writings, none in those of his closest friends or advisers.

There came no open breach, in 1680 or 1681, to mark a dénouement. The estrangement between the King and Mme de Montespan was not new, dated back long months past; they had not met in private since the spring of 1680; and if the King continued his custom of going to her apartments for the *medianoche*, he insisted on going in the company of the entire court; and if he partook of the midnight collation, he may well have insisted that it be prepared and served by his own staff. It was no secret to the court that Mme de Montespan had, months earlier, been superseded in the King's favor by Mlle de Fontanges and by Mme de Maintenon.

Bussy describes a violent scene of mutual recrimination. For what "faults and failures" the King reproached Mme de Montespan, Bussy does not specify, noting only that "Beside herself with fury . . . she lashed back with the words: 'At least, I do not stink to high heaven as you do!' . . . to which charge, Bussy says,

"His Majesty was extremely sensitive" (as well he might be; his baths, most infrequent, on doctors' prescription only; his morning ablutions confined to a mere dab at hands and lips with a cloth dipped in spirits of wine).

If any one person at the court would have known the King's personal judgment on Mme de Montespan's guilt or innocence, his reaction to the revelations reaching him from Vincennes on the subject of the former Favorite's involvement in a series of sordid crimes, that one person would have been Mme de Maintenon, the new Favorite, favored over the puling Mlle de Fontanges, "favored by attentions from her admirer such as few admirers lavish on their ladies," according to Mme de Sévigné, who had had opportunity to observe the lot of them.

Whatever Mme de Maintenon may have known, she had confided—it was once thought—to a friend in far-off Quebec in two letters which appeared in La Beaumelle's biography in the mid-eighteenth century. These letters of Mme de Maintenon's to Mme de Frontenac, wife of the Governor of New France, furnished a precious insight into the moment of truth between the King and Mme de Montespan—until late in the nineteenth century, when they were discredited, categorized as expert literary forgeries. Under the dateline of August 25, 1680 (whether by La Beaumelle's hand or by Mme de Maintenon's) the letters are poignant even if apocryphal:

"Monsieur de Louvois arranged a tête-à-tête for Mme de Montespan with the King. . . . They are having it out, at this writing, but love may well win the day. So far, the King stands firm, but Mme de Montespan is irresistible in tears. Mme the Dauphine is saying her prayers; her piety has given the King occasion for serious reflection. But the flesh needs only a moment's opportunity to destroy the work of Divine Grace. . . ." (And continued in the next installment): "The King's session [with Mme de Montespan] hardened his resolve, and I congratulated him on his victory over so formidable an adversary. . . . Mme de Montespan first wept, then launched into bitter recriminations, ended up in an avalanche of words, at her most arrogant!"

X

The Case Proceeds

MONTHS HAD PASSED, the new year of 1681 had rolled around, and still the King—a normally decisive man—had arrived at no decision regarding the disposition of the Poisons Affair trials.

"The greatest problem confronting us is the decision as to how to proceed with this case. How to know" (La Reynie debated with himself and Louvois) "what is to the best interests of the sovereign and the state, to the cause of justice and the glory of God?"

La Reynie called it "a travesty of justice" that criminals such as these should escape trial for the reason that their crimes were "too monstrous" to be allowed to come to public knowledge—"The very enormity of their crimes proves their safeguard!"

"There are one hundred and forty-seven prisoners in the Bastille and at Vincennes," the Lieutenant-General of Police wrote in one of his memoranda: "All charged with serious crimes . . . all engaged in the poison traffic and in sacrilegious and impious practices. . . . Yet if the course of justice is interrupted, most of them will escape the punishment they deserve. Indeed, this crime wave must be attributed to lackadaisical prosecution in the past. . . . Poison is the common solution to people in desperate dilemmas. . . . Abominations of sacrilege and impiety are widespread in Paris, in the countryside, in the provinces . . ."

By letter of January 23, 1681, the Lieutenant-General of Police declared to Louvois that he considered it "of utmost importance that His Majesty deign to permit the Chamber of the Arsenal to proceed immediately with the trial of these prisoners."

Louvois was inclined to agree with La Reynie; the only problem, as he could see it, being how to recall the judges while withholding vital information from them; namely, the whole secret dossier involving Mme de Montespan. How to prosecute the Poisons Case without opening up the Montespan Case?

For Minister of War Louvois to favor the continuation of the prosecution was reason enough for Minister of the Marine Colbert to oppose it, although, in this instance, Colbert had additional motives. The King encouraged these arch enemies in their ferocious tug of war for power and favor, "playing off one against the other," as Visconti observed, "to keep them on their mettle—the better to serve him."

There are historians who see in Louvois not only the King's "evil counselor" but also the machinator of the Poisons Affair, using it to wreak his vengeance on his enemies and Colbert's friends; certainly the Comtesse de Soissons, the Duchesse de Bouillon, and the Duchesse de Vivonne come under that category. As for the Duc de Luxembourg, he had incurred Louvois's wrath in disputes over military matters. But Louvois's motive for an attack on Mme de Montespan is less easily discernible. Why would he have sought to bring about Mme de Montespan's downfall, only to encourage Mme de Maintenon, obviously in the line of succession as Favorite, obviously hostile to Louvois?

Colbert, surveying the impasse to which the Poisons Affair had come, pointed out to His Majesty that there were three lines of action open: the first was to reconvene the Chamber of the Arsenal, resume the trials of all the prisoners, and continue those prosecutions to their legitimate conclusions. But "this," Colbert noted, "is a method which His Majesty expresses an unwillingness to adopt." The second possible method of procedure was to try only the principals in the case: the Voisin Girl, the Abbé Guibourg, La Trianon, La Chapelain, Le Sage (the Abbé Mariette had died at Vincennes during the winter); and to use their own denegations "to prove their calumnies." But this group included the three criminals who had most loudly denounced Mme de Montespan . . . and the mention of her name was taboo. The third and last alternative—the one advocated by Colbert—was to pronounce the Chamber of the Arsenal permanently closed, and to exile "that whole criminal rabble" from Vincennes and the Bastille to the far ends of the earth: to Canada, to Cayenne, to the island of Santo Domingo. Finally, "To burn it all! . . . Burn all the papers of the secret dossier . . . to make sure that no record of such abominations, such obscenities, such ordures should survive."

If La Reynie balked at that alternative, so did Louvois.

The King had not yet announced himself, still wavered, still listened—as was his custom—to the arguments, now of Louvois, now of Colbert.

By mid-April, La Reynie thought he had hit upon a solution which might satisfy both Colbert and Louvois—even the King—a way out of their embarrassing predicament: The King could reopen the trials, recall the judges to the Chamber of the Arsenal, on one condition, "That the Chamber be not deceived."

That meant that the Chamber must be formally notified, through its proper officers, that certain evidence was being withheld.

That meant that there would have to be a resort to royal justice, in some instances; that the King himself would have to sit in judgment (as it was always the prerogative of the King of France to do) on the fate of a certain number of the accused; those, to wit, whose testimony comprised the secret dossier. ("A violation of all the rules of justice," "A dishonor to justice," La Reynie knew, for judges to sit in judgment without all the evidence before them. Himself a magistrate, the stab of his conscience provoked the cry: "We are dealing here with flesh and blood, with living men!"— With human beings and the rights of man, he almost said, an inflammatory and well-nigh revolutionary proposition coming from a functionary of the seventeenth-century monarchical regime.)

La Reynie now found himself standing, in defense of justice

and legal tradition, against his benefactor and patron, Colbert, and against his sovereign, the very source of all law and justice in the realm, the monarch-magistrate by ancient royal tradition. La Reynie, scion of a long line of magistrates, stood up to the might of the state. Not that justice or the process of law in *Ancien Régime* France was much to boast of, but such as it was—such few rights and privileges as had been established by the Parlements of France throughout the course of centuries—La Reynie fought to defend against personal and political interests, against further encroachment of absolute authority.

La Reynie requested an audience of the King and was granted it: he was to be heard in the Council Chamber, at a date set for mid-May.

Courtiers, visitors, and diplomats in greater number than usual thronged Versailles that day (according to a May issue of the *Mercure Galant*); lined the Hall of Mirrors to see the exotically costumed envoys of the Czar Fëdor III prostrate themselves before King Louis XIV as he passed by on his way to the chapel from the Council Chamber.

During the meeting in the Council Chamber, La Reynie had presented his case direct to the King, taking four hours to do it.

The formula for the new law which La Reynie proposed recommended itself to the King by reason of its flexibility: the state secret, the King's secret, would be kept inviolate while only a minimal violation would be done the traditional legal process.

On May 14, 1681, the King's Council promulgated a decree by which

HIS MAJESTY HAS ORDERED THAT THE COURT CLERK—IN THE PRESENCE OF THE CHANCELLOR, THE TWO CHAIRMEN OF THE ARSENAL COMMISSION AND THE SOLICITOR-GENERAL —ACT TO EXTRACT CERTAIN SPECIFICALLY DESIGNATED TRANSCRIPTS FROM THE TRIAL DOSSIER. . . . THESE PARTICULAR INTERROGATIONS AND DECLARATIONS TO BE PERMANENTLY SEQUESTERED FROM THE MAIN BODY OF THE EVIDENCE . . .

As subtle and confusing as a prestidigitator's patter: Here before your very eyes, Most Honorable Judges—but never to be put into your hands—are the secrets of La Filastre's Question. Presto chango! Here you have the transcript . . . minus the pages on which La Filastre inculpates the Marquise de Montespan. That page, those pages of La Filastre's testimony, all pages whereon the Marquise's name appears, whether in La Filastre's testimony or that of any other prisoner—have been removed from the official dossier of the trial, to form a special dossier, the *Faits Particuliers*. That special material is being set aside and will constitute the basis of a separate and special investigation, a secret investigation to be conducted by Monsieur de La Reynie, acting on his own.

The royal decree of May 14 concluded with a royal lie, to the effect that "the evidence so sequestered has no bearing upon the cases to come before the Chamber of the Arsenal." Whereas, of course, it emphatically did: even those prisoners who had not named Mme de Montespan and whose cases could therefore come before the court for judgment, even those were to some extent involved with their accomplices, their fellow criminals whose cases had been removed from the jurisdiction of the court to that of the King.

Still, on May 19, 1681, court clerk Sagot could record that the court was back in session "after seven months and nineteen days' interruption": "The King, during this recess, found himself under considerable pressure to discontinue permanently the sessions of this Chamber; numerous courtiers, including personages in very high places, sought to persuade him to this course, under a variety of pretexts, the most specious of which was to the effect that further inquiry into the poison traffic and the poison crimes must impair French prestige, at the international level. . . . Monsieur de La Reynie had audience with the King in his study, in the presence of the Chancellor, Messieurs Colbert and Louvois, on four different occasions, each session four hours long, and it was after these conferences that His Majesty determined to continue the sessions of the Chamber, commanding that the trials proceed forthwith in accordance with regular procedure, save with respect to the sequestered material or special dossier, including the Filastre declaration under torture, which His Majesty, for reasons of state, cannot allow to be divulged. . . ."

After sixteen hours of conference at the highest level, La Reynie had won his point, and a semblance of justice was to be preserved.

The reassembled court went to work with a vengeance on those prisoners left under its jurisdiction. Interrogations multiplied. La Joly admitted fashioning figurines out of wax as love charms for Mme de Dreux, who was back at her old tricks less than a year after her release from the Fortress of Vincennes in April, 1680. That charmer would not risk a second hearing in the Chamber, would not rely on being shown such leniency a second time—not even with two cousins on the bench—and so, set out at once for the nearest border.

La Trianon was failing fast, and the Curé de Saint-Laurent (who had been so successful in obtaining a retraction from La Filastre, *in extremis*) was dispatched to La Trianon, now in hers. But she, like her coven sister, La Voisin, kept her secrets, and rather than risk making confession under torture, chose to strangle herself with a cord (a traditional form of suicide among witches, according to the Inquisitional records).

Things began to move so fast that La Reynie fell behind in his reports to Louvois, who took the Lieutenant-General of Police to task for his remissness, reminding him that the King expected "punctual" notification of "what was going on at the Royal Chamber and at Vincennes."

Louvois and the King were anxious to know what a prisoner named Mme de Villedieu was saying about the Demoiselle des Oeillets, His Majesty's occasional mistress, Mme de Montespan's onetime handmaiden.

Madame de Villedieu was a not-so-lonely widow, who had taken up, long ago, with Le Sage and La Voisin, seeking guidance from the stars, the Tarot cards, and the Sibyls before choosing her next mate.

This time, La Reynie reported punctually: what La Villedieu

had said was "that it was strange, indeed, that she should have been arrested for her one visit to La Voisin, whereas *that other person* [des Oeillets is never referred to by name], who had made more than fifty visits to the sorceress, was still at liberty! Of course, when she [La Villedieu] had asked *that other person* whether she was not afraid of being apprehended, *that other person* had replied that she had no cause for fear, that 'they' would never permit her to be arrested . . ." ("The King would never permit it" was what des Oeillets had actually said, according to La Villedieu's statement to Police Captain Desgrez).

"There is no doubt," La Reynie continued in his report to Louvois, "that orders reached Mme de Villedieu at Vincennes immediately thereafter; for, from that day forward, she point-blank refused to talk, refused to answer any of my questions—no matter how inconsequential—having to do with *that other person.*"

Mademoiselle des Oeillets's sense of security may have been shaken by repeated visits from the Minister of War, in person; by his repeated interrogations.

Louvois reported to La Reynie that Mlle des Oeillets categorically denied all the charges, claiming to have paid La Voisin "only one," one innocent visit only, "in company with five or six young girls of her neighborhood, and that ten years ago." To prove her innocence, she proposed a confrontation, at Vincennes, with the prisoners who claimed to know her, defying them to recognize her. When they did, she insisted that it was a case of mistaken identity, and produced a dozen theories to prove it: a woman named Teriague was her double, they were "alike as two drops of water"; it must have been Teriague these people took her for! Or her niece . . . or her cousin . . . both of whom ran to fortunetellers all the time, and probably used des Oeillets's name. And then there was a maid in the Comtesse de Soissons's retinue, almost exactly des Oeillets's height and size; both maid and mistress hated des Oeillets and her mistress, and would happily have done them both a disservice. Last but not least, out of the twenty servingwomen in Mme de Montespan's household, at least eighteen were jealous of des

Oeillets, and might well have played her the scurvy trick of using her name at La Voisin's!

La Reynie indicated that he thought the lady did protest too much: "The firm stand evidenced by the person in question," he wrote Louvois, "is the product of either a clear conscience or of the fact that La Voisin, the principal actress in this drama, is no longer with us. . . ."

The question of Mlle des Oeillets's guilt or innocence has intrigued a score of investigators, from Louvois's and La Reynie's day to this; has inspired a score of books in debate of the question. It is difficult to see the logic in the assumption that Mme de Montespan's guilt or innocence hinges upon Mlle des Oeillets's; yet, so Mme de Montespan's apologists have assumed time and time again. (After all, Mlle des Oeillets may have been acting on her own and not necessarily as an agent of her mistress; while Mme de Montespan was, according to the charges made against her, in direct contact with La Voisin and company, and did not rely entirely on La des Oeillets as go-between.)

Among Mme de Montespan's apologists, the most ardent, Jean Lemoine, devoted half a lifetime to research into the Poisons Affair and to the roles played in it by Mme de Montespan and her confidential maid. The strongest blow he was to strike in their defense was to exhume, early in this century, out of the city's Archives, the Last Will and Testament of Mlle des Oeillets, filed in her Paris *quartier*; proof that she had died peacefully in 1687, in her own bed, in her own handsome Paris residence, a free woman and a woman of substance, disposing of a considerable estate to family and friends—and not, as had been previously believed, a prisoner in a remote provincial cell to which she had presumably been committed for her guilt in the Poisons Affair. The assumption stemmed from a letter addressed by Louvois to La Reynie, dated September 22, 1686, which reads: "The attached letter is to advise you that La des Oeillets, who was incarcerated on orders from the King in the Charity Hospital at Tours, died there on the eighth of this month." (Either a slip of the pen on Louvois's part, or the coincidence of a homonym, as Lemoine believed—Mlle des Oeil-lets, even in death, a victim of mistaken identity?)

"The Chambre Ardente is beginning to quicken the pace of the executions, more burnings now than ever before. . . . Three poor devils went up in flames yesterday," the English Attaché d'Affaires reported to London on June 21, 1681.

The first three death sentences to be pronounced by the court after its long recess fell upon two poisoners, Debray and Deschault, and upon La Chanfrain, concubine and acolyte to the Abbé Guibourg. (If the Abbé could not be put on trial lest he mention the name of the unmentionable, La Chanfrain did not enjoy the same immunity.) All three victims had been sentenced to the Water Torture prior to execution, but the Boot was substituted in La Chanfrain's case when the doctors in attendance declared her to be too fat to endure the water treatment without choking to death and thereby interrupting the questioning. At the Eighth Corner of the Extraordinary Question, she lost consciousness, but was re-vived in time to mount the scaffold to the gibbet awaiting her on the Place de Grève. In a variation of the usual program, that afternoon, she was hanged while the other two were burned alive.

All the breezes off the Seine, that summer of 1681, could not dispel the pall of smoke overhanging the Place de Grève. A Dame de Carada was burned alive on June 25, convicted of sacrilege and impiety with murderous intent, of having attended Black Masses with the Abbé Guibourg, of having stuck needles and pins into a wax image representing the woman who had alienated the affec-tions of her fiancé, a Monsieur de Vise, brother of the editor of the *Mercure Galant* (though not a word appeared in print on those pages).

Next came an abjured priest, Father Davot, from the church of Notre-Dame de Bonne Nouvelle, to be hanged by the neck and then set afire. But not by chief executioner Guillaume, who had to beg off again: Davot had been his father confessor, as well as La Voisin's.

The crimes were not all hanging crimes; the judges, not all

hanging judges. La Cottard was "admonished" by the court and condemned to pay a 100 livres Amend. La Bigenne, La Unziesme, and La Sylvestre were all three acquitted. As were a couple named Jourdain, herbalists, with a sideline in bats and toads which were delivered neatly packaged in carnation pots to their clients—an innocent enough profession, to hear them tell it, except for the fact that those clients were all professional poisoners.

The case of Mme de Dreux came up again. The Chambre Ardente tried her, this time, *in absentia*: pronounced a sentence of perpetual banishment on this *femme fatale*.

Then, another bonfire on the Place de Grève; standing room only for the crowd, which had come to watch the hanging of Lalande, convicted as a Satanist and habitué of Black Masses—though he denied the charges with his dying breath. As grand finale, his corpse was removed from the gibbet and tossed on the pyre.

La Vertemart could thank her lucky stars that La Voisin had turned down her bribe of a string of pearls to help her get a place in Mme de Montespan's household. The Chamber let La Vertemart off lightly enough: she was banished for life, never to set foot again in the kingdom.

In June came word of the death of Mlle de Fontanges, and coming in the very midst of the Poisons Affair trials, this touched off a fresh flurry of rumor, a new wave of alarm.

What next? Who next? No one was safe. Everyone was edgy. The Abbé Guibourg had reported on a client who was out for revenge on Colbert (the latter's bookkeeper Pelissari may have died the victim of a dose intended for his master); the minister would partake of food only at his own solitary table, losing his appetite for even his own chef's *chef-d'oeuvres*. Le Sage fluttered the parliamentary bench by insinuating that Lamoignon, former Premier President and presiding judge at the Brinvilliers trial, had died no natural death, but had been poisoned. The police department itself was uneasy at the rumor of a plot afoot to poison La Reynie's adjutant, Captain Desgrez; the captain's maid was hauled in for questioning. (At Louvois's sudden death, ten years later in

1691, the cry of poison would go up again; the Duchesse d'Orléans crying the name of Mme de Maintenon as murderess, although the antipathy between the King's last Favorite and his Minister of War hardly seemed a sufficiently compelling motive.)

Mademoiselle de Fontanges had been moved, moribund, from Versailles to the Convent of Port-Royal in Paris, where Louis XIV may or may not have paid her one final visit: the stories of the deathbed scene are touching but unreliable; and her famous last line, "Having seen tears in the eyes of my King, I can die happy," entirely out of character for "the Beautiful Idiot," as Mme de Sévigné called her.

Bussy's wicked, widely quoted quip was more realistic: "To the sick, upon whom His Majesty lays hands" (in the ancient royal thaumaturgic rite performed upon the scrofulous), "His Majesty speaks the words, 'The King touches thee, may God heal thee,' To the demoiselles he fancies, the formula should be changed to: 'If the King kiss thee, God help thee!' "*

Not all La Fontanges's fabulous jewels could buy her her young life (she had just turned twenty); nor all her diamonds, believed in those days to be amulets: "A protection against poison, witchcraft, madness and the terrors of the night," according to De Boots, a seventeenth-century authority on precious stones.

Although the King made clear his preference in writing, that "It would be better if an autopsy could be avoided"; even so, Mlle de Fontanges's family insisted. The transcript of the official report is missing from the Archives of the Bastille, but a résumé by the chief commissioner refers to "the cause of death as dropsy of the chest, gangrene of the right lobes of the lung . . . and liver damage." (Modern medical opinion endorses the diagnosis that Mlle de Fontanges died a natural death; and attributes it, variously, to "In-

---

* On five high holy days a year, immediately after Mass, the King was awaited by hundreds, often by thousands, of sufferers of scrofula, the disease known as the King's Evil. The King spoke a blessing: "The King toucheth thee, may God cure thee," made the sign of the cross on the patient's forehead, then applied his fingers to the sores. Saint-Simon assures us that His Majesty, after such laying on of hands, promptly scrubbed up with vinegar, water, and orange water.

flammatory pulmonary edema of tuberculous origin" and "Hemorrhage due to placental retention.")

No one believed it, at the time.

Bussy temerariously proclaimed that "the King's grief was so
keen that he could not conceal it, and he would have visited stern
retribution upon Mme de Montespan's head, had not cogent reasons compelled him to dissimulate his resentment."

Madame, the Duchesse d'Orléans, brutally frank, as usual,
expressed it as her opinion that "Mme de Montespan was a devil
incarnate, whereas La Fontanges was kind and simple. . . . The
latter died, so it is said, because the former poisoned her in a glass
of milk. I do not know whether this is true, but what I do know is
that two people in her employ died, and it was publicly said that
they had died of poison. . . ." Later, the Duchess had increased
Mme de Montespan's score: "I know of three persons whom she
has poisoned—Mlle de Fontanges and her infant son and one of
her maidservants. . . . Heaven only knows how many other murders that have not come to light!" *Madame* even thought the King
in danger: "Outraged as he was by then . . . at the things she [Mme
de Montespan] had perpetrated . . . it was no longer safe for him to
keep her around: She lost all self-control when her tantrums seized
her."

Madame de Caylus, more responsible than *Madame*, weighs
her every subtle word: "At the death of Mlle de Fontanges, rumors
flew . . . to the discredit of Mme de Montespan, but I am convinced
that they were baseless."

Even Mme du Noyer, writing from far-off Toulouse, swelled
the chorus of accusation: "Many people believed that a jealous
rival lent a hand to Fate in cutting short her life" (that of Mlle de
Fontanges), "and the rumor was rampant in Provence as well as in
Paris. God only knows the truth of it all!"

In all justice to Mme de Montespan, it should be said that if the
seven surgeons who performed the autopsy on Mlle de Fontanges
knew their business, and if they were honest in attributing her
death to natural causes, then not a single rival of Mme de Montespan's can be said to have fallen victim to her: not La Vallière,

not La Louvigny, not La Théobon, not La Gramont, not La Ludres, not La Soubise, and certainly not Mme de Maintenon.

And yet, a cloud of suspicion had fallen upon Mme de Montespan, in her own time, as a sampling of contemporary opinion indicates—and this despite the fact that none of her contemporaries ever learned of the charges brought against her in the course of the Poisons Affair trials.

The one possible exception, the King's one confidante, was Mme de Maintenon, and she made clear her suspicions in a letter to her brother: "Mme de Montespan seeks me out, and invites me to Clagny for visits. Nanon [Mme de Maintenon's maidservant] expresses fears for my safety." (The King would surely have passed on to Mme de Maintenon the warning La Reynie had given him.)

But, for the sake of appearances, for the sake of the exquisite courtly politesse, the former Favorite and the new Favorite maintained a surface cordiality designed to take in all but the best informed.

On May 27, 1681, Mme de Maintenon wrote to her old friend, the Marquis de Montchevreuil (to whom she would shortly entrust the care and education of her pet pupil, the Duc du Maine): "Mme de Montespan and I took a walk together today, arm in arm, laughing merrily . . . but things go none the better between us, for all that . . ."

Madame de Caylus also tells the story of the vicious contest raging behind the scenes: "Often thrown together . . . they found themselves, one day, traveling in the same carriage, tête-à-tête. Mme de Montespan made the suggestion that they call a temporary truce, and enjoy one another's conversation. . . . 'Not that we will love one another any the better for it, not that we will not resume our contest where we left off, at the journey's end'—a suggestion to which Mme de Maintenon agreed."

Actually, the contest was over; victory, Mme de Maintenon's: "No one ever better than she vis-à-vis the Center of the Universe" (another of Mme de Sévigné's code names for His Majesty): "Every night from six to eight, he spends in her apartment"—the magnificent new Versailles apartment assigned to her on the second floor of the recently completed section of the château, at the top of the Queen's staircase, just across the way from Her Majesty's; on the same floor, and not too far removed from His. (Mme de Montespan was shortly to lose hers, in the shuffle; shortly to come down from the Olympian heights of that second floor, down in the world, to ground level.)

At just about this time, Racine and Boileau, coming as they did regularly to read the latest installment of their official History of the reign to the King and Mme de Montespan, were astonished to find Mme de Maintenon instead: "Installed in an armchair close beside the King, in intimate conversation with His Majesty, who was confined to bed with some indisposition, on that occasion. They had begun their reading" (according to the Racine Memoirs, written by Racine's son) "when Mme de Montespan, who was evidently not expected, made her entrance. . . . After profuse and protracted compliments to the King and Mme de Maintenon, she was finally invited by the King to take a seat. . . . For, as His Majesty remarked, it was not fair that she should miss the reading of a work of which she, herself, had commissioned the writing. . . . From that day forward, Mme de Maintenon's favor evidenced itself every day more strongly. . . ."

Madame de Maintenon's relation to the King—whether or not she had yet become his mistress, whether or not she was still managing to hold him off with her chill piety and moral exhortations— provided material for a debate that would rage, at the time, and then drone on for generations, through countless dusty volumes.

If Mme de Maintenon's own version is to be trusted, the Queen expressed to her her gratitude not only for the King's conversion but for his return to the marital bed, ostensibly at Mme de Maintenon's urging.

Heaven (with some temporal assistance) had convinced Mme de Maintenon that hers was the divine mission of bringing His Most Christian Majesty of France back to the paths of righteousness. ("God has entrusted into your hands the interests of the Church and State, along with the salvation of a great monarch," the Bishop of Chartres wrote to Mme de Maintenon.) The monarch, in his forties, with a few aches and pains to remind him of his own mortality, was ready for conversion; and this, in turn "strengthened Mme de Maintenon's hold over him" (in Voltaire's cynical analysis); if he was now ready to renounce "his attachment for a married woman—this was, to great extent, due to the fact that his ardor for her had considerably cooled."

Even so, in her official capacity as superintendent of the Queen's household, Mme de Montespan accompanied the King and court, in October, on their solemn entry into Strasbourg for the celebrations attendant upon the annexation of that strategic city on the Rhine. "FRANCE CLOSED TO GERMANS" was the legend engraved, somewhat prematurely as it developed, on the gold medal struck to commemorate the glorious occasion.

It had been too long between glories, between victories, between wars: not one fresh triumph to mark the Sun King's monuments since 1678, the year of the signing of the Treaty of Nijmegen. Armed *cap-à-pied*—to the teeth! for the peace, while the rest of Europe had demobilized, Louis XIV was in excellent position, in 1681, to establish and enforce legal claims (based on obscure medieval covenants and enfeoffments) on some ten Alsatian cities, including prized Strasbourg.

The Minister of Marine could show off as well as the Minister of War, that October; Colbert happily demonstrated the new power of the French navy by blasting Algiers into rubble with an offshore bombardment, from mortars mounted on five especially designed ships; a sensational "first" in naval warfare, a revolutionary new technique of death and destruction (invented by a mariner named Renaud), as well as a fiery warning to the Algerian and Tripoline pirates to keep hands and grappling hooks off French vessels, in the future.

Upon his return to Saint-Germain from the six-week Alsatian expedition, Louis XIV took time off to attend to personal business, to legitimize his last two children by Mme de Montespan: to bestow on their four-year-old daughter the name of Mlle de Blois; and to entitle their three-year-old son Comte de Toulouse.

The Case Proceeds

In September, the King had joined with Mme de Montespan in polite sighs and platitudes over the death of their seven-year-old daughter, Mlle de Tours; in October, they conferred on the selection of a site and design for a handsome arcaded mausoleum to be erected in the child's memory.

The King called Mme de Montespan into conference again, that season, to deal with an emergency arising over the latest folly perpetrated by the lady's husband: the Marquis de Montespan proposed to send a letter to the Pope to petition for a divorce in order to be free to marry a young lady he was courting in Toulouse. The Marquis's friend, Mme du Noyer, advised her Paris correspondents of developments in that ancient capital of Languedoc: "The Pope would surely have granted a special dispensation had he ever received that letter, had not Monsieur de Louvois . . . warned him that if he dared to send it off to Rome, the King's patience would be exhausted; and he, Monsieur de Montespan, would be a lost man! Not only would he be jeopardizing his own life and limb, but the career and fortune of his son, the Marquis d'Antin, as well! Intimidated by the minister, poor Montespan backed down . . ." (Mme du Noyer clucked her sympathy with the Marquis; he was her idea of "the noblest seigneur imaginable! . . . And if he permits himself to pillory his wife's reputation, he puts up with no such liberties from any other!")

But not all these distractions could long distract the attention of the King (nor that of Mme de Montespan) from the business being transacted in the Chambre Ardente and the Fortress of Vincennes.

"His Majesty awaits with impatience your reports on this latest affair," Louvois wrote La Reynie, in the autumn of 1681.

"This latest affair" shaped forth as an extensive conspiracy, involving partisans of the late Fouquet (dead in 1680 after twenty years of solitary confinement in a distant fortress-prison).

"A conspiracy on the grand scale," Louvois called it: a plot on foot not only against Colbert but even against the King, in revenge for their severity toward the once-powerful superintendent of finance. (A relative of Fouquet's, using an alias, had availed himself of the Abbé Guibourg's Black Masses: "Death powders and death spells designed to do away with the King," Guibourg admitted: "Poison passed under the chalice and a wax image representing His Majesty melted down on the altar.")

The investigation could never discover the identity of the ringleaders, never fathom the mystery.

A prisoner named Jean Maillard seemed to hold the key to it, but it was never wrested from him. He died sneering at death and at all the instruments of torture; all the torturer-interrogators got for their pains—or rather his—was a blast of sarcasm and a stream of curses. Maillard was mixed up with the worst of the poisoners and the alchemists; the late Sainte-Croix and the Marquise de Brinvilliers had been his intimates.

Two noblemen turned up among the late arrivals at Vincennes: the Marquis de Monteran and the Marquis de Termes, both under suspicion as pro-Fouquet agents; the latter, a cousin of Mme de Montespan's (charged by La Voisin in her petition as the nobleman holding her "gallant" Blessis under durance).

"That's the affair on the carpet presently," a contemporary letterwriter reported to a friend, upon the arrest of Mme de Montespan's kinsman: "No one knows what it's all about, for everything that goes on at the Chambre Ardente is kept very quiet, but de Termes's equerry, who was arrested with him, was put to the Question yesterday. By next week, we should have some news on this intrigue, which has something to do with poison. . . ."

Poisoned wine bottles! Six of them, delivered by the Marquis's equerry, so the accusation reads, to Mlle de Fontanges at the Abbey of Chelles. Not that he ever admitted to the charges, dying, as he did, under torture; which was just as well, for had he named Mme de Montespan, as it was feared he might, his interrogation would have had to have been set aside, sequestered, added to the secret dossier.

On September 9, 1681, the first of the so-called "Fouquet gang" went to the Place de Grève: a poisoner named Debray was strangled and then burned. On September 13, the mode of execution was varied once again: a shepherd named Moreau, accused of preparing poison to be used on the King, was broken alive on the wheel. A man named Barenton, who admitted under torture to having supplied poison pellets to a cousin of Fouquet's "for the murder of the King," was sentenced to be strangled; his body burned to ashes, and the ashes scattered to the wind. Just before his execution that week, another man named Perceval named the Marquis de Monteran as the ringleader of this conspiracy.

Maillard, condemned to death "for having known but not revealed dastardly criminal plots against the person of the sovereign," happened to be the subject of another sovereign state and, as such, was entitled to the privilege of execution at the hands of the headsman. His paramour, La Baliron, was banished; his accomplice, La Guesdon (formerly in the service of the Marquise de Brinvilliers), imprisoned for life.

Throughout the fall and winter, the countryside was combed and a clutch of rustics thrown into jail with inmates from the city: a shepherd and a laborer from Lérinville, a carpenter from Nogent, a weaver from Maintenon were charged with "casting death spells on man as well as beast"—proof that the practice of witchcraft was still widespread throughout the land.

"The Place de Grève is blazing away again," in the words of one Parisian, in a letter dated January 5, 1682: "Burnings and sometimes hangings are scheduled there, these days, according to the verdict of the Chamber. . . . La Joly, the famous poisoner . . . who was just as slippery as La Voisin . . . did plenty of talking before her execution, seventeen days ago." Under the Water Torture on December 19, 1681, La Joly had confessed to a string of poisonings and ritual murders, but she might have cheated justice and escaped the stake, had not the jailers—in the very nick of time—discovered the vial of poision she had secreted in her hair, against just such an eventuality.

On the twenty-first of December came the turn of La Bouffé, a midwife-abortionist; and after her, La Méline, both condemned to both the gibbet and the stake. La Poignard, accused of having sacrificed her own baby on the Devil's altar, enjoyed the mercy of the court—a mere three-year term of banishment. La Desloges was the first victim of the New Year, hanged on January 17, 1682.

On March 13, 1682, the Chamber of the Arsenal acquitted the Marquis de Termes, releasing him from Vincennes. The explanation of the leniency shown him may well lie in his relation to Mme de Montespan; as may that of the missing interrogations—no documents relating to his case to be found today among the Archives of the Bastille.

A number of other prisoners, against whom the charges did not seem to warrant further detention, were also released at this time.

The King was showing himself eager, now, to wind up the business at the Chamber of the Arsenal, as Louvois advised La Reynie: "His Majesty requests that you submit a list of those prisoners whom you think we would be justified in releasing; those whom you think should be confined in state institutions; those whom you think we must continue to hold at Vincennes. . . ."

XI

The Case Is Closed

B Y 1682, THE JUDGES OF THE CHAMBRE ARDENTE, along with
the King and Louvois and Colbert, were all eager to have
done with it, to finish up the Poisons Affair trials, dragging on into
a third year.

La Reynie attributed the judges' *malaise* "not merely to the
nationwide mood of criticism but to a natural aversion, a distaste,
such as all decent men must suffer as the agents of doom . . . and
this in addition to the resentment they feel at seeing justice cheated
of the main offenders. . . ."

La Reynie agreed that the case should be brought to a close,
but warned against doing so "on a note of indifference or disillusionment, lest the remaining criminals, both known and
unknown, lose their respect for the law and continue in their
license . . ."

The Vanens Affair was revived: Vanens—along with his maid
and mistress; his valet, La Chaboissière; and his confederates
Cadelan, Clausel, and Bachimont—had been among La Reynie's
earliest arrests; all of them were languishing, half forgotten, in their
cells, four years later.

Le Sage accused Vanens of complicity in the poisoning of the
Duke of Savoy in 1675; while La Chaboissière brought charges of
counterfeiting and of complicity with La Chapelain. But Vanens
escaped both the Question and the scaffold; was sentenced, instead,

to the galleys for life; although, dangerous as he was, it was later decided to immure him forever in a provincial prison.

Early in April, 1682, Louvois instructed La Reynie to take the necessary legal steps to prepare the official dissolution of the Chamber.

In a hurry, the judges set out to dispose of the cases left on their docket: on April 14, La Simon was condemned to perpetual banishment; the Abbé Deshayes to five years' exile; La Saloman and the Abbé Lemeignan banished, forbidden to set foot again in the viscountcy of Paris. Bault drew a sentence of six months' imprisonment; Muble (La Bosse's husband), Merville, and Blessis (La Voisin's paramour) were condemned to the galleys.

"There are still some eighty prisoners left to be tried," a contemporary correspondent noted in a letter, early that summer: "The judges are rushing things along as fast as possible . . ."

On the sixth of July, La Chaboissière, Vanens's valet, necessarily less guilty than his master, paid a steeper penalty—was hanged on a gallows in the Place de Grève; his, the distinction of suffering the last public execution in the Poisons Affair.

La Reynie began to draw up statistics on the case; clear proof that it constituted the most extensive legal process of the reign. During the three years since the appointment of the Chamber of the Arsenal, between the dates of April 7, 1679, and April 8, 1682, that court had held 210 sessions; 319 arrest warrants had been authorized; 218 persons had actually been taken into custody; and these subjected to 856 interrogations. Eighty-three prisoners had been tried; 108 yet to come to trial (27 of the 108 would be judged along with Vanens, subsequent to the date of La Reynie's balance sheet). La Reynie computed that there were 21 prisoners who could be released from custody without further investigation.

That left a total of 60 prisoners yet to be dealt with. Actually, however, that figure was reducible to 46, as La Reynie noted, if one deducted the 14 prisoners "removed by the King from the jurisdiction of the court"—the 14, that is, including the worst villains of the piece; including the three accusers, the three principal

Louis XIV. Portrait by
Charles Le Brun.
Musée de Versailles.

Louis XIV at the Academy of Science. Detail of a painting by Henri Testelin.
Musée de Versailles.

Marie Mancini, the Sun King's
first *grande passion*.
Portrait by Pierre Mignard.
Bibliothèque Nationale, Paris.

The King's Favorite, Mademoiselle de La Vallière, with her two children.
Painted by Schmitz after Mignard. *Musée de Versailles.*

Marie Thérèse, Queen of France, wife of Louis XIV.
Portrait by Charles Beaubrun. *Musée de Versailles. Photo: Giraudon.*

The Marquis de Montespan.
Portrait by Nicolas de Largillière.
*California Palace
of the Legion of Honor.*

The Marquis d'Antin,
son of the Marquis and
Marquise de Montespan.
Bibliothèque Nationale, Paris.

Madame de Montespan. Miniature by Louis de Châtillon.
Formerly in the collection of the Duke of Buccleuch and Queensbury.

Two daughters of Louis XIV and Madame de Montespan: Mademoiselle de Blois and Mademoiselle de Nantes. Portrait by Philippe Vignon. *Musée de Versailles.*

Madame de Montespan and children. After Mignard.
Musée de Versailles.

The Duchesse de Fontange.
Bibliothèque Nationale, Paris.

Henrietta of England, the first *Madame*,
holding a portrait of her husband,
the Duc d'Orléans.
Portrait by André Matthieu.
Musée de Versailles.

Madame de Sévigné.
Portrait by Mignard.
Musée Carnavalet, Paris.
Photo: Bulloz.

Elizabeth-Charlotte of
Bavaria, the second *Madame*.
Portrait by Hyacinthe Rigaud.
Musée de Versailles.

Mademoiselle de Montpensier,
the *Grande Mademoiselle*.
After a portrait by Mignard.
Bibliothèque Nationale, Paris.

Two portraits by Mignard
of Madame de Maintenon.
Upper photo: Giraudon.
*Lower photo: Service de
Documentation Photographique
de la Réunion
des Musées Nationaux.*

LE PORTRAIT DE LA VOISIN.

Source de tant de maux maudite creature
Qui par mille poisons destruisois la Nature,
Si la parque en fillant tes detestable jours
A fait regner la Mort, en prolongeant leur cours,
Vn suplice effroyable et plein d'Ignominie
A sceu trancher le fil de ton enorme vie .

Portrait of the sorceress, La Voisin, by Antoine Coypel.
Bibliothèque Nationale, Paris. Photo: Giraudon.

The principal methods of execution
in seventeenth-century France.
Etching by Jacques Callot.
Bibliothèque Nationale, Paris.

The Marquise de Brinvilliers
undergoing the Question.
Print by Bourdet.
Musée Carnavalet, Paris.
Photo: Bulloz.

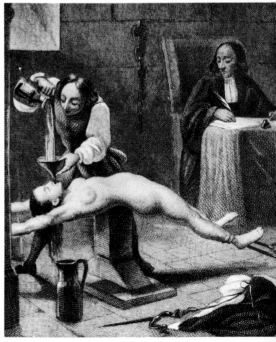

Gabriel Nicolas de La Reynie,
Lieutenant-General of Police,
whose fastidious records
of the Affair of the Poisons
survive. Engraving by Van Schuppen
after a painting by Mignard.
Bibliothèque Nationale, Paris.

L'EXECVTION

REMARQVABLE,

DE MADAME DE BRINVILLIERS,
qui a esté condamnée à faire Amande honorable de-
vant Nostre-Dame, & de là conduite à la Gréve,
pour y estre Décollée & ensuitte jettée au feu, pour
avoir empoisonné son Pere, ses Freres, & quantité
d'autres gens de Condition.

IL faut mourir ma Sentence est renduë;
Mais ce seul mot me rend toute esperduë,
Me faut mourir dessus vn échaffaut,
C'est pour punir mes trop cruels deffauts,

The execution of the Marquise de Brinvilliers shown in a contemporary cartoon.
Bibliothèque Nationale, Paris.

A prisoner being drawn and quartered. Etching by Jacques Callot.
Photo: Bulloz.

Louis XIV at a council of state. *Musée de Versailles*.

witnesses against Mme de Montespan: namely, the Voisin Girl, the Abbé Guibourg, and Le Sage. The eleven others were involved in the criminal activities of, and by the testimony of, the aforementioned three; namely, Romani, Bertrand, Galet, La Chapelain, La Delaporte, La Bergerot, La Pelletier, La Bellier, Latour, Renard, and La Vautier.

La Reynie made one last plea that these, the prime offenders, not be allowed to escape the due process of the law, insisting that their cases had definite bearing on the cases of the others who would come before the court; that it was inequitable to pass judgment on the others without considering the evidence contained in the testimony of these.

His efforts were commendable, but in vain; reasons of state prevailed, and the fourteen were never to be turned over to a regular court of justice; but were subjected, instead, to royal justice; their fate to be decreed by His Majesty (who had "a genuine understanding of the spirit of the law," according to Voltaire); the sentences in these cases to be effected by *lettres de cachet*, letters under seal (that ultimate expression of arbitrary royal authority which would constitute one of the chief grievances of the Revolution).

On July 21, La Reynie submitted to Louvois the formula for a decree discontinuing the Poisons Affair trials and dissolving the Chamber of the Arsenal.

Louis XIV and Louvois lost no time: the decree was drawn up, signed by the monarch, and promulgated by the Royal Council on that very day of July 21.

The Chamber of the Arsenal emptied. One hundred and four judgments had been rendered there; of these, 36 had been death sentences (two, *in absentia*); 34 of these sentences had been carried out in the public square by either fire, cord, or ax. Four life sentences to the galleys had been pronounced; 34 sentences involving banishment or financial amends. There had been 30 acquittals in the course of the three-year sessions.

No official report on the trials had ever appeared in print, but with 34 public executions—the Place de Grève running with blood and thick with smoke—the Parisian public must have been aware of what was going on, while those close to the source of power and authority had more than an inkling of the mystery behind it all.

The Venetian Ambassador to Paris, for example, reporting to the Doges on July 29, 1682, would write: "Much whispering goes on about the severity of the sentences and the underlying reasons. There are strange and mysterious facets to this case which I would like to be able to point out to you, but upon which discretion prescribes my silence . . . as it prescribes my putting off a full report until a later date."

The task of disposing of the remaining prisoners devolved upon La Reynie, whose first step was to loose some 40 criminals, though the most innocuous of the lot, back into the Paris underworld.

In August, the Bastille and Vincennes were further cleared. Among those who had never come up for judgment was La Bosse's son, who was shipped off to the army; while Lemaire, La Verte-mart's brother, who had been discovered in the King's wine cellars, was marched across the border at Peronne, with a 50-*pistoles* annual subsidy, on condition that he never set foot in France again, never talk about what he had heard as the Abbé Guibourg's cellmate.

There were other prisoners in the Bastille and at Vincennes, in no way connected with the Poisons Affair, innocent of any other crime than that of having heard the mention of the name of Mme de Montespan from an indiscreet cellmate. It was a crime to be expiated with long years, if not life, imprisonment.

Manon Bosse was such a casualty: "Under the name of Manon Dubosc, she was sent to a convent at Besançon," as La Reynie recorded her case: "The King paid a pension of 250 livres a year for her there. She was never released for the reason that she had shared a cell [at Vincennes] with the Voisin Girl, who had told her everything."

In October, six female prisoners were sent for safekeeping behind convent walls in various regions of France; others were transferred from Paris to Lyon or to Rouen or to Tours, to charity hospitals, for confinement. The state institution at Tours was named as the place of detention for Mme de Villedieu, less fortunate than her friend, Mlle des Oeillets, still at liberty in Paris, despite her camaraderie with La Voisin.

On December 15, 1682, in his Council Chamber at Versailles, Louis XIV signed general orders for the deportation of the last lot of criminals, the worst of the lot, including the fourteen prime culprits who had never come to trial. Letters under the King's seal were made out in the names of that sinister triumvirate: the Abbé Guibourg, Le Sage, and the Voisin Girl.

The remotest, darkest dungeons and the strongest keeps were selected as their destination. They would not burn, they would not hang; but their stratagem—if it was a stratagem—in naming Mme de Montespan, to avoid judgment, would assure them a penalty scarcely preferable to the supreme penalty, a life scarcely preferable to death.

The Citadel of Besançon was selected to entomb eleven desperadoes, headed by the Abbé Guibourg, Le Sage, Romani, Galet, and Cadelan.

Louvois himself sat down to write to Monsieur Chauvelin, Intendant of the province of Franche-Comté; to instruct, in minute detail, "the preparation of two cells in the Citadel, each to hold six prisoners in maximum security; each prisoner to be attached by hand or foot to an iron chain . . . the chain to be affixed to a ring in the wall . . . the chain just long enough to permit the prisoner to lie down on his straw pallet. . . . Since these are the most dangerous of criminals, the King wants them secured in this fashion so that they cannot injure the guards assigned to come to feed them and to remove their ordures. . . . You will see to it that these cells are located in an isolated part of the Citadel where nothing these scoundrels say can be overheard. . . ."

Louvois made his warning even stronger in December of 1682, advising Chauvelin that Romani was the worst of the incorrigible lot: "Above all, insist that the guards take measures to prevent all others from hearing the rubbish this gang is capable of talking, sometimes at the top of their lungs. They have been known to speak infamies about Mme de Montespan . . . wild tales with no foundation whatsoever in fact. . . . Issue warning to these prisoners that they will be mercilessly punished at the least word on such a subject. . . . And make it strong enough, so that they are afraid to open their mouths. . . ."

Watch out for Le Sage as well as Romani, Louvois wrote in December, in reply to Chauvelin's report that the prisoner had dared take the name of the King in vain: "Le Sage is an habitual, hardened criminal and a liar, who never spoke a word of truth the whole time he was at Vincennes." Even so, Chauvelin was ordered to quiz him further on the implications of his reference to the King, to "put Le Sage on bread and water and flog the hide off him from morning to night until he comes out with it. . . ."

Louvois's instructions to Chauvelin further included the preparation of maximum-security accommodations at the *château-fort* of Saint André-de-Salins, in the Jura Mountains, for fourteen female prisoners being shipped to Franche-Comté from Paris.

The provost-marshal of the Île-de-France sent his guards to escort the Voisin Girl, over land and sea, to the Citadel of Belle-Île-en-Mer, in the Bay of Biscay, off the coast of Brittany. Three members of her mother's coven, La Pelletier, La Poulain, and La Delaporte, made the long one-way journey with her.

La Chapelain (La Filastre's crony) was sent south, to the Mediterranean, to be shut away in the keep of the Château of Villefranche, with La Guesdon, Vanens's and La Brinvilliers's accomplice, to keep her company.

La Guesdon was to have the distinction of being the last survivor of the Poisons Affair's cast of criminal characters.

In 1717, the Villefranche commandant reported to the proper government authority (Louvois twenty-six years dead, by then) that out of "the original lot of four prisoners of state connected with the poison crimes, who were sent here for confinement thirty-six years ago . . . La Guesdon was the last to die; died here the 15th of this month [of August], leaving 45 livres in silver which she had saved out of her 8 sols daily food allowance. . . . So, there's one less pensioner for the King to provide for!"

Many of these "pensioners" of the King's were still alive in

1691, La Reynie noted: sixteen still chained up at Fort Saint André in the Juras; thirteen, at the Citadel of Besançon. The Abbé Guibourg had been cut loose, in death, from his chains at Besançon in 1686, as Louvois's correspondence file reveals; Romani from his, in 1714. The date of the death of Le Sage, as that of the Voisin Girl, is nowhere to be found on record.

There were some few instances of clemency shown toward Poisons Affair survivors: in 1693, Anne Robert, coven sister of La Bosse and La Vigoureux, was transferred from the fortress at Nantes, at the intervention of "certain pious parties" to a convent at Le Mans. At Angers, however, in 1712, four Poisons Affair prisoners were still vainly imploring their liberty. And Blessis (paramour of La Voisin of not so blessed memory) made several pleas for mercy, all rejected by the King. At the time of the last one, in 1702, His Majesty decreed that Blessis was not only "to remain in the galleys," he was forbidden henceforward to submit "any further *Mémoires* on the subject of his liberation." (Despite the brutality of the torture, despite the ruthlessness of the punishment, despite the inequities and inadequacies of the legal process in *Ancien Régime* France, in what is categorized as a despotic regime—an absolute monarchy where the monarch's word was law, where neither the word "citizen" nor the word "rights" had yet been enunciated—one cannot but marvel at the restraint of the monarch in the employ of his infinite authority. The most dangerous of these "pensioners" of the King's might easily and silently have been dispatched by knife or sword or cord, deep within their prison fastnesses, at a word from His Majesty or Louvois. Clearly, that word was never spoken in all the long years of the imprisonment of the Poisons Affair criminals.)

Although the doors of the Chamber of the Arsenal were closed and the Paris prisons empty in 1682, La Reynie could not feel that his duty had been done until adequate anti-crime legislation had been formulated and promulgated. His correspondence with Louvois reveals his concern for the public safety, his anxiety to design a criminal code that would discourage the repetition of such hideous crimes as had recently plagued the nation.

Colbert appointed La Reynie to draw up such an ordinance, which the King promptly signed, and submitted to the Parlement of Paris for registration on August 30, 1682.

This edict has survived several centuries, numerous wars and revolutions and regimes, and may be said to constitute the basis of the poisons regulations of the French legal code to this day.

The preparation, manufacture, sale, distribution, and application of known poisons such as arsenic, realgar (arsenic monosulfide), orpiment (arsenic trisulfide), and sublimate (mercury chloride) were restricted to individuals identified with certain specified professions or trades, to wit: "Doctors, surgeons, apothecaries, goldsmiths, silversmiths, blacksmiths, dyers, and other persons known to be publicly engaged in callings which may require such usage. . . ." All of these designated professionals and tradesmen were to be officially registered. The operation of alchemical laboratories or distilleries was outlawed to private individuals. Article VI of the edict betrayed seventeenth-century science's uncertainty about certain mysterious animal, vegetable, and metallic substances: "Included under the category of poison will be not only those known poisons which cause instant and violent death, but also those which work more slowly, causing gradual deterioration in health or lingering illness . . . whether these poisons be used in their natural state or as ingredients in a manufactured compound. . . ." The final article of the edict forbade the medicinal use of "Venomous insects, toads, vipers, serpents and other such creatures . . . without special authorization. . . ."*

Article I of the edict proscribed the magical arts; specifically, the arts of divination: fortunetellers, who played on "the vain curiosity and superstition" of the general public, were banished from the realm by the edict of 1682.

For "Sacrilege, impieties and malefices," the penalty of death

---

* There are animal venoms, such as snake venom, which have powerful poisonous qualities, but most of these are not poisonous when taken orally. Strange ideas of cause and effect were still prevalent in the seventeenth century.

was prescribed. Thus, it was an offense against the state religion that was to be prosecuted, not witchcraft *per se*.

The prosecution of witchcraft had been striken from the statute books in France by decree of Louis XIV, by edict of the Parlement of Paris, in 1672.

"In the times of Henri IV or Louis XIII, they would not have dared to take such a step!" Voltaire boasted: "The spirit of reason and reasonable doubt, which was just dawning in men's minds, began almost imperceptibly to erode superstition. . . . In those earlier reigns, the standard test for witches had been to throw them into the water, bound hand and foot. If they managed to stay afloat they were convicted of witchcraft; if they sank, they were declared innocent. . . . In the country, every shepherd practiced magic. In the city, amulets, talismans and zodiac rings were popular. No one doubted the efficacy of the divining rod to locate underground springs or buried treasure. . . . Everyone had to have his horoscope cast. All the talk was of the magic arts. It was all a delusion, yet savants and magistrates wrote learned treatises on the topic. Superstition was so deeply ingrained in mens' minds that, even as late as 1680, a comet could create panic . . ."*

But there was a distinct change, there was progress, Voltaire implied, in Louis XIV's Splendid Century; his royal decree and the parliamentary edict of 1672 furnished proof that the Age of the Inquisition was past and the Age of Reason straight ahead.

The judges of the Chamber of the Arsenal had not acted as inquisitors, had shown reluctance at even hearing cases of sorcery. La Voisin, La Grange, La Bosse, La Vigoureux, La Trianon, La Filastre, La Joly, La Chapelain, La Chanfrain had not been tossed into the Seine to sink or swim, had not been tried as members of the witch cult, but as members of a crime ring, murderesses, poisoners, cutthroats, kidnappers, abortionists; incidentally, but not primarily, as defilers and desecraters of the Christian altar.

---

* Voltaire meant 1682, the year of Halley's Comet, as it came to be called in honor of Edmund Halley, the astronomer who observed it and was the first to calculate its orbit and predict its return.

Not that Paris had heard the last of witches and sorcerers: charges against the practitioners of the black arts—against poisoners, diabolists, magicians, horoscopists, fortunetellers, seekers after buried treasure and after the philosopher's stone—were preferred and are recorded in the Archives of the Prefecture of Police, as late as 1709, 1711, 1775. Nor were the witch trials in the American colonies in 1692 the last. The last public execution on the charge of witchcraft took place in Scotland in 1722.

With the legislation in prohibition of witchcraft persecution to his credit, Louis XIV had proven himself a man before his time. His "cousin" of England, George II, would not repeal anti-witchcraft laws until 1751.*

The doors of the Arsenal Chamber locked, the last of the Poisons Affair prisoners dispersed by the end of 1682, there remained only the mountain of legal documents to be disposed of. This whole vast mass of material—the official minutes of every court session, the record of every judgment pronounced and of the execution of every sentence, the copies of every warrant issued, the transcripts of every interrogation of every prisoner in the courtroom, in the interrogation hall, or in the torture chamber; the entire body of official court correspondence, intra- and extramural—all these Chamber of the Arsenal Papers were gathered up, folded, and stacked into "twenty-nine large packets and eight chests" to be turned over to court clerk Sagot for safekeeping; and at Sagot's death in 1690, to Sieur Gaudion, clerk of the Châtelet Court, who recognized the official transfer by proper notice, including a meticulous inventory, dated January 25, 1691.

* Not that the world had heard the last of witches or of witchcraft, of the supernatural or of magic, even then, even in the Age of Reason, the Age of Enlightenment, the Age of Voltaire. In what Jung calls "the collective unconscious"—the deepest level, the one common to the entire human race throughout history—"exist the deep instinctual tendencies which produced, in primeval man, his concrete belief in the supernatural." And, "If the veneer of civilized skepticism sometimes reduces that response to a weak half-belief," even so, "Jung and Freud . . . along with a great many psychologists, sociologists and anthropologists . . . would agree that there remain in men's minds certain elements which tend to produce . . . responses and practices akin to those of primitive man."

The Case Is Closed

Alongside—but separate from—this official dossier of the Chamber of the Arsenal trials, reposed the black leather coffer containing what La Reynie termed *"Les Faits Particuliers"* or special, secret material; this coffer under lock and key and seal, just as it had been transmitted from La Reynie to Louvois by special messenger Desgrez in January, 1681. Sieur Gaudion duly acknowledged receipt and accepted responsibility for the safekeeping of this coffer, to which La Reynie kept the key.

The records of the trial proper repose today in Paris's Library of the Arsenal, in the collection of state papers known as the Archives of the Bastille. Although the Archives of the Bastille were originally classified in alphabetical order by the name of the prisoner in question, they have been reclassified in chronological order —the Chamber of the Arsenal Papers occupying sixteen full files, under sixteen reference numbers: No. 10,338 through No. 10,354, under which they may be located today by researchers interested in consulting them.

Les Faits Particuliers, the special, secret material consigned to the sealed black leather coffer, has long since, as we know, disappeared into thin air, gone up in smoke.

XII

Dénouement

THE CASE WAS CLOSED. The Poisons Affair trials, the most sensational of the seventeenth century, had come to an end, although the Chamber of the Arsenal had never been asked—had never been permitted—to sit in judgment on the guilt or innocence of Mme de Montespan. Her name was never to be spoken before the tribunal once the King had intervened.

The court of Versailles had heard even less than the court of the Arsenal. Only the King, the Chancellor, Louvois, Colbert, and La Reynie—and possibly Mme de Maintenon—had ever seen the *Faits Particuliers* containing the testimony in which Mme de Montespan had been mentioned.

Of all her contemporaries, of all the seventeenth-century memorialists or commentators, only one—the Italian Visconti—ever connected Mme de Montespan's name with the Poisons Affair, with La Voisin: "La Voisin bragged," Visconti wrote in his Memoirs, "that it was by her [magical] arts that Mme de Montespan and Louvois managed to maintain themselves in royal favor."

If the tribunal was never to pronounce itself on the matter of Mme de Montespan's involvement in the Poisons Affair, neither was the King.

What history has denied us—the script for the dénouement of the affair, the lines of the grand finale as spoken by the two protagonists, the libretto for the last great scene played out between Louis XIV and Mme de Montespan—the playwright Victorien Sardou has supplied.

Where La Beaumelle, biographer of Mme de Maintenon and editor of her correspondence, might have been expected to adhere to the strict confines of historical fact, a dramatist such as Sardou might give free rein to his imagination in his play, *L'Affaire des Poisons (The Poisons Affair)*, a great success on the Paris boards toward the close of the nineteenth century.

As it deserved to be, for not only does it provide a rousing climax to that passion-ridden adventure of Mme de Montespan's and Louis XIV's—there is a better than even chance that it happened just this way. The playwright's version of the nature and the extent of Mme de Montespan's involvement in the case coincides with that of the majority of responsible historians. After intensive research into the period and the trial, and working well within the framework of history, Sardou takes only slight poetic—or dramatic —license with years and dates, adding only one character, the Abbé Griffard, to the original cast; only one item, a goblet of lemonade, to the original stage properties. The time, as set by Sardou, is late 1680 or 1681, as the trial before the Royal Chamber of the Arsenal draws to a close. On stage, in the King's private apartments at Versailles, as the curtain rises on the last act, are the King, La Reynie, and the one fictitious character, the Abbé. The last has assured La Reynie that he can identify Mme de Montespan as the principal participant in a Black Mass, and that he can provide irrefutable proof thereof if he is given the opportunity of a confrontation with the lady. Mme de Montespan responds to the King's summons but protests at the suggestion of a confrontation with the Abbé, referring to it as "a test beneath my dignity." The King's reply is: "Then you must hasten to confound him, Madame, by proving your innocence."

. . .

THE KING [*Addressing Abbé Griffard*]*

You claim to be a witness to Madame's presence at the ceremony you have described?

ABBÉ GRIFFARD

I do, sire.

THE KING

You have incontrovertible proof, you claim, of what you say?

ABBÉ GRIFFARD

As incontrovertible as any proof can be . . .

[*Pointing to the trial dossier on the table*]

The Voisin Girl's confession is there . . . these love potions were prepared subsequent to the Mass celebrated at La Voisin's for that purpose . . . the same kind to which Madame has resorted, for many years now, to retain Your Majesty's favor.

MADAME DE MONTESPAN

[*Rising from her* tabouret, *threatening, as if to rush at him*]

These are lies. . . . All lies!

ABBÉ GRIFFARD

What Madame did not know was that friends of Monsieur Fouquet's, despairing of his liberation from prison, had plotted, with La Voisin, for the death of Your Majesty!

[*Mme de Montespan draws away, back of the chair*]

What Madame did not know was that these love potions contained poison.

[*A muffled exclamation from the King, another from La Reynie. Mme de Montespan, trembling, leans for support upon the chair.*
Griffard goes toward the table where a bottle of lemonade and a goblet are arranged upon a tray]

If the Voisin Girl never delivered such potions to Madame . . .

If Madame never played the leading role in a ceremony such

* NOTE: Extensive deletions have been made in the Sardou text here.

as I have described, if Madame has never sent such powders to be poured into His Majesty's beverages by the hand of a lackey placed by her on His Majesty's staff . . . as in the case of this beverage. . . .

> [*He pours the lemonade into the goblet*]

If these things are not true, then all I have said is a lie, a libel, a calumny . . . in which case Your Majesty can drink of this brew without repugnance and without fear.

> [*He pushes the goblet to the other side of the table where His Majesty stands*]

But if there is any truth in what I have said, then this goblet may contain a fatal dose. . . . There may be death in it. . . .

THE KING   [*Looking at Mme de Montespan*]

Do you hear, Madame?

> [*The King takes a step toward the table, reaches out his hand for the goblet*]

MADAME DE MONTESPAN   [*Throwing herself in his way to stop him*]

No! No, do not drink!

> [*She collapses, weeping, upon the* tabouret *in front of the table. Silence*]

THE KING   [*Pointing to the door at the left, addressing La Reynie and Griffard*]

Use that door, please, Messieurs, and leave us.

> [*La Reynie and Griffard exit*]

SCENE IX
(*The King and Mme de Montespan*)

THE KING

What this man says is true, then? The charges in these documents, true, too? You actually patronized that poisoner? Went to her house and lent yourself to those ignoble practices? You have had me drink these vile concoctions? Is it true? Answer me!

MADAME DE MONTESPAN   [*In a low tone of voice, choked with tears*]

If it is true, it is all your fault! You have yourself to blame! You forced me to it. If I am guilty, you share the guilt along with me because it was you, who by your constant betrayals . . . pushed me to the brink of despair and condemned me to the use of such base means of self-defense.

THE KING

I forced you to it?

MADAME DE MONTESPAN

Have you not been cruel enough? . . . Have you not humiliated me before a succession of rivals . . . rivals whom I have had to face with a smile? Not to mention your passing fancies, your lights of love, your hole-and-corner assignations. Those we will skip. I will confine myself, instead, to those who gloated over me . . . La Louvigny, La Rochefort, La Ludres, La Gramont, La Soubise . . . who knows how many others? I have lost count by now. . . . Last of all, your Fontanges. And now, your Maintenon! It was to hold your love against these others that I had recourse to that Voisin woman! Yes, it is horrible, it is shocking. I admit it. But if it is a crime, think well before you pronounce judgment on me. . . . Can you withhold your pardon for a crime committed out of love for you?

THE KING

You would dare ask my pardon for such abominations as are written there?

> [*He picks up the trial reports from the table, hands them to Mme de Montespan*]

Read them! . . . Such infamies as these are indelibly imprinted on my mind's eye. Our liaison is at an end. You evoke in me only scorn and disgust.

MADAME DE MONTESPAN

Come, then, be honest and say straight out that you are tired of me . . . only too happy to have found a pretext!

THE KING [*Pointing to the dossier*]

A pretext—this?

MADAME DE MONTESPAN

Should I have allowed myself, then, to be superseded, dis-

Dénouement

missed like that sheep of a La Vallière who merely bleated her distress as she made her exit?

THE KING

It ill becomes you to mock at the woman I sacrificed to you. . . . In her distress, she turned—not to the devil—but to God!

MADAME DE MONTESPAN

To whom you yielded her, willingly enough. Do you expect me to cloister myself as she did?

THE KING

It would be the best thing for your sins.

MADAME DE MONTESPAN

And for yours! But don't count on it. Resignation is not my long suit. I am no repentant sinner. I cannot see myself as a nun.

THE KING

No, not such a supreme egoist as you, supremely ambitious, supremely vain. You have never loved me; you have loved only the King. What you have loved have been the honors I have heaped upon you, the gold I have lavished on you to indulge you in your mad prodigality, your extravagance, your splendor.

MADAME DE MONTESPAN

My splendor was a source of pride to you . . . another reflection of your own glory. At that, I have cost you less than the water-spouts for your Versailles fountains.

THE KING

Tomorrow you will leave the court . . . and go to live in the retreat I shall designate for you. . . . I have means to compel your obedience.

> [*The King strides to the table to ring a bell*]

MADAME DE MONTESPAN

I challenge you to try it. . . . You will not run me off, like a servant . . . not me, the mother of your children . . . of whom the eldest may one day mount the throne . . .

> [*The King, his hand on the bell,*
> *freezes into immobility at the mention of*
> *the word "children," and returns to his armchair*
> *as she continues speaking*]

MADAME DE MONTESPAN

The whole world, agasp at the disgrace of a person of my position, would search for the cause . . . and perhaps would find it . . . which would mortify your pride! You would never risk such a scandal. You will stifle this whole affair. You will burn those bundles of parchment. You will find some means to silence those criminal wretches so that they will never divulge our shame—mine and yours! . . . And I will stay on at the Palace, retaining my rank, my titles, my posts, my properties, my fortune. As for the homage paid me heretofore by the court, it will be assured me hereafter because you will set them the example. As for love, there I will let you off lightly. We have had enough of love, you and I . . . yet, come what may, I will go down in history as the radiant companion of the most glorious years of your reign: the official mistress of the young King—the handsome, gallant and victorious Sun King . . . who, now, behind the somber skirts of La Maintenon will emit only fading sunset beams . . .

> [*She crosses toward the door*]

Go, then, and rejoin your Duenna. Do penance with her for your delights with me. You will have time to regret them.

THE KING   [*Ringing the bell*]

Remorse, perhaps. Not regret.

> [*Addressing the Usher, who*
> *opens the door for Mme de Montespan*]

Light the way for Madame.

> [*Mme de Montespan makes her exit as*
> THE CURTAIN FALLS]

Nothing remains to be said except that they deserved one another.

PART THREE

The Fall

I

The Fall of Madame de Montespan

IF THE POISONS AFFAIR had embarrassed the Sun King in his private
life, he brazened it out on the international scene—never such
bullying, such bravado, such thrust toward empire since the campaigns of Alexander and of Caesar.

If the Poisons Affair had revealed a glimpse of a somewhat less
than splendid aspect of this Splendid Century—a momentarily dim
view of French glory—a brilliant display of bombs was shortly to
burst over Algiers, Genoa, and Luxembourg, diverting public
attention from Versailles' and Paris' sordid secrets.

The attack on the Barbary Coast came as a chastisement for
the corsairs preying on French merchant vessels; Genoa's offense,
in French eyes, was to have supplied galleys on Spanish orders; the
bombardment of Luxembourg was a land grab, pure and simple—
Louis XIV, like every French ruler after him, seeking to bulwark
the vulnerable northeastern angle of the French hexagon.

To that same purpose, France assaulted the Spanish Netherlands, seizing Courtrai and Dixmuide, ravaging Bruges and Brussels—1683, a very good year for the King of France to go on the
offensive, while the Emperor of Austria and the King of Spain were
busy defending the gates of Vienna against a Turkish siege.

The ultimate expression of Louis XIV's vainglory came in
1688, with his challenge to the Pope: the seizure of Avignon (time-
honored papal enclave on the Rhône) was in retaliation for His

Holiness's excommunication of the French Ambassador to the Vatican.

The period between 1678 (the date of the Treaty of Nijmegen) and 1686 (the date of the origins of the League of Augsburg) marks the time at which Louis XIV's star reached its zenith; never since Charlemagne had a French monarch so far extended the nation's dominion and frontiers; never again, save briefly in the heyday of Napoleon, would France's borders be spread so wide.

Probably Louis XIV did not fully appreciate the significance of the rout of the Ottoman hordes at the Kahlenberg: thenceforward Austria was free to face westward, to oppose the French rampage across the Continent, to rally all the other nations there to the banner of the League of Augsburg. Even the Protestant sovereigns would join up with the Catholic as a consequence of Louis XIV's persecution of the French Huguenots, his revocation of the Edict of Nantes in 1685. Protestant William of Orange, Louis's dogged enemy, acceding to the throne of England after the Glorious Revolution of 1688, would bring that nation along with Holland into the League against France.

From then on, France was to stand—or fall?—alone, in a great and ultimate test of strength which lasted throughout the next two decades. Except for one brief truce, all the remaining years of Louis XIV's reign, some twenty-six of them, would be taken up in a national struggle for survival.

In the spring of 1683, Louis XIV and his entire court made another splendid but arduous royal progress through Alsace and the Franche-Comté—an inspection tour of Vauban's new fortifications girdling the new frontiers*—not returning to Versailles until the end of June.

The Queen returned in a state of utter exhaustion. A month later, she was dead ("The first trouble she has ever caused me," His Majesty deigned to pay faint praise).

But "he was touched rather than grieved," Mme de Caylus

---

* Marshal Sébastien Vauban, the great military engineer, was to inspire a national trust in fortifications which would crumble only with the Maginot Line.

commented, and by the beginning of the next week, when Mme de Maintenon arrived with the Dauphine at Fontainebleau to join the King, "He could not resist twitting her, good-humoredly, on her deep mourning and somber air."

Mme de Montespan wept copiously, although Mme de Caylus somehow mistrusted that lady's "flood of tears"; she could not quite make out the reason: "Perhaps Mme de Montespan feared she might be turned back to her husband?"

The reason was obvious: the end of Marie Thérèse meant the end of Mme de Montespan's tenure of office as superintendent of the Queen's household, the end of all the prestige and prominence inherent in that lofty post.

Mme de Maintenon's grief may have struck her cousin, Mme de Caylus, as "sincere" but it was Mme de Maintenon who was to be the chief beneficiary at the demise of the Queen.

It had been Mme de Montespan—with her exalted lineage and her brood of royal bastards—who had aspired to become the morganatic wife of the French sovereign, in the event of his wife's death; but she had missed her chance, or bungled it, possibly through her involvement in the Poisons Affair.

For it was assumed that the King could not live in a solitary state; the Duc de Luynes, in his Memoirs, quotes Mme de Montespan as saying: "Thought should be given promptly to an appropriate remarriage for him. Knowing him as I do, I know that he will marry soon. It may be an ill-advised match he makes, but marry he will."

"A *mésalliance* so shocking," in Saint-Simon's opinion, that "posterity will never believe it": the King of France and of Navarre —and the Widow Scarron! ("How can she believe that Chapter One of her life will be overlooked or condoned?" Mme de Sévigné had inquired several years earlier, unable to credit the fact that the Sun King would overlook or condone the widow's undistinguished origins, her grotesque union with a scabrous minor poet, or her putative liaison with the Marquis de Villarceau. Mme de Montespan's malicious whispering campaign against her rival was apparently launched too late to put off the King.) Saint-Simon was right: His Majesty's choice of a mate was almost incredible . . . this woman almost fifty, three years his senior! And, actually, not a taste in common with him, whereas Mme de Montespan had shared them all; certainly the most royal of his tastes, such as hunting, gambling, building. (Mansart's genius was dismissed by Mme de Maintenon with a wry "We shall all die of symmetry!" a complaint uttered as she shivered in a thousand drafts between the thousands of pairs of tall French windows, aligned with flawless symmetry, one directly across from the other, the length and breadth of the château.)

Mme de Caylus considered it indelicate "to pry into the mystery" surrounding the marriage ceremony. Saint-Simon's guess as to the date seems the best: January of 1684; as does his guess at the list of those in attendance—Père de La Chaise as officiant, the Archbishop of Paris as diocesan; Bontemps, the King's Man Friday, valet-panderer; Nanon Balbien, Mme de Maintenon's confidential maid from her early and impecunious widowhood; possibly the Montchevreuils, one or both of those pious intimates of the bride; probably Louvois (whose opposition to the publication of the banns earned him Mme de Maintenon's undying hatred, to quote Saint-Simon further).

As late as late 1684, Mme de Montespan still had not yielded one inch of her high ground, not one of her semi-royal prerogatives. Racine and Boileau, in their official History of the reign, relate that: "On December 31, 1684, at the supper table, Mme de Montespan made presentation to the King of an album bound between solid gold covers, illustrated with hand-painted miniatures of all the towns of Holland taken by His Majesty in the campaign of 1672. This book cost 4,000 *pistoles*, she advised. Racine and Boileau wrote the text, including an historical eulogy of His Majesty. Such was Mme de Montespan's New Year's gift to the King; nothing ever seen to compare with it, neither in the excellence of its composition nor the lavishness of its production; nothing more pleasing to the recipient could have been devised. . . ."

To return the pretty compliment, on January 5, 1685, the Eve of the Epiphany (the Eve of Twelfth Night, or Feast of Kings, as it was called in France), "The King ordered that a King's Cake be delivered from his table to that of Mme de Montespan." Thus the Marquis de Dangeau in his stale and stodgy daily Journal,* which tells us further that His Majesty, throughout the year 1685, continued to give his former mistress continuing proof of his consideration and his homage by two visits every day—one in the early afternoon after Mass; one in the late evening, after supper; formal, semi-public calls paid upon mother and children, the three remaining under her wing, Mlle de Nantes, Mlle de Blois, and the Comte de Toulouse. (The Comte de Vexin had died in 1683, at eleven. "A blessing," in Mme de Caylus's opinion, in view of his "myriad infirmities"; the Duc du Maine, aged fifteen, had been established in his own household, in the Princes' wing, with Mme de Maintenon's friend, the Marquis de Montchevreuil, as his governor.)

In 1685, Mlle de Nantes, the first of the royal bastards to go to the altar, was united in marriage with the house of Condé, wed to the Duc de Bourbon-Condé, a grandson of the Grand Condé. "But since she had just turned twelve," as Mme de Caylus explains, "they were not put together for several years" (at the King's decision; the bride's mother, eager for the consummation of the prestigious union, would have been less considerate of the girl's tender years). "The nuptials were celebrated at Versailles in the King's state apartments" (Mme de Caylus continues) "with a glorious illumination of the gardens and with all that magnificence of which the King was capable. The Grand Condé and his son left nothing undone to signal their delight in the consummation of the betrothal which they had made every effort to bring about" (and if anyone wondered that the first Prince of the Blood should have sought out a royal bastard as bride for his heir, it must be remembered that the Condés' disloyalty to the throne in the days of the Fronde had never been fully expiated or forgiven).

---

* The Marquis de Dangeau's diary of life at the Sun King's court—daily entries, in infinite detail, made over a period of thirty years—could hold no interest for the average reader, but proved invaluable to that other assiduous courtier, the Duc de Saint-Simon, who came upon the scene much later. He not only annotated Dangeau's Journal, he shamelessly plagiarized it.

The two girls, Mlle de Nantes and Mlle de Blois, ranked as Bourbon Princesses, but the Mortemart strain predominated: like mother, like daughter, in wit and beauty and capriciousness; the willfulness may have been a Bourbon streak. "Their art of raillery and mockery was perfected by their mother and their aunt. . . . No one was safe from their ridicule . . . and all this under the pretext of amusing the King," according to *Madame*, herself a broad target for their malicious shafts.

"A love child," Saint-Simon called the new Duchesse de Bourbon-Condé, carried away by that "beauty of hers which attested to it . . . a child born of love and made for love, as well" (although elsewhere his natural waspishness reasserts itself when he wonders whether she has "a gizzard in place of a heart"). *Madame la Duchesse*, as the court called her, was endowed with total grace and charm, in the eyes of the Abbé de Choisy, and a great favorite of her father's, "who was infinitely diverted and stimulated by her high-pitched gaiety." (Not to mention the Dauphin, half in love with this enchanting half sister.)

With the wedding gala of this eldest daughter, in July of 1685, "Mme de Montespan had enjoyed her last great triumph at the court of France" (Voltaire).

But thanks to her wit, whimsy, and imagination, her salons remained the most entertaining of any in the court. One never knew what to expect upon entering there. One May day in 1685, the Marquis de Sourches came upon "an atelier of cabinetmakers and upholsterers creating magnificent pieces of furniture before one's every eyes! . . . She [Mme de Montespan] had a positive genius for inventing just such schemes as this to attract and hold the King's interest. . . ." Another day, it might be white mice Mme de Montespan turned to for diversion: "She hitched up a team of six to a tiny silver filigree carriage . . . oblivious to the blood their sharp little teeth brought to her shapely hands . . ." Another time it might be white piglets or white kids, perfumed and beribboned, parading along her marble halls. Once, it was a pair of bears that roamed at will (although not "palace-broken").

Her talents as a partygiver were unsurpassed in her day. In

February of 1685, the King lent her the Royal Orchestra, the Royal Ballet, and the Royal Opera to grace a masquerade she planned. On another occasion, her apartments were transformed into a village fair, the prettiest ladies and girls of the court staffing the stalls. At Marly, she was hostess to the court at a fête announced as the Boutique of the Four Seasons; she and the Dauphin presided at the booth of Autumn; Mme de Maintenon and the Duc du Maine at that of Winter. "There were all sorts of magnificent fabrics and 15,000 *pistoles'* worth of silver articles. . . . Everyone drew lots . . . and took away what he won," Dangeau reports toward the end of that year.

And so it went, according to Dangeau's Journal, on into 1686, Mme de Montespan hanging on for dear life:

> January 17, 1686—A Masquerade at Mme de Montespan's . . . the Duc and Duchesse de Bourbon, the Duc du Maine and all their company in attendance. . . . Singing and dancing until midnight.

> February 20—A Comedy performed tonight. . . . Later, *Monseigneur* [the Dauphin], *Monsieur, Mademoiselle,* and Mme de Montespan donned masks and came into the King's Chamber to show their costumes before going on to the main square of the town where a Masquerade was in progress. . . . "

"The Sultan Queen, the Reigning Mistress," "The real Queen of France" (as Visconti and La Fare had once called Mme de Montespan) would never abdicate; her life inextricably bound up with that of the court, she was unable to envisage a world beyond —or, rather, beneath it; unwilling to descend from the heights of Olympus where she had reigned for a decade or more, unwilling to depart the earthly paradise, the seat of power in France and epicenter of glory; the hub of the universe.

Mme de Maintenon recognized the fact that Mme de Montespan "dearly loved the court . . . not only because of the many persons established there to whom she was attached by bonds of blood or of friendship . . . but also because she so greatly loved court life, itself."

Mme de Montespan was even willing, now, to make concessions to stay on there, even to the point of falling in, in the ranks of the *nouveau* righteous, the newly devout, as Mme de Maintenon also recognized, observing tartly: "The King's conversion sets an example to the entire court, and the ladies who seemed the most unlikely candidates for reform simply live in church nowadays . . . Sunday services as crowded, now, as at Easter! . . . Mme de Montchevreuil, Mesdames de Chevreuse and Beauvilliers and the Princesse d'Harcourt—all the original band of the devout—are less assiduous, today, in the performance of their religious duties than Mesdames de Montespan and de Thianges, the Comtesse de Gramont, the Duchesse de Lude and Mme de Soubise."

Try as she would, Mme de Montespan could not always hold that wicked tongue of hers, not even with Mme de Maintenon; as on the day she found the curate and the Gray Sisters of Versailles all gathered at the new Favorite's door. "Whereupon [according to Mme de Caylus] she remarked to her: 'You could not hope for a better attendance, Madame, in your antechamber, were it the day of your funeral!' . . . Mme de Maintenon, appreciative as she was of wit . . . was highly amused by Mme de Montespan's *bons mots*. . . ."

Here Mme de Caylus taxes our credulity. Mme de Maintenon could scarcely have relished her former rival's malice. She would suffer Mme de Montespan's presence yet a little longer; a few more months, a few more years, biding her time, counting the days, hastening the one when she would finally bring her down.

The King procrastinated. For a dozen reasons—the first four of which were his four dearly beloved children by her—His Majesty could not bring himself to the final break with his long-established mistress. If the physical attraction between them was no longer operative, she had become a habit with him; he had grown accustomed to her special brand of humor, her taste, her originality; he depended on the stimulus, the *élan* she lent to any occasion she graced; the tone she set, the excitement she added to any company she joined.

He was loath, too, to disrupt the pattern and the rhythm of the

court—a collection of satellites revolving about his sun in movements as fixed as those of the stars in their courses. To dismiss
Mme de Montespan would be to displace one of the major celestial
bodies.

Mme de Maintenon would have to find a way to bring about
her eclipse.

Saint-Simon said it was "the Devil" Mme de Maintenon summoned up, "to affright the King with hellfire" on the score of his
early transgressions with the Scarlet Woman. The other weapon
Mme de Maintenon would have found ready to her hand would
have been the reference to Mme de Montespan's involvement in
the Poisons Affair: reminders to the King of Mme de Montespan's
love philters, love powders, love charms; the abominations to
which she had lent herself on the Abbé Guibourg's altar.

It would best serve Mme de Maintenon's game—and the
King's—to have Mme de Montespan retire from the court of her
own volition. Mme de Maintenon's every move would be calculated to that purpose: a rebuff, here; a disparagement there—a
slight, a snub, a slur—barbs designed to penetrate even that satiny,
thick hide, and provoke Mme de Montespan to depart Versailles,
on her own.

II

In Exile

IT WAS A DELIBERATE AFFRONT, a slap in the face to Mme de Montespan, to be omitted from the select group invited to accompany the ailing monarch, in May of 1686, to the spa of Barèges, a journey contemplated in the hope that those curative waters might spare him from the last resort of primitive seventeenth-century surgery.

The year 1686 was the Year of the Fistula. (Michelet divides the reign of Louis XIV into the pre- and post-Fistula eras; the latter, the beginning of the decline in personal as in national power. And a supreme perversity of fate, in Michelet's opinion, that Louis the Great should have been afflicted in the region of the anus—"to all men, great and small, the most humiliating!")

Insult was added to injury, in the case of Mme de Montespan, the Abbé de Choisy thought, when "She was obliged to hear the announcement of her exclusion" (from the Pyrenees expedition) "from the lips of her detested rival. . . . For it was Mme de Maintenon who was chosen to relay to her, in unambiguous terms, the King's message that he wanted to break off all personal relations with her, and that he advised her to start thinking about the salvation of her soul, as he was giving thought to his."

Dangeau breaks in to say that "the message sent Mme de Montespan into a violent fit of the vapors"; followed by a violent fit of temper, in which she departed suddenly, without so much as a by your leave to anyone at Versailles.

The Barèges journey was abandoned: it was to be the scalpel, after all, instead of the waters; but the insult to Mme de Montespan was compounded, in November, when Mme de Maintenon barred her way to the King's bedside where he lay recovering from the barbarous surgery, as he had somehow recovered from the dental surgery—the extraction of his upper teeth—the previous year, likewise without benefit of anesthesia: a clumsy job resulting in a fracture of the jaw, resulting in a slack one; a sunken look to mouth and chin, and a newly sharp and predatory look to the nose. (If Mme de Montespan could no longer play Venus, with all her extra *embonpoint*—"What a lot of flesh she has added lately!" Mme de Maintenon commented nastily to her brother—neither could Louis XIV play Apollo, in this his fiftieth year.)

Mme de Montespan had only begun to discover the taste of humble pie in 1686. "Mme de Maintenon would accustom her to a steady diet of it," as Saint-Simon pointed out. In September, Mme de Montespan's name was dropped from that most exclusive of all guestlists—the forty-odd "intimate" friends invited to join the monarch, the royal family, and Mme de Maintenon for a few days of "private" and "informal" country living, at a short remove from Versailles, at His Majesty's lavish new woodland retreat, his latest building folly, his hideaway château and dozen guest pavilions at Marly.

The Abbé de Choisy quotes Mme de Montespan in a bitter jest with the King at this social cut in September, "telling His Majesty that she had a grace to ask of him, that she be included [on the Marly list] if only to entertain the guests in the rear carriage or the antechamber. . . . These acrimonious brushes with the King should have proven to her that it was time to make a retreat, but that hour had not yet struck, and meanwhile, she would swallow more and more affronts. . . ."

A cruel public affront came from an unexpected source, from good courtier Racine, ready to sacrifice his earliest patroness as a pretty compliment to his latest, Mme de Maintenon. Or so the lines of his biblical drama *Esther* were interpreted: lines in the mouth of the holy Esther [Mme de Maintenon]:

> *Perhaps you have heard of the sudden disgrace*
> *Befallen haughty Vashti [Mme de Montespan], whose place*
> *I occupy since the King visited his wrath on her head,*
> *Ordering her off his throne and from his bed.*

Mme de Montespan had declined the King's suggestion that she take jurisdiction over the affairs of their son, the sixteen-year-old Duc du Maine, probably because the mother-son relationship was less than cordial: the Prince's foster mother had done a thorough job of weaning him from his natural mother. Actually, Mme de Montespan was not an unnatural mother if she is viewed in the context of her times. Strong maternal sentiment was seldom evinced by the *grandes dames* of the *Ancien Régime*; their children went from wet nurse to nurse to governess or tutor. Mme de Sévigné's assiduities and devotions to her daughter were commented upon as extravagant, as abnormal. Louise de La Vallière, like most noble mothers, addressed her daughter as "Mademoiselle." When Michelet accuses Mme de Montespan of disliking children, he is taking the word of her arch enemy, Mme de Maintenon, and that of a highly prejudiced Mme de Caylus; whereas Saint-Simon declares that "She loved them all [all her children] with a passion, except the Duc du Maine."

Whether or not she loved this eldest of her children by the King, she had secured for him one of the greatest fortunes in France by inducing the *Grande Mademoiselle* not only to make the Duc du Maine her heir but to make him a gift, in 1681, of her principality of Dombes, her county of Eu—all this as the price (though never so crassly stated) for the release of the *Grande Mademoiselle*'s insolent, bantam lover, the Duc de Lauzun, rotting now for some ten years in solitary confinement in Pignerol Fortress for the effrontery of having dared to aspire to the hand of a Daughter of France.

In Exile

The Duc du Maine—at seven a published author; at ten, a child prodigy—had not lived up to his early promise, but "no one had more wit than he," Saint-Simon conceded, despite his savage animosity toward that Prince: "No one was ever endowed with more subtle and insinuating graces, while he was all the more disarming for his natural, naïve, even innocent air. No one had ever been born with vaster ambition!" (except, perhaps, his future Bourbon-Condé wife, who would ceaselessly connive with him after power).

The young Duke was "too close to the King" (again by Saint-Simon's analysis) "not to have early discerned Mme de Maintenon's rising favor . . . and the inevitable decline of Mme de Montespan's. . . . From that time on, his mother could only be a millstone around his neck, while he had everything to hope for from his preceptress."

Nor did she disappoint him, Saint-Simon observed: "Her influence would open up to him the most incredible grandeurs . . . one after the other, until he was within reach of the throne itself!" (Only a small frail child, the future Louis XV, standing ahead of him, in 1714, subsequent to four deaths in the legitimate line:* although Saint-Simon was certain that a civil war would have broken out before such a shameful, illegitimate succession would have been countenanced in France.)

Saint-Simon, who tells this story and his own proud role in it, announces with a well-nigh orgasmic delight ("with a voluptuous surexcitation never experienced before or since") the bastards' downfall in the Regency Council in 1718 when the Duc du Maine was divested of the powers with which Louis XIV had invested him as superintendent of the education of young Louis XV. The Regent (the Duc d'Orléans), the Princes of the Blood, the Dukes and peers of the realm (Saint-Simon among them) all joined together on that occasion to demote the Duc du Maine and his brother, the Comte de Toulouse, from the rank of Princes of the

* Three Dauphins had died between 1711 and 1712; the Duc de Berry, the Grand Dauphin's third son, died in 1714.

Blood to that of simple peers, to remove them from the line of succession—"To pluck their false plumage from their bosom!" in Saint-Simon's exultant phrase.

With the Duc du Maine and the other royal bastards off in the upper regions, in the abode of demigods, it was curious that a sibling rivalry should have anguished their lowly half brother, the Marquis d'Antin, a mere mortal—the only child of Mme de Montespan by her lawfully wedded husband, conceived and born before she had been promoted to the couch of Jupiter. (Ironically enough, it would be the legitimate d'Antin for whom she would blush, not for her brood of semi-divinities.)

D'Antin's mother would try in vain in later years to compensate for the neglect of the early ones: every page of his Memoirs (the strangest kind of document, never intended for publication; actually, an examination of conscience) breathes a smoldering resentment against his mother, reveals the traumatic effect of her abandonment upon his formative years ("It seemed a kind of persecution . . . the treatment I suffered at Mme de Montespan's hands"). After his one meeting with her in 1679, at the age of fourteen, he had had only rare glimpses of his mother, "and then in secret."

The Marquis d'Antin had learned early, even at the isolated Montespan Château de Bonnefons in the Pyrenees, of his mother's anomalous position at court and the scandal to the family: "My nurses talked constantly to me—out of my father's earshot, to be sure—about the King and the court, about the great career and great fortune certain to be awaiting me there. . . ." (What he and they were too naïve to realize was that his mother's place at court was to constitute the greatest obstacle to his advancement there—his person a living, breathing reminder to the King of the shameful state of sin, of double adultery, in which he and his concubine were living.) "Impressionable child that I was, I yielded to this love of grandeur . . . and joined my nurses in building a thousand castles in the air . . . the beginning, though I did not realize it then, of a lifelong enslavement of my heart and of my senses" (his lifelong career as fawning courtier is what he meant, and for which he would express his self-contempt, spattering it across all the pages of his Memoirs; in his case, an effective form of catharsis).

D'Antin was "a handsome and clever man," Choisy thought, and Saint-Simon commented that "he had inherited the Mortemart flair for wit and conversation, seasoned with the Gascon spice of his father's race," a considerable endowment.

From the best of tutors to the best of colleges (for rhetoric and philosophy) to the Academy (for the military arts), by eighteen d'Antin was ready, like most young noblemen, to serve his King and country on the field of battle.

Whereupon his mother stepped in for the first time to forward his career. It was already late, in 1683, her favor on the wane, her influence diminished; but she could arrange for a junior grade lieutenancy for him in an elite corps, the King's Regiment—an appointment that carried with it the honor of presentation to the King.

D'Antin's paternal great-uncle, the Duc de Bellegarde, performed the honors on September 4, 1683, at Fontainebleau—his mother conspicuous by her absence.

"I thought the Gates of Heaven had opened before me, when I was finally received at court!" the young man confided to his Memoirs.* "At that time, I had yet to discover the cruel disillusionments to be encountered there."

The King was curt with the new young officer come to swear his fealty. He could not be expected to give warm welcome to the son his ex-mistress had deserted for his sake.

It would take young d'Antin the rest of his natural life to break down the King's reserve and win his favor, but he was willing to dedicate it to that end, ready to spill his entire fortune in the ruinous extravagance incumbent upon the court nobility (though less prodigal with his blood, as some of his fellow officers were to reproach him). D'Antin would exemplify "the perfect courtier," a

---

* "The court consists of a small coterie of men and women with whom one can spend the days of one's life more agreeably than with any other," d'Antin wrote in his Memoirs: "And here at court, as nowhere else; for nowhere else could such a group as this be assembled."

title Saint-Simon conceded him. (Paying court was an art unto itself, and there were books wherein to study it: Castiglione's *The Courtier* and Gracian's *The Courtier's Manual* dating back to the sixteenth and early seventeenth centuries respectively.) The Duc d'Orléans made the cruel gibe that "D'Antin has the makings of a true courtier—having neither humor nor honor to hold him back."*

By the time he was twenty, the Marquis d'Antin had his own regiment (purchased at a staggering sum), and had been named a gentleman in waiting to the Dauphin, for which he gives his mother grudging credit, terming this "the sole grace and favor" she had obtained for him. She was showing him "good will" by then, he admitted, but strictly "after her own fashion."

In 1686, she arranged an excellent marriage for him with the daughter of the Duc d'Uzès, and settled "a 2,000-écu pension" on the young couple: "The only contribution she ever made to my subsistence," d'Antin noted sourly, still dissatisfied with her good offices in his behalf. Dangeau was impressed, if d'Antin was not, at "the magnificent apartments she furnished for the newlyweds, at the trousseau basket for the bride, brimful of ribbons, fans, perfumes, gloves, and a handsome diamond and emerald parure. . . . No less than 40,000 francs' worth!"

Despite his constant grumbling at fate and at his mother, the course of d'Antin's career was up, up, up . . . an appointment to Maréchal de Camp; shortly after, one to Lieutenant-General.

* The famous story of the Perfect Courtier is the one told about d'Antin and the *allée* of chestnut trees at his estate of Petit Bourg, where His Majesty did him the supreme honor of stopping off for the night en route from Versailles to Fontainebleau, in 1707; and of complimenting him upon the perfection of the property—with the sole exception of the centuries' old, towering chestnuts which seemed to cut off a fine view from the King's apartment. The next morning, the King could look out his windows in an uninterrupted view across the countryside; the Perfect Courtier had ordered the offending trees chopped down silently and swiftly during the night. "We can all be grateful, Mesdames," the irrepressible and irresistible young Duchesse de Bourgogne exclaimed, "that the King did not ask for our heads. Monsieur d'Antin might have chopped those off, too!"

Of Mme de Montespan's three sons, only the Comte de Toulouse showed her much affection. None of the Duc du Maine's fierce ambition gnawed at this youth, who would develop into an attractive man, although aloof, reserved, undecipherable; "A man of honor, integrity and judgment . . . an excellent Admiral . . ." (dour Saint-Simon cannot praise him highly enough).

The King removed him from his mother's aegis in 1690, ostensibly to take the twelve-year-old on his first military expedition into Flanders, where the Duc de Luxembourg was to rout the allied armies—Dutch, Spanish, English, Swedish, German—of the League of Augsburg.

If the Duc du Maine enjoyed "successes" on that campaign (the victory of Fleurus, one of the last he and France were to enjoy), he shared them regularly with Mme de Maintenon, writing her in July: "I am really ashamed at all the praise and compliments . . . showered on me . . . for having simply done my duty. . . ."

Louis XIV could now point with pride to all three of his sons in the field: the Dauphin having been given command of the armies invading Germany in 1688 (commander in name if not in fact; "exposing himself as much as necessary," according to Voltaire, "though not temerariously; an unadulterated joy to the King to see himself imitated but not outdone").

By 1691, only Mlle de Blois, aged fourteen, remained in her mother's charge. The girl's removal—her transfer to the guardianship of that pious dragon, the Marquise de Montchevreuil, Mme de Maintenon's creature—was the most telling blow of all, and carefully premeditated.

Mme de Montespan reacted with a flash of her former temper and departed Versailles abruptly for a visit to Paris.

A variety of other expedients had been attempted to that purpose, but in vain. All Mme de Maintenon's Jesuit cohorts had tried their hand at persuading Mme de Montespan to remove herself from the vicinity of His Most Christian Majesty while he sought to make atonement for his numerous sins—a list headed by her name.

"The Bishop of Meaux [Bossuet] was finally delegated by the King to tell her that, for both her own sake and his, she must retire. . . ."

Thus Mme de Caylus; whereas Saint-Simon gives credit to the Duc du Maine "for undertaking what no one else would dare, what the King could not bring himself to do . . . for delivering to Mme de Montespan His Majesty's final, peremptory order for her dismissal. . . . Monsieur de Meaux finished up the job. . . . Mme de Montespan departed in tears and rage, and never forgave the Duc du Maine . . . refusing for a long while to see him . . . though, that was the least of his concerns for, by this strange service, he had endeared himself forever to the all-powerful Mme de Maintenon. . . ."

Mme du Noyer, that indefatigable letterwriter from Toulouse, is the only contemporary to describe a fiery scene between the monarch and his former mistress, before her carriage careened out of the Marble Courtyard and through the Versailles gates: "She [Mme de Montespan] asked one last audience of the King, and realizing there was no further point in mincing words, she let herself go in a fury, reproaching him for his ingratitude in the face of the sacrifices she had made for him. The King endured this tantrum because she was a woman, and because it was the last he would have to put up with from her. . . . "

Madame, the Duchesse d'Orléans, is the only contemporary to describe an amazing scene laid on the Versailles terrace, at an hour shortly after La Montespan's exit: "The Duc du Maine made haste to send all his mother's baggage after her, to Paris, without giving her so much as a word of notice. As for her furniture, he ordered that it all be thrown out of the windows . . . to make sure she would not return!"

To make sure that he would come into possession—as had been promised him—of that prize ground-floor apartment of hers (known as the Apartment of the Baths, once the site of marble bathing pools), his own apartment in the Princes' wing having already been assigned to his sister, Mlle de Blois.

Gone was the Scarlet Woman of the Scriptures, which was how

Mme de Maintenon saw her, "arrayed in purple and scarlet . . . and decked with gold and precious stones and pearls, having a golden cup in her hand full of abominations and filthiness of her fornication."

Enfin. At last. To take Saint-Simon's word for it: "At last, she had relegated her rival from the court! . . . With Mme de Montespan's departure, Mme de Maintenon experienced a supreme sense of relief . . . at long last delivered of her enemy. . . ."

III

The Way of the World

A<small>FTER THE FALL</small> (according to Mme de Caylus): "Mme de Montespan spent some time at Clagny, where I saw her quite often with [her daughter] Mme la Duchesse. She continued also to come to Versailles to see the Princesses [her daughters] who had remained behind when the King went off to the siege of Mons [in April, 1691; another sterile French victory]. It was said that Mme de Montespan wandered like a lost soul, doomed to return again and again to the scene of a former life, in expiation of former sins. . . . Actually, it was difficult to recognize, in such conduct, that proud spirit of hers, that grandeur of soul to which I have made reference earlier. . . . She seemed devoured by ambition, tormented by irresolution. . . ."

"She ate her heart out," was how the Abbé de Choisy saw and said it, "and still could not quite make up her mind to quit the field. . . ." (The court her element; away from it, she floundered, gasped, like a fish out of water.)

"Mme de Montespan has returned to Paris after a few days at Clagny," Dangeau's Journal reports in April of 1691: "But she has not wholly renounced the court. She will see the King from time to time and, in truth, it would appear that there was undue haste in stripping her apartments. . . ."

"The [ex] mistress retired to the Convent of Saint-Joseph

which she had built [in the *quartier* Saint-Germain], but she was slow to make the readjustment . . ." (by Saint-Simon's account) "She was at a loss to know how to occupy the empty days and hours that stretched before her; she dragged herself and her discontent from Bourbon [the spa] to Fontevrault [her sister's Abbey] to the estates of d'Antin. . . ."

If Mme de Montespan found difficulty adjusting to her new role, the world goggled to see her in it, as a lay Mother Superior at Saint-Joseph's, in which capacity she served that religious community, of which she was chief patroness and benefactress—one of her numerous philanthropies; this, a refuge for one hundred destitute orphan girls, where they were taught a means of livelihood and prepared for marriage.

In a maternal role, Mme de Montespan is reported briefly at Fontainebleau, nursing the Duchesse de Bourbon through an attack of smallpox; performing the same service for Mlle de Blois, at Clagny—which château, as it was shortly suggested to her, was situated uncomfortably close to Versailles and would constitute an appropriate wedding gift for the Duc du Maine.

His marriage to Anne Louise Bénédicte de Bourbon, daughter of the Prince de Condé, was to take place in March of 1692 in the chapel of Versailles—Mme de Montespan not among those present.

"None of the King's legitimized children suffered in any way whatsoever by the absence of Mme de Montespan," from what Mme de Caylus could see: "Mme de Maintenon served their interests better . . . than their natural mother could have done. . . . Indeed, to be frank, I must admit that Mme de Maintenon may have gone too far in her ambitions for them. . . . In the end, she herself came to agree with the rest of France that His Majesty had tried to raise them up too high."

The marriage arranged for Mlle de Blois with the Duc de Chartres did seem presumptuous—the King's bastard daughter and the son of his own, his only brother. *Madame*, the Duchesse d'Orléans, was outraged if her husband was not. When she heard the news that her son had agreed to the shameful alliance, the slap she struck him across the cheek resounded the length of the Hall of Mirrors (where Saint-Simon heard it)!

It may have been that the regency of France was well worth a slap; Louis XIV would appoint this obliging nephew of his to head the government that would have to be set up at Louis XIV's death to function during the minority of his great-grandson, Louis XV.*

So flagrant were the corruptions of the future Regent that any mud, any charge slung at him could be made to stick: even the charge of incest with his daughter, Mlle de Valois (the most scandalous figure of all that scandalous age, who would eventually be wed to the Duc de Berry, third son of the Dauphin): even the charge of poison, in 1712, when his three throne-heir cousins died off in rapid succession. (The King believed his nephew innocent of these poison charges and, wishing to spare him the stigma and ordeal, refused to allow him the public trial he demanded to clear his name.)

Mlle de Blois would be addressed by her husband as "Madame Lucifer" ("Proud as Lucifer" was the popular expression); proudest of that prideful lot of royal bastards, her mother-in-law, *Madame*, would add in outright "exasperation." And no wonder: "All those children of Mme de Montespan's and the King's were raised to consider themselves superior to everyone else in the world!" Her daughter-in-law was furthermore "the laziest woman in the world," so lazy there could be no official court at the Palais Royal during the regency; too lazy to reproach her husband for his succession of mistresses, too lazy to take on lovers of her own,

---

* The house of Orléans would finally attain to the Crown of France in 1830, after the Revolution, after the First Republic, after the first Napoleonic Empire, after the Bourbon Restoration, after the last of the last two Bourbons—Louis XVIII and Charles X. If Louis Philippe (of the house of Orléans), King of the French between 1830 and 1848, could boast of his resemblance to Louis XIV, it was thanks to the marriage between Mlle de Blois and the Duc de Chartres in 1692. The Comte de Paris, present Pretender to the throne of France, belongs to this house of Bourbon-Orléans, a direct descendant of Louis Philippe.

which contributed to the relatively smooth course of their marriage. She was "always reclining on a *canapé* . . . even to eat" (*Madame* again); always eating, "always drinking," like her mother and sister, who "could down floods of wine as if it were water . . . without ever once falling under the table."

The King outdid his own magnificent self in the magnificence of the dinners, concerts, and balls celebrating the marriage in 1692 between his daughter and his nephew, both aglitter with jewels; she, in a gown of gold and silver, tiny black flowers embroidered all over the lamé bodice; the skirt all striped with silver and ruffled with gold Spanish needlepoint; diamonds and rubies twined through her luxuriant chestnut tresses.

The mother of the bride did not appear in the Versailles chapel; her name did not even appear on the marriage contract.

The bridegroom, the Duc de Chartres, distinguished himself, that summer of 1692, on the bloody field of Steenkerke, and again in the summer of 1693 at the still bloodier field of Neerwinden (which was more than could be said of his brother-in-law, the Duc du Maine).

The 1690's were years of bloody, inconclusive battles: "The devastation no longer confined to Europe," as Voltaire noted, "but extending now to far-off Africa [Senegal] and America" (Santo Domingo, Jamaica, Newfoundland, Hudson Bay, Quebec; Franco-Indian raids threatening even Boston and New York). The Magnificent Wars were over. After 1693, Louis XIV would no longer go campaigning in the midst of his dazzling courtly caravans.

The King had "broken" shockingly, as he approached sixty, *Madame* noted sadly: "He has visibly deteriorated, looks old and heavy, seems even to have shrunk. . . . His face has changed as well. . . . He is scarcely recognizable."

Almost the entire burden of the direction of the war and state now bowed the monarch's shoulders. With the deaths of Colbert and Louvois, France had seen the last of her great administrators; and with the death of Maréchal Luxembourg, the last of her great commanders.

After nine years of death and desolation, by the terms of the

Treaty of Ryswick signed in 1697, the net results were nil: France's frontiers remained those of 1679, plus only Strasbourg.

The last decade of the seventeenth century was scourged by war's concomitants: economic collapse set in in France, and a decimation of the population (the loss of an estimated two to three million, at least) occurred between the famine years of 1693 and 1694.

Fénelon, Archbishop of Cambrai, addressed so bold a letter to the King that its authenticity was doubted until the day the manuscript was discovered:*

"Your people, Sire, are dying of hunger. . . . Town and country are being depopulated. . . . Industry languishes. . . . Commerce flags. . . . You have destroyed half the strength within the nation to make and defend vain conquests outside it. . . . They [the ministers of state] have made your name hateful . . . and that of the whole French nation odious . . . to all neighboring peoples . . ."

This letter Fénelon delivered to Mme de Maintenon for delivery to the King, but she demurred.

Mme de Montespan, at this time, may have found her only comfort in Mme de Maintenon's discomfiture; the somber, retiring, pious figure became more unpopular than any of the King's flamboyant Favorites. She was more pernicious than they, by *Madame*'s indictment: "Not all the King's mistresses together did as much harm as she!"

Justly or unjustly, Mme de Maintenon was charged with the King's mistakes, which multiplied.† "Destiny is decided in her

---

* Fénelon spoke for the palace peace party, headed by his devoted pupil, the Duc de Bourgogne, eldest grandson of the monarch—the hope and promise of the nation, full of intelligence, compassion, vision: but for whose untimely death in 1712, the story of the Bourbon dynasty in France might have had a different ending.

† This parody of the Lord's Prayer was to be heard in the streets in the 1690's and early 1700's:

> Our Father which art at Marly,
> Thy name is no longer hallowed;
> Thy will no longer done,
> Neither on earth nor on the sea,
> Give us, this day, our daily bread

chamber," Mme du Noyer charged, and it was true that the King consulted there with his ministers—she, huddled out of the draft in her hooded (*tonneau*) chair, "Her glasses slipping down over her nose while she worked at her tapestry" (Mme du Noyer again). If she was reported to sit silently by, even so the King was reported to value her opinion, her good sound common sense: "*Votre Solidité*," "Your Solidity," he called her.

There were those who said that Mme de Maintenon was far more to be feared than her predecessor ever was, for all the wicked Mortemart tongue. Mme de Montespan may have cheerfully sacrificed her victims for the sake of a laugh from the King, but all she had ever asked was a laugh at their expense; she was not vindictive, had never asked the King for a *lettre de cachet* to be used against an enemy. "She never sought to do harm to anyone," François de Gaignières, the journalist, said of her, implying that as much could not be said of Mme de Maintenon.

Mme de Maintenon soon gave Mme de Montespan to understand that all communication between them was to cease: "She has let me know that she wants no further contact with me," Mme de Montespan confided by letter to the Duchesse de Noailles: "So, silence it shall be, on my part as well as on hers, now that I know that is what she wants."

Mme de Maintenon evidenced an occasional qualm of conscience for her rigors toward her former benefactress, as in this letter to the Abbesse de Fontevrault, sister of Mme de Montespan, dated September, 1691, just six months after the latter's dramatic exit from Versailles: "I am delighted to have had a message, through you, from Mme de Montespan. I feared she was angry with me, although God knows I have done nothing to incur her ill will; God knows I have only good will for her. . . ." and, again in 1701, to the same correspondent, further protestations of benevo-

---

Before we starve to death.
Pardon Thine enemies whom Thou hast vanquished
But not Thy generals who have ravaged Europe.
Lead us not into the temptation of changing masters
But deliver us from La Maintenon.

lence: "Your letter omits any mention of Mme de Montespan; mine could never make such an omission. She is too often in my thoughts, and I take this, as every occasion, to wish her well. . . ."

Her relations with the woman whom she had superseded in the monarch's affections form the subject of a lecture or "Discourse" (as they were known) given by Mme de Maintenon in her St. Cyr classroom, intended surely to point a moral, although those ingénues may have found it a difficult one to ferret out, as does the reader (pondering the text today in a collection entitled *Edifying Letters of History*):

"Mme de Montespan and I were the greatest friends in the world. She took a strong liking to me and—naïve as I was—I gave her my affection. She was a woman of great intelligence and charm. She confided in me without reserve, told me her inmost thoughts. Yet here we are on bad terms, though neither of us intended it so. It came about surely through no fault of mine and yet, if anyone has cause for complaint, it is she; for she can assuredly say: 'It is I who am responsible for her elevation. It is I who introduced her to the King and brought him to like her. Then she became the Favorite and I have been chased off.' But, now, to look at it from my point of view: Was I wrong to have accepted the King's friendship—on such terms, please note, as I accepted it? Was I wrong to have given him good advice and to have urged him to break off his sinful liaison? And, now, back to my original thesis: Close as I was to Mme de Montespan, had I entered with bad faith into her intrigues; had I given her improper counsel . . . whether from a divine or a worldly point of view . . . had I shown her the way to retain the King's friendship instead of urging her to renounce it, then would she not presently have evidence to use against me, by which to bring about my downfall . . . were she of a mind to take vengeance against me?"

Communications had been severed between Mme de Maintenon and Mme de Montespan; far more grievous for the latter, she now lost touch with the King.

Out of touch with the court but unable to put it out of her mind, still restless, still pacing in her exile, Mme de Montespan acquired the Château de Petit Bourg in the Forest of Fontaine-bleau. "When the King went to Fontainebleau for the hunting," Mme de Caylus said, "she would go running to Petit Bourg to watch her faithless lover, from a distance, happy even to catch sight of his pack, on the gallop. She always hoped that the King would stop one day, at her château, but he was no sentimentalist, never one to look back."

Madame de Caylus offers another insight into Mme de Montespan's state of mind in her exile: "In the years after Mme de Montespan had left the court . . . I saw her at the Carmelite convent where she went to visit Mme de La Vallière, who had become a kind of spiritual guide to her . . ." (Sister Louise de la Miséricorde was named as the author—and Bishop Bossuet as the editor—of the anonymous pious work, entitled *Reflections on the Mercy of God*, first published in 1680, running into many editions. In such an odor of sanctity did she live her last years and die, in 1710, as to create a strong tide of sentiment favoring her canonization.)

But there was not, as yet, any sign of true Christian humility in Mme de Montespan, none Saint-Simon could detect: "She never lost her regal air. That queenly demeanor she had arrogated unto herself clung to her even in her retreat. Everyone had become so used to paying her homage in her heyday that there was no demur in later times. . . . All France came to call. . . . It had somehow become an established custom. . . . She greeted them all, like a Queen holding court—one who does honor to any guest by addressing him. . . . There was an air of grandeur about her and her abode [in her apartments at the Convent of St. Joseph]. . . . Still beautiful as the dawn. . . . Still the best of company, and endowed with such graces as to make even her hauteur acceptable. . . ."

Saint-Simon contradicts himself; one sign of Christian humility he did detect in the Marquise de Montespan—an act of contrition in the direction of the Marquis: her official spiritual guide, Father de La Tour, "exacted a terrible penitence of her, that she ask pardon of her husband and submit herself into his hands. She wrote to him, by her own pen, in terms of total submission, offering to return to his roof if he deigned to receive her; and if not, to betake herself to whatever destination he should prescribe to her. For anyone who knew Mme de Montespan, this constituted the most heroic of sacrifices. She got credit for the gesture without having to suffer the consequences. Monsieur de Montespan sent back word that he wanted neither to receive her under his roof nor to make any prescription to her; neither to hear from or of her ever again in his life."

Now that the Marquise was removed from the court, who should appear there, in the late 1690's, but her husband, the Marquis? Suddenly *persona grata* (thanks to his son's nascent favor) after thirty or more years' exile; a situation to strike *Madame* as exceedingly funny: "Nothing could have been more amusing than to see him and his son, d'Antin, playing cards with Mme d'Orléans and Mme la Duchesse de Bourbon [his wife's two illegitimate daughters by the King], deeply respectful as he kissed the hands of these Princesses and handed them their cards. Even he must have seen the humor of the situation because he would occasionally turn around and give a little smirk. . . ."*

Removed from the court and the vortex of power, Mme de Montespan may have been touched more lighly than might otherwise have been the case by the grave national and international problems—France, with all Europe, in suspense to discover what disposition the heirless, moribund Charles II of Spain would make of his empire.

The last decade of the seventeenth century could be only less terrible than the first decade of the eighteenth; the brief truce of the

---

* The court had occasion to laugh again at Montespan's vain pretensions to the title of his maternal uncle, the Duc de Bellegarde, who had died without male issue, the duchy and the peerage hereditary, however, only on the sword side. If not the title, Montespan did enjoy the late Duke's estates near Toulouse, abandoning his own grim and craggy Bonnefons for the Château de Saint-Élix, a Renaissance jewel with the most beautiful orangerie in the Midi, elaborate French gardens, and a vast park; the gift, according to family tradition, of Francis I to a Gascon ladylove—his salamander emblem carved in the central façade to prove it.

Treaty of Ryswick ending as the War of the Spanish Succession began.

When the last Will and Testament of the cretinous, impotent, monstrous Spanish monarch was opened in 1700, Louis XIV could see only the splendor of his grandson's inheritance: the Spanish Empire in its entirety, in all its vast extent, going to the Duc d'Anjou.

The bequest was catastrophic to France if glorious to the Bourbons. The war to maintain the young Bourbon Duke upon the throne of Spain pitted France against all Europe through twelve long and critical years.* At the turn of the century, as the seventeenth gave way to the eighteenth, it seemed that Louis XIV and his grandson and the Bourbon *Gloire* had brought France to the brink of disaster, under the threat of invasion and disintegration— to her knees in defeat, in starvation, in economic collapse, in bankruptcy.

Cracks appeared in the Pharaonic mask: Louis XIV sued for a peace the coalition would not grant him; he deigned to explain their plight to the people in a public letter; he set the nobility an example by cutting expenses at Versailles, by sending his gold plate and silver furnishings to the mint—stripping the Hall of Mirrors of its silver orange-tree tubs, its massive silver tables, its silver chandeliers which had flickered with four thousand tapers. The allowances of the royal family were reduced; and so was that of Mme de Montespan.

She shrugged off a two thirds cut in her annual remittance from the Royal Treasury with the remark that "she regretted it less for her own sake than for that of her wide charities."

She was far from indifferent to personal tragedies, such as the loss of her sister, the Marquise de Thianges, who died in 1693 in

---

* The Spanish house of Bourbon would occupy that throne long after the French line had lost its own. Alfonso XIII would hold on a full century longer in Spain than Charles X in France, taxiing out of the Royal Palace in Madrid only in 1931; and his grandson, today, apparently Franco's heir-designate, destined to remount the throne at the General's demise.

the handsome Princes' wing apartment adjoining the Dauphin's—to the end, even after Mme de Montespan's *disgrâce*, a privileged character at Versailles. By the time the Duc de Saint-Simon met her there, in 1691, "her eyes were rheumy, puffy, with green crepe bags beneath them. The large linen bib tied beneath her chin was to catch the profuse and constant drooling. Even in such a state as that, she gave the impression . . . by her air and by her manner . . . of being Queen of the Universe. And every night, in her sedan chair, she had herself carried—bib and green crepe bags and all—up to the top of the King's back staircase, into his private apartments, where she joined him and the royal family . . . after supper . . . taking her seat in an armchair and staying on there until the hour of His Majesty's retirement. . . . The King liked to tease her; while she, in the best of spirits and high good humor, stood her ground against him gloriously and imperiously. . . . It was said that she was even wittier, even wickeder than Mme de Montespan. . . ."

Spitfires though they both may have been, and frequently quarreling, still Mme de Montespan mourned her sister, writing to a friend: "One is never prepared for death . . . but this one came when I least expected it. . . ."

She had mourned her amiable and congenial brother, the Duc de Vivonne, whom she had lost in 1688.

In 1701, she had the death of *Monsieur* to grieve—no matter how she felt about that of her husband, which occurred the same year.

Monsieur had been her first friend in the royal family when she came to court, and remained her friend even after she departed it. (Her son-in-law, the Duc de Chartres, inherited his father's title, and her daughter now became Duchesse d'Orléans. *Madame*, the dowager Duchess, trembling lest she be relegated to a convent through Mme de Maintenon's ill will, implored pardon for her slanders and incivilities in the past, and promised to control both her tongue and pen in the future.)

Whether or not Mme de Montespan mourned her husband, she was conspicuous in her observation of the conventions after his death, "donning widow's weeds, like any other." Could Saint-Simon have been right when he went on to say that the Marquis de Montespan had "lived and died enamored of her"? His will named her executrix, requesting her to act in this capacity "for the sake of the genuine friendship and tenderness he had always felt for her." Still, some doubt arises as to the sincerity of Montespan's sentiments upon perusal of his two final testamentary requests, to wit: that his widow "pray for his soul" and "pay off all his debts"—which were considerable.

But it was the loss, in 1704, of the Abbesse de Fontevrault—her one remaining and her dearest sister, her confidante and her companion—that left Mme de Montespan bereft and shook her to her foundations.

Father de La Tour was delegated to break the news to her in Paris. She rushed from the city to the estates of her niece, the Duchesse de Lesdiguières ("to seek refuge from her sorrow," as a correspondent notified Dangeau), and then rushed off again, away again, in one direction and then another, it made little difference where, apparently; whether to Bourbon l'Archambault (the spa) or to d'Antin's Château de Bellegarde, to Petit Bourg or to Oiron, just so she kept moving. She was "running hard" (Mme de Maintenon's word for it), running away from sorrow, from herself.

In 1700, Mme de Montespan had purchased the Château d'Oiron, one of the most magnificent domains in Poitou, her natal province (where, as Mme de Thianges had been wont to boast to the King, "The Mortemarts had once ruled like Kings"). At Mme de Montespan's direction, the Holy Family Hospital ("dedicated to the maintenance, sustenance and care of one hundred needy aged of both sexes") would be constructed adjacent to the château and so handsomely endowed as to be self-sustaining for generations.

"It would take her long years to get hold of herself," Saint-Simon commented after Mme de Montespan's repudiation by the King; by the time she moved to Oiron, she may have been coming close to it.

"Most of the time, here, I comprise my own society," she wrote to a friend, "but, even alone, I have converse with a multitude of passions, yearnings, projects, prejudices. . . . A tumult still agitates and troubles me . . . keeps me from hearing the voice of God. . . ."

An inventory of her library at Oiron reveals that it was devoted to religious texts: multivolume sets, *The Lives of the Saints, The Confessions of Saint Augustine, The Sinner's Guide* (no copy, oddly enough, of La Vallière's *Reflections on the Mercy of God*).*

In permanent residence at Oiron, Mme de Montespan maintained contact, by letter, with the great world where she once had reigned supreme: with the Duchesse de Noailles, for one; with Daniel Huet, Bishop of Soissons (later Bishop of Avranches), for another. It was popular in that day and time, among the literary-minded, to set themselves subjects for debate by mail. The Bishop chose to take the affirmative of the subject he suggested: "Resolved that the written word is superior to the spoken." Celebrated conversationalist that she was, Mme de Montespan was surely humoring him when she conceded that, "what you have stated about the written word reveals advantages I had not hitherto perceived . . . I had always felt that the vivacity and spontaneity of conversation— the excitement of actually seeing ideas dawn on the face of the speaker—weighted the scales in favor of conversation against the chill detachment of a letter, which can be composed at leisure . . . and who knows with what outside assistance! . . . But you have made me change my mind . . . made me see the vulgarity, the deceptions, the perils of conversation. . . . Often the conversationalist is carried away by the sound of his own voice to the point of saying things he does not really mean. . . . Audience reaction can influence us . . . and sometimes we speak to court approbation

* Mme de Montespan's library included few secular titles: *A Gardener's Manual, A Universal Pharmacopoeia, The Poor Man's Surgeon and Physician, The Alimentary Guide, A Study of Chemistry, New Fairy Tales or Fairies à la Mode, Tale of Tales, Memoirs of the Court of Spain.* Mme de Montespan's copy of Bossuet's *Sermons* was found at the Abbey of Fontevrault, marked with her armorials, dogeared from frequent reference; one passage significantly underscored refers to "the most shameful weakness of human nature . . . concupiscence, which fastens the soul down to the body with bonds as strong as they are tender. . . ."

rather than out of the true sentiment of our hearts. . . . Sometimes we cast pearls before swine and see our thoughts debased in the process. . . . While, at other times a delightful thought is suppressed for the reason that one has not yet had time to phrase it gracefully. . . . By letter, on the other hand, one can reveal oneself to one's single, chosen confidant without danger of being overheard by others. . . . Yet, in my eyes, the supreme advantage of correspondence over conversation is that the precious words of one's correspondent may be preserved . . . are not gone with the wind . . . not evaporated into thin air. . . ."*

Voltaire says, speaking of "those later years of her life," that Mme de Montespan "found diversion in reading aloud, to her friends, from her Memoirs . . . reminiscences about the court which she and Mme de Maintenon had earlier agreed to compile, each from her own point of view." If Voltaire knew whereof he spoke, a fascinating document has been lost to history—one surmise being that the Marquis d'Antin destroyed the Memoirs after his mother's death, among a number of other items, as a courtesy to Mme de Maintenon.

Mme de Montespan had waited too late to cultivate d'Antin's trust and affection. "If she finally acted a mother to him," Saint-Simon reflected, "it was after long years in which she had acted more like a [cruel] stepmother. . . . Finally, she set out to endow and enrich him. . . ." Petit Bourg was bequeathed to him; Oiron to his son, the Marquis de Gondrin; and upon Gondrin's marriage, in 1707, to Marie Victoire de Noailles, Mme de Montespan lavished 100,000 francs' worth of jewels on the bride.

"But it was penitence which inspired her liberality toward d'Antin," Saint-Simon continues: "She could never really seem to open her heart to this son of hers by her husband. . . . It was always an effort for her. . . . Her heart was preoccupied with her other children, and the fact that there was constraint, now, between her and them, further complicated her relation with him. . . . Any man other than d'Antin might well have avoided contact with a mother

* This is a literal translation of Mme de Montespan's phrase: *"Des paroles que le vent emporte . . . et que l'air dissipe. . . ."*

who had brought shame upon his name and that of all his family; but such was not his character. . . ." ("Servility stood him in the place of character," Saint-Simon said of d'Antin, in reference to his relation to the King. And *vis-à-vis* his mother's other children, "His humility was excessive; he displayed infinite patience under their rebuffs.")

As for these half brothers and sisters, Mme de Montespan "lavished gifts on all of them, as well," Saint-Simon remarked, "acting on a natural maternal instinct but also motivated by a desire to preserve their affections in order to maintain—through them—some sort of link with the King with whom she no longer had any contact whatsoever . . . not even indirectly through these children of theirs. Their attentions to her had slackened; they saw her only rarely, now, and then only at her request."

It had not been so, earlier: earlier, they had been "assiduous in their attentions to her . . . flattering themselves with the same hope she cherished. . . ."—the hope that, in the event of Mme de Maintenon's death (a good possibility "in view of her age and infirmities"), the King would turn back to his former mistress, now that she was "widowed, free . . . with no further obstacle to prevent, no further religious scruple to interfere with a reunion, the resumption of an ardent relationship . . . to which both might be prompted by tender sentiment for one another as well as by mutual interest and ambition for their common children. . . ."

There is more than Saint-Simon's word for it: there is further proof of this vain illusion in the "King's Chamber" at Oiron, thus designated, thus furnished—as if His Majesty could be expected any day, any hour, to rejoin his true mate, his wife in all but name, and mother of his favorite children. That is how she must have regarded it when she set the room aside for him; when she set up the great oaken bedstead behind a gilded railing, its canopy topped by a crown, its counterpane and bed curtains of black velvet, lavishly embroidered in gold and silver thread; when she arranged the massive gold-pedestaled, green chalcedony table and the ten armchairs of gilded wood, upholstered in magnificent tapestries representing the twelve Sibyls; when she named it the King's Chamber, and dedicated it to his occupancy.

Pictures of the King adorned every wall of the château: there were four in Mme de Montespan's room alone. There were miniatures of the King as a boy, of the King on a white charger. The Beauvais Manufactory had woven tapestries, to her order, representing conquests of the King, on land and sea. There was a unique and extravagant bust of the King executed in solid silver—all except for the hair, which was wrought of solid gold (happily spared from the patriotic contributions to the mint in 1689 and 1707).

There were portraits of the royal family, legitimate and illegitimate, in gold and silver frames, by the dozen, and as many more of the châtelaine of Oiron herself, no less than two as Mary Magdalene—Mignard showing her as more voluptuous than repentant; reclining on a bed of rushes, diaphanously clad, barearmed, barefooted, flowing golden locks barely draping a bare bosom, flowers bursting into bloom all about her.

"At last, God touched her," Saint-Simon intones: "From that time on, until her death, she was unfaltering in her conversion, and ever more rigorous in her penitence. First, she had had to renounce the secret bonds that attached her to the court as well as the hopes, chimerical as these may have been, with which she had so long flattered herself. . . . Gradually, she came to the point where she gave away all she possessed to charity. She devoted many hours of the day to good works for the poor; lowly and menial tasks, such as sewing chemises and other such garments . . . and she set all those about her to doing similar work. Her table, which she had loved to excess, became the most frugal imaginable; her fast days, more and more frequent. She deserted her guests and the little card games which were her diversion to go to her oratory for prayer.* She took

* Backgammon was obviously another favorite diversion: the Château d'Oiron inventory made after Mme de Montespan's death lists two boards, one of morocco leather, one of ebony. The inventory shows four snuffboxes —silver, tortoise-shell, crystal, and ivory; evidently, Mme de Montespan was a user. (*Madame*, the Duchesse d'Orléans, complains of the prevalence of "the nasty habit" among the ladies of the court.) The château boasted two

to mortifying her flesh unceasingly; her sheets and chemises were of coarse, rough unbleached linen, although she concealed them beneath regular sheets and chemises. She constantly wore bracelets, belts, and garters with iron spikes which often left lacerations. And even her tongue, once so dreaded, was made to do penance, too. She lived, moreover, in such utter terror at the approach of death that she hired a number of women whose sole duty was to keep vigil while she slept—her bed curtains left open; candles burning bright to dispel the shadows of the night and the tomb; the women of the night watch gathered round her . . . so that whenever she wakened, she would find them chatting, playing games or eating . . . to make sure they would not doze in their chairs and leave her unattended."

If Saint-Simon had any idea of Mme de Montespan's involvement in the Poisons Affair—which he had not—he could not have more vividly described what might be construed as the torments of a guilty—a perhaps criminally guilty—conscience; he goes on to describe her psychosomatic ailments, her increasing hypochondria: "In good health, but always thinking herself to be ill. . . .

"The last time she went to Bourbon—and she went out of no real need for such a cure—she must have had some premonition of impending death for she made mention of that possibility . . . paying two years' pension in advance to her long list of pensioners, mostly impoverished noblemen . . . and doubling the amount of her annual alms distribution."

Reports on Mme de Montespan's final, fatal visit to the watering resort reached the Duc de Saint-Simon, firsthand, from his mother, likewise at Bourbon, who went promptly to call on her notorious cousin, the Marquise, and found her looking very well.

It was the next report which brought the shocking news of Mme de Montespan's mortal illness: "She was stricken suddenly,

---

spinning wheels and a harpsichord, although there is nowhere a hint as to whether Mme de Montespan could play the instrument (one portrait shows her playing the lute).

one night, without warning. The women on night vigil with her wakened all the household."

An emetic—another panacea of the age—was administered, and it was this which was deemed, by Saint-Simon as by Dangeau, to be the fatal dose (by the *Mercure Galant* reporter, as well, in an obituary column published in June of 1707, the only newspaper to take account of the demise of the former Favorite; the official *Gazette de France* preserving a total silence).

"She died a highly edifying death," was Saint-Simon's accolade: "She summoned her entire domestic staff, down to the humblest, and made public confession of her publicly sinned sins, asked pardon for the long and open scandal of her life. The terror of death which had so long obsessed her was suddenly dissipated. . . . She gave thanks to God that He had permitted her to die far removed from her children, the fruits of her adultery . . . and after that made no further mention of their names. . . . D'Antin, for whom a courier had been sent, arrived as she approached her end. . . . But, as soon as she had expired, only a few hours later, he took off again for Paris, having left orders which were either strange . . . or strangely executed. . . . That once so perfect body fell prey to the unskilled hands of some apprentice surgeon. . . . The obsequies were left to the discretion of the lowliest valets, the rest of her entourage having apparently deserted . . . her body was left for quite some time outside the door of her residence while the priests of the parish church disputed possession with the canons of Sainte Chapelle Cathedral. The parish church finally won out, and there the coffin was deposited as casually as if it had been that of some insignificant provincial *bourgeoise*; nor was it removed until quite some time later [August 3] for transport to Poitiers, to the Mortemart family crypt [marked by a magnificent black marble cenotaph in the vermeil choir of the Church of the Cordeliers] —and then in a funeral cortège remarkable for its shameful parsimony."

"Before setting out [for Bourbon], d'Antin had sent a message to Marly to notify his mother's natural children. The Comte de

Toulouse advised the King and asked permission to go to his mother. Permission granted, he set out at once, but had gone no farther than Montargis when he met another courier, who brought him the news of his mother's death . . . upon which notice, he— along with all the doctors and medical attendants in his train— turned back. Nothing could have exceeded the grief manifested by the Duchesse d'Orléans and the Duchesse [de Bourbon] and the Comte de Toulouse. . . . The grief of the Duchesse [de Bourbon] was all the more striking for the reason that she had always prided herself at showing emotion for no one. . . . All this evidence cannot but confirm my theory that the children entertained high hope for their mother's restoration to royal favor. . . ."

Not the Duc du Maine, "who could not conceal his joy" at his mother's death!

Not the Marquis d'Antin, "What had he to gain from a woman who had shown him neither affection nor esteem?"

And if Mme de Maintenon stood between him and the sun, "he flattered himself that—his mother once out of the way—he could win over the all-powerful enemy. . . ." (And did so: from the day of the funeral on, he began to bask in the full sun of royal favor. "Here I am, at last—thawed out!", he crowed in the privacy of his Memoirs: Duc d'Antin, by 1711!* The d'Antin marquisate elevated by royal brevet to a dukedom peerage. Governor of the Orléanais! Superintendent of royal properties—a prize post in which he succeeded Mansart.)

But up to the very hour of his mother's death, as Saint-Simon reminds us, d'Antin had been obliged "to truckle vilely" to his mother's natural children. "In the future, he intended to fly on his own wings. . . ."

Temporarily, he found himself embarrassed: if he felt obliged to affect "an exaggerated mourning" in the presence of his half brother and sisters, he felt simultaneously the need to avoid any

* A dukedom peerage, ironically enough, to be enjoyed by only three generations of d'Antin's family; the third Duke dead without issue in 1757; the line and title extinct.

show of filial grief in the presence of the King and Mme de Maintenon.

"He could not maintain the delicate balance required to carry it off," a sharp-eyed Saint-Simon observed, "and the world—accustomed to pay respect to Mme de Montespan—never forgave her son. . . . There was a general outcry against the indecency of the obsequies, the niggardly sums distributed to her large domestic staff at dismissal. . . . But all this was as nothing in comparison to the affair of the testament. It was widely known that Mme de Montespan had made a will; she made no secret of it, referring to it on her deathbed without, however, giving any indication as to where she kept it. . . . It was never to be found. . . ." (She being intestate, her one legitimate child was sole heir to her vast fortune.) A hue and cry went up . . . the loudest protests coming from Mme de Montespan's servants . . . dependents, who were left without resources. Her children were indignant at such procedures, and let M. d'Antin know it. . . . He had expected some such reaction . . . but hoped that they would work him no great harm. . . .

"It might have been expected that Mme de Maintenon would have felt an infinite relief at long last to be delivered of a former benefactress whose place she had usurped, whom she had chased from the court, of whom she had continued to be jealous and fearful. But it was not so [to Saint-Simon's amazement]. Remorse for the ingratitude with which she had rewarded the other's benefactions now overwhelmed her; tears overtook her, and for lack of a better refuge, she went to hide herself on her *chaise percée* [close stool]. But Mme the Duchesse de Bourgogne, who had followed and discovered her there, stood speechless in astonishment. She was no less astonished at the utter insensibility of the King, in the aftermath of a passionate love affair of such long years' duration. She could not restrain herself from expressing this surprise. But he replied calmly that, since the day he had given Mme de Montespan her *congé*, he had never expected to lay eyes on her again; thus, she had been, from that day on, dead to him. It is not difficult to comprehend that the exhibition of grief on the part of their children was displeasing to him. . . .While they dared not wear mourning for a mother no longer recognized . . . still, despite the awe in which they held their father, they did not abridge their sorrowing. . . . The whole court came visiting, though not a word was said about the event which had occasioned the visits . . . certainly a curious performance. . . . A common loss served, temporarily, to reconcile Mme the Duchesse d'Orléans and Mme the Duchesse [de Bourbon]. . . . Their sorrow endured quite some time. . . . But when it was over, the sisters' rapprochement was over, too. . . . Gradually, they resumed their normal attitudes toward one another . . . and to the world in general . . . gradually slipped back into their customary way of life. D'Antin was not so easily nor so soon restored, as he might have hoped, to the good graces of his mother's children but, in the end, passions subsided, tensions eased, bygones were bygones. It was over and done with, out of mind. And that's the way of the world."

Bibliography

THE TRIAL DOCUMENTS

PARIS'S BIBLIOTHÈQUE DE L'ARSENAL is the repository for the Archives de la Bastille, wherein is included the official dossier of the Poisons Affair trials: here are all the legal papers emanating from the Royal Chamber of the Arsenal, the court clerk's minutebook covering the entire legal procedure of the Royal Chamber from the issuance of the arrest warrants to the pronouncement and execution of the final judgments; here are copies of all the arraignments, all the interrogations and declarations— except, of course, for those sequestered by order of the King.

François Ravaisson, archivist of the Library of the Arsenal during the latter half of the nineteenth century, compiled, annotated, and published the major—certainly the most interesting—portion of the Archives of the Bastille, with Volumes IV through VII covering the Poisons Affair trials. Ravaisson included numerous other documents pertinent to the Poisons Affair, such as letters of Louvois's from the Archives of the Ministry of War, and notes and letters of La Reynie's from the police official's own personal papers and notebooks, which have now been deposited in the French Manuscript collection of the Bibliothèque Nationale, Paris's great national library.

Records of the trial of Le Sage and the Abbé Mariette before the criminal court of the Parlement of Paris in 1668 are filed in the Archives Nationales in Paris.

Numerous documents pertaining to the trial of the Marquise de Brinvilliers before the supreme court of the Parlement of Paris in 1676 are to be found in the Bibliothèque de l'Arsenal: the trial dossier and the manuscript copy of the Abbé Pirot's account of the Marquise's last days are in the French Manuscript collection at the Bibliothèque Nationale.

CONTEMPORARY SOURCES

Anonymous: *Lettres historiques et anecdotiques* (a collection of chronicles published during the reign of Louis XIV). Bibliothèque Nationale, Paris.

Antin, Duc d': *Mémoires autographes.* Société des bibliophiles, Paris,. 1821.

Aumale, Mlle d': *Mémoires.* Paris, n.d.

Boileau-Despréaux, Nicolas: *Oeuvres complètes.* Paris, 1873.

Bossuet, Jacques: *Oraisons funèbres et sermons.* Paris, n.d.

Bussy, Roger de Rabutin, Comte de: *Histoire amoureuse des Gaules, La France galante.* Paris, 1868.

——: *Correspondance avec sa famille et ses amis.* Paris, 1857.

——: *Mémoires.* Paris, 1857.

Caylus, Mme de: *Souvenirs.* Paris, 1804.

Choisy, Abbé de: *Mémoires pour servir à l'histoire de Louis XIV.* Utrecht, 1727.

Colbert, Jean-Baptiste (ed. Pierre Clement): *Lettres, instructions et mémoires de Colbert.* Vol. VI, Paris, 1869.

Condé, Louis II de Bourbon, Prince de: *Lettres inédites à Marie-Louise de Gonzague, reine de Pologne.* Paris, 1920.

Coulanges, Marquis de: *Mémoires.* Paris, 1820.

Dangeau, Marquis de: *Journal de la cour de Louis XIV.* Paris, 1854–60.

Fénelon, François de: *Lettre à Louis XIV.* Paris, 1825.

——: *Oeuvres.* Paris, 1820–28.

Feuquières, Marquis de: *Memoirs, Historical and Literary.* London, 1735–6.

La Beaumelle, Laurent de: *Mémoires pour servir à l'histoire de Mme de Maintenon.* Amsterdam, 1755.

La Fare, Marquis de: *Mémoires et réflexions sur les principaux événements du règne de Louis XIV.* Paris, 1838.

La Fayette, Madame de: *Histoire d'Henriette d'Angleterre.* Paris, 1839.

——: *Mémoires de la cour de France pendant les années 1688 et 1689.* Amsterdam, 1731.

——: *La Princesse de Clèves.* Paris, 1678.

Languet de Gergy, Archevêque de Sens: *Mémoires inédits sur Mme de Maintenon.* Paris, 1863.

La Vallière, Louise de: *Réflexions sur la miséricorde de Dieu.* Paris, 1680.

Bibliography

Le Dieu, Abbé: *Mémoires et journal sur la vie et les ouvrages de Bossuet.* Paris, 1856.

Louis XIV: *Mémoires écrits par lui-même, composés pour le Grand Dauphin, son fils, et addressés à ce Prince, suivis de plusieurs fragments de Mémoires militaires, de l'instruction donnée a Philippe V, de 17 lettres addressées à ce Monarque.* 2 vols. in 1, Paris, 1806.

————: *Oeuvres de.* 6 vols., Paris, 1806.

———— (ed. Girardet): *Manière de montrer les Jardins de Versailles (1690–1699).* Paris, 1951.

————: *Mémoires et lettres.* Paris, 1927.

Louvois, Marquis de: *Lettres.* Archives du Ministère de la Guerre.

Luynes, Duc de: *Mémoires sur la cour de Louis XIV.* Paris, 1862.

Maintenon, Marquise de: *Conseils et instructions aux demoiselles de Saint-Cyr.* Limoges, 1875.

———— (ed. T. Lavallée): *Lettres historiques et édifiantes.* Paris, 1856.

———— (ed. T. Lavallée): *Correspondance générale.* Paris, 1865.

———— (ed. M. Langlois): *Lettres.* Paris, 1935-9.

Mancini, Marie: *Apologie, ou les véritables Mémoires de Marie Mancini, connétable de Colonna, écrits par elle-même.* Paris, 1881.

Mazarin, Duchesse de (Hortense Mancini): *Mémoires.* Cologne, 1675.

Montpensier, Mlle de (the *Grande Mademoiselle*): *Mémoires.* Paris, 1776.

Motteville, Mme de: *Mémoires.* Amsterdam, 1739.

Noyer, Madame du: *Lettres historiques et galantes de deux dames de condition, dont l'une était à Paris et l' autre en province.* Cologne, 1723.

Orléans, Duchesse d' (second *Madame*): *Correspondance.* Paris, 1891.

Ormesson, Olivier d': *Journal.* Paris, 1860–62.

Patin, Gui: *Correspondance.* Paris, 1901.

Pirot, Abbé Edmé: *La Marquise de Brinvilliers, récit de ses derniers moments.* Paris, 1883.

Racine, Louis: *Mémoires de la vie de Jean Racine.* Paris, 1844.

Saint Maurice, Marquis de: *Lettres sur la cour de Louis XIV.* Paris, 1911–12.

Saint Simon, Duc de: *Mémoires.* Paris, 1879.

Scudéry, Mlle de: *La promenade à Versailles.* Paris, 1669.

————: *Lettres de Mlle de Scudéry et de Mmes de Salvan et de Saliaz.* Paris, 1806.

Sévigné, Marquise de: *Lettres.* Paris, 1862.

Sourches, Marquis de: *Mémoires sur le régne de Louis XIV.* Paris, 1882–92.

Spanheim, Ezekiel: *Relation de la cour de France*. Paris, 1900.
Tallemant des Réaux: *Historiettes*. Paris, 1840.
Visconti, Primi: *Mémoires de la cour de Louis XIV*. Paris, 1909.
Voltaire: *Le siècle de Louis XIV*. Paris-Lille, 1925.

GENERAL BIBLIOGRAPHY

André, L: *Le Tellier et Louvois*. Paris, 1942.
Anonymous: *Aventures de l'Abbé de Choisy, habillé en femme*. Brussels, 1880.
Audiat, Pierre: *Madame de Montespan*. Paris, 1939.
Baguet, Henri: *Une maîtresse du Roi Soleil en Bourbonnais*. Moulins, 1914.
Belin, Camille: *Nicolas de La Reynie*. Limoges, 1874.
Bertrand, Louis: *Louis XIV*. Paris, 1923.
Boissier, Gaston: *Madame de Sévigné*. Paris, 1888.
Boulenger, Jacques: *The Seventeenth Century*. New York, 1920.
Chapman, Hester W.: *Privileged Persons*. London, 1966.
Clement, Pierre: *La police sous Louis XIV*. Paris, 1866.
———: *Madame de Montespan et Louis XIV*. Paris, 1868.
———: *Lettres, instructions et mémoires de Colbert*. Vol. VI, Paris, 1869.
Cordelier, Jean: *Madame de Maintenon*. Paris, 1955.
Cornu, Maître: *Le procès de la Marquise de Brinvilliers*. Paris, 1894.
Coulon, Marcel: *Racine et la mort de la du Parc*. Mercure de France, June 1, 1940.
Cousin, Victor: *Madame de Sablé*. Paris, 1854.
Cronin, Vincent: *Louis XIV*. London, 1964.
Delavaud, Louis: *La cour de Louis XIV en 1671, Mme de Montespan, Colbert et Louvois*. Paris, 1912.
Durant, Will, and Ariel Durant: *The Age of Louis XIV*. New York, 1963.
Émard, Paul, and Suzanne Fournier: *Les années criminelles de Mme de Montespan*. Paris, 1939.
———: *Monsieur, frère de Louis XIV*. Paris, 1953.
Erlanger, Philippe: *Louis XIV*. Paris, 1965.
Funck-Brentano, Frantz: *L'Ancien Régime*. Paris, 1926.
———: *Le drame des poisons*. Paris, 1902.

————: *Les lettres de cachet à Paris*. Paris, 1903.

Gallotti, Jean: *Mademoiselle de Fontanges*. Paris, 1939.

Goubert, Pierre: *Louis XIV et vingt millions de Français*. Paris, 1966.

Gréard, O.: *Madame de Maintenon: Extraits de ses lettres, avis, entretiens, conversations, proverbes sur l'éducation*. Paris, 1905.

Guérard, Albert: *The Life and Death of an Ideal*. New York, 1956.

Hallays, André: *Madame de Sévigné*. Paris, 1922.

Houssaye, Arsène: *Mademoiselle de La Vallière et Madame de Montespan*. Paris, 1860.

Irwin, Margaret: *Madame Fears the Dark* (play). London, 1930.

Iung, T.: *La vérité sur le masque de fer (Les Empoisonneurs)*. Paris, 1873.

Jacquemont, André: *Nicolas de La Reynie*. Paris, 1900.

Jourdy, G: *La Citadelle de Besançon, prison d'état au XVIIe siècle, épisode de l'affaire des poisons*. Gay, 1888.

Lacroix, Paul: *XVIIe siècle, institutions, usages et costumes*. Paris, 1880.

Lair, Jules: *Louise de La Vallière et la jeunesse de Louis XIV*. Paris, 1902.

Langlois, Marcel: *Madame de Maintenon: Lettres*. Paris, 1935–9.

Laulan, Robert: *La mort de Mlle de Fontanges*. Mercure de France, April 1, 1940.

————: *Un diagnostic rétrospectif sur la maladie mortelle de Mlle de Fontanges*. Presse Medicale, June 4, 1952.

Lavallée, T.: *Madame de Maintenon: Lettres historiques et édifiantes*. Paris, 1856.

————: *Madame de Maintenon: Correspondance générale*. Paris, 1865.

Lavisse, E.: *Histoire de France, des origines à la Révolution*. Vols. VII and VIII, Paris, 1911–12.

Legué, G.: *Médecins et empoisonneurs aux XVIIe siècle*. Paris, 1896.

Lemoine, Jean: *L'Affaire Montespan, réponse à MM Sardou et Funck-Brentano*. Paris, 1908.

————: *Madame de Montespan et la légende des poisons*. Paris, 1908.

————: *Les des Oeillets*. Paris, 1939.

————, and André Lichtenberger: *De La Vallière à Montespan*. Paris, 1902.

Lemonnier, H.: *L'art Français au temps de Louis XIV*. Paris, 1911.

Lewis, W. H.: *The Splendid Century*. London, 1953.

————: *The Sunset of the Splendid Century*. London, 1955.

Locard, Edmond: *Le XVIIe siècle médico-judiciaire*. Paris, 1902.

Loiseleur, Jules: *Trois éngimes historiques*. Paris, 1882.

Magne, Émile: *Scarron et son milieu*. Paris, 1924.

Mallet-Joris, Françoise: *Marie Mancini*. Paris, 1964.

Mandin, Louis: *Racine, le Sadisme et l'affaire des poisons. Mercure de France*, June 1, 1940.

Mandrou, R.: *Introduction à la France moderne, Essai de psychologie historique, 1500–1640*. In *L'Evolution de l'Humanité*. Paris, .

Masson, A.: *La sorcellerie et la science des poisons au XVIIe siècle*. Paris, 1904.

Michelet, Jules: *Histoire de France*. 1843–67.

Mitford, Nancy: *The Sun King*. New York, 1966.

Mongrédien, Georges: *Madame de Montespan et l'affaire des poisons*. Paris, 1953.

————: *Madeleine de Scudéry et son salon*. Paris, 1946.

————: *La vie litteraire au XVIIe siècle*. Paris, 1947.

Montifaud, Marc de: *Racine et La Voisin*. Paris, 1878.

Mousnier, R.: *Les XVIe et XVIIe siècles in L'histoire générale des civilizations*.

Nass, L.: *Les empoisonnements sous Louis XIV*. Paris, 1898.

Nicolson, Harold: *The Age of Reason*. New York, 1961.

————: *Kings, Courts and Monarchy*. New York, 1962.

Noailles, Duc de: *Histoire de Madame de Maintenon*. Paris, 1848–58.

Nolhac, Pierre de: *Versailles, résidence de Louis XIV*. Paris, 1925.

Phelps, Ruth S.: *Amphitryon and Madame de Montespan*. Chicago, 1927.

Praviel, Armand: *Madame de Montespan, empoisonneuse*. Paris, 1934.

Rat, Maurice: *La royale Montespan*. Paris, 1959.

Ravaisson, François: *Archives de la Bastille*. Vols. IV–VII, Paris, 1870–1874.

Robert, Henri: *Les grands procès de l'histoire*. Paris, 1928.

Sackville-West, V.: *Daughter of France*. New York, 1959.

Sainte-Beuve, C. A.: *Causeries du Lundi*. Paris, 1851–62.

————: *Portraits de femmes*. Paris, 1844.

Sardou, Victorien: *Théâtre complet*. Paris, 1934–59.

Ségur, Pierre de: *Le Tapissier de Notre Dame, les dernières années du maréchal de Luxembourg (1678–1695)*. Paris, 1903.

Steegmuller, Francis: *The Grand Mademoiselle*. New York, 1956.

Thuillat, L.: *La Reynie*. Limoges, 1930.

Tilley, Arthur: *Madame de Sévigné*. Cambridge, 1936.

Truc, Gonzague: *Madame de Montespan*. Paris, 1936.

Wilhelm, Jacques: *La vie quotidienne au Marais au XVIIe siècle*. Paris, 1966.

Ziegler, Gilette: *Les coulisses de Versailles*. Paris, 1963.

Bibliography

BIBLIOGRAPHY OF MAGIC AND
THE OCCULT ARTS

This list offers no more than a hint at the vast bibliography of magic, which begins with the earliest recorded civilizations—the Assyro-Babylonian, the Egyptian, the Semitic, and continues on to include the Iranian, the Greco-Roman, the Islamic, the Celtic . . . to mention only a few, at random, in the western world. In the twentieth century, interest in the subject flourishes rather than flags, as anthropologists, ethnologists, and sociologists pursue the study of magic and religion on every continent.

The foremost manual of inquisition is the *Malleus Maleficarum* (The Witches' Hammer), published in Cologne in 1486, compiled by the Dominican Jacob Sprenger, the Holy Office's High Inquisitioner for the German witchcraft trials in the late fifteenth century. Other authorities on the judgment of witches are the French jurisconsult Jean Bodin, who wrote *Démonomanie des sorciers*, published in 1588, and Pierre de Lancre, inquisitor in the Basque witchcraft persecutions of 1609, whose textbook is entitled *Le Tableau de l'inconstance des mauvais anges* (1613). Another prominent and zealous prosecutor of witchcraft was King James I of England and Scotland, author of an anti-witchcraft tract, the *Daemonologie* ("Newes from Scotland, declaring the damnable life and death of Doctor Fian, a notable sorcerer who was burned at Edenbrough in January last") (1591).

Blau, J. L.: *The Christian Interpretation of the Cabala in the Renaissance*. New York, 1944.
Bosman, L.: *The Meaning and Philosophy of Numbers*. London, 1932.
Cavendish, R.: *The Black Arts*. New York, 1967.
Frazer, Sir James G.: *The Golden Bough, A Study in Magic and Religion*. New York, 1922.
Michelet, Jules: *Satanism and Witchcraft* (trans, of *La Sorcière*). New York, 1939.
Murray, Margaret A.: *The Witch Cult in Western Europe*. Oxford, 1921.
———: *The God of the Witches*. New York, 1933.
Givry, Grillot de: *A Pictorial Anthology of Witchcraft, Magic and Alchemy*. New York, 1958.

BIBLIOGRAPHY

Hill, Douglas, and Pat Williams: *The Supernatural*. New York, 1966.

Jung, C. G.: *Psychology and Alchemy*. London, 1953.

Lethbridge, T. C.: *Witches; Investigating an Ancient Religion*. London, 1962.

Lowe, J. E.: *Magic in Greek and Latin Literature*. Oxford, 1929.

Robbins, Russell H.: *The Encyclopedia of Witchcraft and Demonology*. New York, 1959.

Rohmer, Sax (A. Ward): *The Romance of Sorcery*. New York, n.d.

Scholem, G. G.: *Major Trends in Jewish Mysticism*. New York, 1946.

Seligmann, Kurt: *History of Magic*. New York, 1948.

Thorndyke, Lynn: *The Place of Magic in the Intellectual History of Europe*. New York, 1905.

Trachtenberg, J.: *Jewish Magic and Superstition*. New York, 1961.

————: *The Devil and the Jews*. New York, 1939.

Waite, A. E.: *The Pictorial Key to the Tarot*. London, 1922.

————: *The Secret Tradition in Alchemy*. New York, 1926.

Wedeck, Harry E.: *Dictionary of Magic*. New York, 1956.

Index

i

Index

Index

A NOTE ON THE TYPE

This book is set in ELECTRA, a Linotype face designed by W. A. Dwiggins (1880–1956), who was responsible for so much that is good in contemporary book design. Although much of his early work was in advertising and he was the author of the standard volume LAYOUT IN ADVERTISING, Mr. Dwiggins later devoted his prolific talents to book typography and type design and worked with great distinction in both fields. In addition to his designs for Electra, he created the Metro, Caledonia, and Eldorado series of type faces, as well as a number of experimental cuttings that have never been issued commercially.

Electra cannot be classified as either modern or old-style. It is not based on any historical model, nor does it echo a particular period or style. It avoids the extreme contrast between thick and thin elements that marks most modern faces and attempts to give a feeling of fluidity, power, and speed.

This book was composed, printed, and bound by The Haddon Craftsmen, Inc., Scranton, Pa. Typography and binding design by Charles E. Skaggs.